From Financial Crisis to Social Change

Torsten Geelan
Marcos González Hernando
Peter William Walsh
Editors

From Financial Crisis to Social Change

Towards Alternative Horizons

Editors
Torsten Geelan
Department of Sociology
University of Cambridge
Cambridge, UK

Marcos González Hernando
Department of Sociology
University of Cambridge
Cambridge, UK

Peter William Walsh
Department of Sociology
University of Cambridge
Cambridge, UK

ISBN 978-3-030-09972-5 ISBN 978-3-319-70600-9 (eBook)
https://doi.org/10.1007/978-3-319-70600-9

Cover illustration: Richard Mehtälä
#explainartist
www.explainartist.org

Printed on acid-free paper

This Palgrave Macmillan imprint is published by Springer Nature
The registered company is Springer International Publishing AG
The registered company address is: Gewerbestrasse 11, 6330 Cham, Switzerland

Preface: The Labyrinths and the Layers of Social Change

Over the longer run, social change may take the form of trend lines, and sometimes even appear as human evolution. But in the short run of some years or a decade, it is more often than not unexpected and surprising. This might be said of the financial crisis of 2008 onwards, though it did have some expected consequences. Chief among these was popular indignation: against soaring economic inequality; against the recklessness of the speculators who caused the crisis; and against the prophets of austerity who said we must pay the price for the errors of greedy elites. However, nowhere has there been any public measures aimed at reining in this galloping inequality.

Rather, looking back from 2016, the main social change since 2008 has gone in a completely different direction, delivering a reinforcement of nationalism and xenophobia. Eastern Europe is full of increasingly shrill, chauvinistic and xenophobic governments, already ahead of Donald Trump in banning Muslims from entry. Similarly, the new regime in the Ukraine is resurrecting from its dark past the "heroes" of ethnic hatred and unrestrained mass violence—Stepan Bandera, Symon Petliura and their kind—while oligarchic corruption is doing its business as usual. In western Europe, xenophobic parties form part of the governments of Denmark, Finland and Norway and are re-defining the political agenda in Austria, Belgium (Flanders in particular), the Netherlands and Switzerland. In France, the Front National has become the prime working class party. In Sweden, only half of the working class now sympathise with the labour parties, the Social Democrats and the Left party. Most notable, though, has been the election of Donald Trump, a living caricature of both the bragging US businessman and the bigoted, provincial White American. His rise is due to the appeal of his nationalist phobias, in the same way that the campaign for Britain to leave the EU became a major force thanks to anti-immigration opinion.

Mass jingoism and hatred of the unfamiliar do not just sprout from evil minds—although the latter may safely be assumed to exist. They have their social reasons. Obviously, there is the challenge of vast flows of refugees to Europe. This is largely if not exclusively the result of destruction across a vast area—from north-western Pakistan and Afghanistan to Libya—by United States and allied invasions and bombardments. The stream of refugees is not accepted into the United States; nor by its admirers in Eastern Europe; and only a few are allowed into the United Kingdom and France, its closest allies. The brunt has had to be borne by less warring countries of the western sub-continent.

However, more interesting from the perspective of the authors of this book is that racism, xenophobia and Islamophobia often function as what late-nineteenth century Marxists, referring to popular anti-Semitism in Tsarist Russia, called a "socialism of idiots": an expression of anger at exploitation and exclusion that is diverted—with the help of evil masterminds—into fear and hatred of another exploited or vulnerable group. There is no doubt that a great deal of the popular anger at the 2008 financial crisis and its consequences has been successfully re-directed against immigrants. It is for this reason that many American working class Whites support a ruthless, narcissistic billionaire.

Frustration that is diverted into scapegoating feeds on the abandonment of the populace by Social Democratic and Liberal elites. When this is not blatantly the case, however, bigotry meets its limits. Consider the May 2016 mayoral election in London, where a Conservative barrage of Islamophobic innuendos and anti-Semitism-smearing fell flat against the Labour candidate Sadiq Khan.

The surge of chauvinism and xenophobia is only part of the story of recent social and political developments, albeit a major part. In point of fact, the political landscape of the North Atlantic area has shown a remarkable overall stability, though with some shifts inside the establishment. The only country where it has radically changed is Greece. Under German orchestration, the whole Eurozone apparatus and, more reluctantly for once, the IMF were mobilised to castrate it. By contrast, in Iceland the governing cartel was ousted, but only temporarily, returning to office in time to face the revelations of the Panama Papers. Similarly, although the Spanish and the Italian establishments have been shaken up, the Spanish protest movement-cum-party, Podemos, has so far been largely neutralised by national issues in increasingly multi-national Spain; while the real social meaning of the Italian Five Stars movement-cum-party remains to be revealed.

As a direct effect of the crisis, some hot new blood has been pumped into the establishment. Jeremy Corbyn's election to the Labour leadership and the large rallies of Bernie Sanders's campaign in the Democratic primaries were very impressive mobilisations, against all (smug Liberal) odds. At the same time, the Portuguese elite has had to accommodate a leftward move, with its Socialist government forming a pact of support with the Communist party.

Nevertheless, the 2008 financial crisis did not have the effects that great optimists like Manuel Castells and Paul Mason imagined. However, beneath the layers of institutions with their inherent inertia, and beyond electoral mobilisations and their ephemerality, there exists another layer of social change: that of *generational experience*.

Generational experience deserves its own recognition and respect; and this book is *de facto* about this layer. Moreover, it is my duty, as an old scholar, to place this particular layer in its broad context. Firstly, as an old '68-er, I learned the hard way. Our political movements were all defeated, some deservedly so. Yet, in retrospect, "1968" appears to be a cultural watershed in western Europe-North America, with major, enduring effects on gender and generational relations and on social hierarchies in general.

Whether 2008 will have a similar impact remains to be seen. But what is important is that the critical perspectives on society and the protest movements reported in this book constitute defining generational experiences of young people, born in the late twentieth century and growing up with the crisis. Allegiances and identities can change over time, but youthful experiences tend to set their life-marks. Even without victories in the short run, the 2008 crisis has produced a new generation of critical thinkers and practitioners, who refuse to take the existing world for granted. That is a significant contribution to future social change.

Social and political commitment should be seen and reflected upon as a learning experience. Thinking about post-2008, what lessons are there? Very tentatively, I would suggest a few.

First of all, social change is best viewed as layers of non-synchronised processes. How many layers we should distinguish depends on the purpose of our analysis and is not fixable *a priori.* But important ones do include governmental, politico-social and cultural change. Because of this complexity and the ever-present contingency of social events, social change—in the midst of struggles—is rarely straightforward. Rather, it is usually labyrinthine.

Second, trans-border migration is unquestionably a major phenomenon of our time; and through xenophobia it is adding a new dimension to politics. However, such intolerance cannot be defeated simply by levelling charges of "racism" or "fascism". The associated fears and frustrations of ordinary people must be recognised and addressed, by developing and showing means to tackle them, other than bashing foreigners, and by demonstrating the hypocrisy and hollowness of the programmes of the xenophobic ideologues.

Third, while a protest movement might sometimes manage to stop a specific, tangible measure, such as the construction of a motorway, movements aiming at social change must develop a political form. Post-2008 has seen several successful examples of this: Syriza in Greece, *Cinque Stelle* (Five Stars) in Italy and *Podemos* in Spain. Crucial to their success seems to have been two factors, both of which operate on a fertile ground of official corruption, as well as anti-popular and ineffective crisis management. In tension with each other, they have been, first, a *charismatic, telegenic leader* and, second, *direct participatory democracy.* The former does not fit very well with an anarchistic movementalist ideology and self-perception. Yet, for the crystallisation of heterogeneous mass protests into a forceful politico-social movement, the respective roles of Alexis Tsipras, Beppe Grillo and Pablo Iglesias seem to have been decisive. The second component of success is that the political formation preserved its movement's participative character—primarily by online voting—and did not try to revive the well-structured hierarchy of the classical labour parties. This can be compared to the flop of a more traditional attempt at a new left alternative, the French *Parti de Gauche*.

A fourth lesson is that when you achieve some substantial political weight, you have to study your hostile context very carefully, always thinking "if we do this, what will others do, and how can we respond to that?" Hence, although the defeat of the Syriza government in Greece might have been unavoidable, its last referendum-cum-surrender should nevertheless serve as a textbook example of the disastrous effects of neglecting strategic thinking.

What lessons on social change, then, will our authors offer, informed by their experiences as young people growing up during the crisis of 2008? As our new generation of critical thinkers and practitioners, what will be their contribution to future social change?

Cambridge, UK Göran Therborn

Contents

Notes on Contributors

Benjamin Anderson is a PhD candidate in the School of Communication at Simon Fraser University where his research involves new subjectivities of work and counter-hegemonic social movements. He earned his MA at Johns Hopkins University where he researched rhetoric and speech in the American labour and socialist movements of the early twentieth century. In addition to research and teaching, he serves as a research assistant in the Centre for Policy Research on Science and Technology. He lives and works in Vancouver, BC, in the unceded territories of the Coast Salish people.

Mike Finn is Deputy Head of the School for Cross-Faculty Studies, Liberal Arts Division at the University of Warwick. Born in Liverpool, he was educated there and at Exeter College, Oxford, Magdalene College, Cambridge and Harvard University, where he was a Kennedy Scholar. A former Bye-Fellow of Magdalene College, Cambridge, and Research Fellow of Lady Margaret Hall, Oxford, he was the recipient of the 2001 Palgrave/*Times Higher Education* Humanities and Social Sciences Writing Prize. His publications include *The Coalition Effect, 2010–2015* (edited with Sir Anthony Seldon, Cambridge University Press, 2015) and *The Gove Legacy: Education in Britain After the Coalition* (edited, Palgrave, 2015).

Torsten Geelan is a Lecturer at the University of Leicester. He holds a PhD and MPhil in Sociology from the University of Cambridge and a Bachelor's degree in Economics and Social Science from the University of Manchester. He is the co-founder and co-chair of a new five-year research network (2018–2022) on

Alternatives to Capitalism at the Society for the Advancement of Socio-Economics (SASE). His doctoral research focused on extending our understanding of how trade unions exercise power by including mass communication—thereby bridging the field of industrial relations with the sociology of media and social movement studies. His research on trade unions, the media and precarious employment has been published in *Transfer: European Review of Labour and Research*, *Industrial Relations Journal* and *Danish Sociology*.

Marcos González Hernando is Affiliated Researcher at the University of Cambridge and Principal Researcher at FEPS-Think tank for Action on Social Change (TASC). He is interested in the sociology of elites, knowledge and intellectuals, particularly in what concerns intellectual change and the modes of public engagement of organisations. His recently finished doctoral dissertation, supervised by Professor Patrick Baert, focused on the institutional and intellectual transformation of British think-tanks in the aftermath of the 2008 global financial crisis.

Eric R. Lybeck is a Leverhulme Early Career Fellow at the University of Exeter researching the long-term changes in university expectations in Britain since 1800. His doctoral research focused on the institutionalisation of the modern research university in Germany and the United States over a similar period, highlighting the emergence of philosophical faculties, like sociology, from pre-existing professional faculties, especially law. He has also published research in the fields of general social theory and the history of the social sciences

Charles Masquelier is Lecturer in Sociology at the University of Exeter. His research assumes an interdisciplinary outlook, crossing over the fields of social theory, political theory and political philosophy, with particular interests in critical theory, social movements, libertarian socialism and the co-operative movement. He has published articles in international journals and is the author of *Critical Theory and Libertarian Socialism* (Bloomsbury) and *Critique and Resistance in a Neoliberal Age* (Palgrave).

Andreas Mulvad is Assistant Professor at the Department of Business and Politics, Copenhagen Business School. He holds a PhD in Political Science (University of Copenhagen, 2016) and MSc degrees in Sociology (Copenhagen) and Human Geography: Society and Space (with distinction, University of Bristol). His current research examines the tension between capitalist development and democratic government in an historical-comparative perspective. He is particularly interested in contributing to the ongoing rediscovery of the radical tradition of democratic republicanism. His work has appeared in journals like *New Political Economy*, *Sociology*, *Capital & Class* and *Jacobin* Magazine.

Mike O'Donnell is Emeritus Fellow at the University of Westminster. He has taught in most sectors of education, becoming Senior Lecturer in Sociology and Education at what is now Bath Spa University in 1990. His early publications included a Sociology textbook and accompanying Reader. He has an interest in progressive and radical thought, stretching back to the anti-Vietnam war demonstrations in 1968. His publications include articles on radicalism, particularly in the United States. He has recently edited two collections of articles and papers: the four-volume Structure and Agency (Sage, 2010) and Sixties Radicalism and Social Movement Activism (Anthem, 2010). He is currently working on a book about the relationship of radicalism to liberalism in Britain and the United States and will soon publish under the name of Frank Lankaster a "social novel" set in higher education titled *Tim Connor Hits Trouble*.

Alice Pearson is a PhD candidate at the University of Cambridge. Her doctoral thesis is based on ethnographic research of undergraduate economics education. She holds an MPhil in Social Anthropology from the University of Cambridge and a BSc in Government and Economics from the London School of Economics.

Alex Simpson is Senior Lecturer in Criminology at the University of Brighton. His work focuses on the criminology of harm, issues of elite deviance, cultural marginalisation and the sociology of political economy. Alex undertook his PhD at the University of York. Supported by the ESRC, his thesis is an ethnography of the City of London that focuses on perceived deviant cultural practices of a structural elite in the context of a neoliberal economic environment. Focusing on the financial services industry, this project looks at the embedded rule systems, normative assumptions and common expectations that speak to issues of morality and financial responsibility. Key themes within this study involve aspects of the constructions of social deviance, the legitimisation of harm production and enacted cultures within a neoliberal economic environment. Prior to undertaking his PhD, Alex obtained a BA in Sociology at the University of Leicester in 2010 and then, in 2012, an MA in Globalisation and Development at the University of Warwick.

Steven Speed is a documentary photographer, writer, digital media artist, lecturer, co-founder of Salford Star and director of Mary Burns Media. His research looks at media, politics and social justice and has also just finished a chapter on the homeless crises. He has been documenting protests and campaigns for over 15 years and has had work published in the local and national press and continues to publish work on various campaigns. He works with various campaign groups, activists, community groups and unions producing and publishing content to help promote their causes.

Rune Møller Stahl is a PhD Fellow at the Department of Political Science at the University of Copenhagen. He holds a MSc in Economic History from the London School of Economics, a Cand.scient.pol in Political Science from the University of Copenhagen and a BA in History of Ideas and Sociology from Aarhus University. He has formerly worked as political advisor in the Danish Parliament. Rune's research is primarily concentrated within the fields of International Political Economy and the History of Economic Thought, with a special focus on the development of liberal economic ideology from the nineteenth century until today. His PhD project is focused on the role of the economics profession in the turn towards neoliberalism in Denmark and the United Kingdom in the period since 1970, and the interaction between development economic science and wider social and political structures.

Goran Therborn is Emeritus Professor of Sociology at the University of Cambridge. Born in 1941, he received his undergraduate education at Lund University in Sociology, Political Science and Economics and was awarded a PhD by Lund University in 1974. He was previously co-director of the Swedish Collegium for Advanced Study in Uppsala and University Professor of Sociology at Uppsala University. He has published widely on the topics of class, ideology and Marxism and is the author of many works including *Science, Class and Society* (1976), *What Does the Ruling Class Do When It Rules?* (1978), *The Ideology of Power and the Power of Ideology* (1980), *Between Sex and Power: The Family in the World* (2004), *From Marxism to Post-Marxism* (2008), The World: A Beginner's Guide (2011) and most recently *The Killing Fields of Inequality* (2013).

Rosa Vasilaki holds a PhD in Sociology from the University of Bristol and a PhD in History from the École des Hautes Études en Sciences Sociales (Paris, France). She is a research associate of the Hellenic Observatory at the London School of Economics and Political Science and a research fellow at the Hellenic Foundation for European and Foreign Policy. Rosa's current research project focuses on policing the crisis in Greece, whereas her broader research interests revolve around aspects of the crisis, such as civil unrest and riots, but also political resistance and the possibility of political change. She has previously conducted research and taught sociology at the University of Bristol and the University of the West of England as well as social history and anthropology at the University of Haifa (Israel), the University of Macedonia (Thessaloniki, Greece) and the Panteion University of Social and Political Science (Athens, Greece).

Peter William Walsh is Affiliated Researcher in the Department of Sociology, University of Cambridge. He holds a PhD, MPhil and BA from the University of Cambridge. His doctoral thesis, *The Legislature in Immigration Policy-Making*, supervised by Dr Thomas Jeffrey Miley, examines the role of the national legislature in shaping the immigration law of liberal democratic states.

Olga Zelinska is a PhD candidate in Sociology at the Graduate School for Social Research at the Institute of Philosophy and Sociology of the Polish Academy of Sciences in Warsaw. She is interested in the broad range of social problems, with special focus on Ukrainian contentious politics. She got her Master's degree in Public Policy from Central European University, Budapest, Hungary, and obtained work experience in Ukraine's non-governmental sector.

List of Figures

Introduction

Torsten Geelan, Marcos González Hernando, and Peter William Walsh

In his preface to this edited collection, Göran Therborn urges us to see social change as *layers* of processes, notably those of government, politics, and culture. To these Therborn adds a fourth, that of *generational experience*: the distinctive history shared by those who grew up within a certain period, such as the 'baby boomers' in the aftermath of World War II. For those born in the late twentieth century in Europe and North America, the 2007–08 financial crisis has been a formative life event, shaping their perspective on politics, the economy, and society. This is especially true for those young people who have been actively involved in political action that questions the status quo. The maturation of this new generation of critical thinkers and activists represents a change in the universe of political subjects, which poses a serious challenge to those regimes shaped by the conjunctures of the past (Therborn 1980, 124). Whether they will have a similar impact to those within the 1968 movement remains to be seen.

T. Geelan (✉) • M. González Hernando • P. W. Walsh
Department of Sociology, University of Cambridge, Cambridge, UK

T. Geelan et al. (eds.), *From Financial Crisis to Social Change*,
https://doi.org/10.1007/978-3-319-70600-9_1

Unlike Therborn, the editors, and indeed most of our contributing authors, are not 'old 68-ers'. We belong to Generation Y, the millennials. Born in the 1980s and 1990s, we were not around to learn first-hand just how considerable were the obstacles faced by the political movements of the 1960s. If it is the duty of Therborn and his contemporaries to elucidate the broad historical context underpinning Generation Y, what responsibility remains for us? The same, suggests Therborn, as ever. Like those who lived through 1968, we too must report the experience of our time, reflect critically upon that experience, and seek to ameliorate the iniquities to which that experience speaks. This last aim reflects a debt owed to an important legacy of Therborn's scholarship: the basic insistence that social scientists strive not only to understand society, but to *improve* it.

With that in mind, the 'diagnoses' of Therborn's preface present both an invitation and a challenge. The invitation is to take up the mantle of earlier protagonists in the struggle for social change while heeding the lessons of their endeavour so that we may avoid repeating their missteps. Given the marked sense of pessimism in Therborn's account, born of long observation and reflection, this is no small task. Yet, while Therborn's picture of the present is gloomy and his prospects for the future are hardly glowing, his narrative nonetheless betrays an underlying optimism. One is reminded of that other great Marxist, Antonio Gramsci, who wrote in a letter from prison to his brother in 1929, 'I am a pessimist because of intellect, but an optimist because of will'. Similarly, a part of Therborn's optimism is buoyed by the hope that this new generation will make a significant contribution to future social change. Therein lies the challenge.

We now turn to the defining elements in the experience of young people in the aftermath of the North Atlantic financial crisis, and how these have catalysed their engagement in politics.

The Millennials: Unemployed, Discontented, Socially Aware, and Politically Active

From 2008, workers in Europe and North America have experienced stagnant or declining wages, together with increasing levels of unemployment, underemployment, and job insecurity. Young people have been hardest hit. With many economies in recession amid a bleak global outlook, many employers have been unwilling to hire young workers, despite them being the best educated generation in history. Moreover, those fortunate enough to be employed are often on temporary contracts with slight opportunity for career advancement. Worse, governments across the political spectrum have pursued austerity and labour market policies that have seen young workers' prospects deteriorate still further. Reductions in unemployment benefits and in higher education funding have exacerbated levels of youth poverty and long-term unemployment, at a time of few job creation initiatives (for an indicative overview of these trends in Europe, see Chung et al. 2012).

In response, young people have voiced their dissatisfaction with their employment situation and with government responses to it (Campos Lima and Martin Artiles 2013). This has involved modes of political action that are both representative (e.g. voting, party activity) and extra-representational (e.g. strikes, demonstrations, boycotting). Those involved in the former use their skills and expertise to build networks and cooperate with politicians, elites, and interest groups, while those partaking in the latter engage in 'do-it-yourself' activities at the grassroots and local levels (Monticelli and Bassoli 2017, 845). Hence, the experience of millennials has two distinct yet entwined dimensions: labour market trajectory and political participation. While these two dimensions vary considerably according to geography, socio-demographic characteristics, and socio-political context, a sizeable proportion of those coming of age in this historical juncture have felt compelled, first, to think and act in ways that question the 'common sense' they have inherited, and second, to push at the boundaries of what is thought politically feasible. More specifically, this population has demanded solutions not only to youth-specific problems, but broader societal ones, too. Chief among these are the dismantling of the welfare state, rampant inequalities in income and power, the alarming rate of climate change, and the hollowing out of democracy.

In this way, our generation has stood at the forefront of the challenge to the dominant ideology of neoliberalism, which has spurred policy shifts towards the privatisation of public services; the liberalisation of trade and financial markets; the weakening of trade unions; and a prioritisation of the interests of business, finance, and white-collar professionals over blue-collar workers (Mudge 2008). In fact, a strong argument can be made that the neoliberal consensus, which has been ascendant for decades, is slowly beginning to crumble, despite its enduring support from many financial and political elites. With the rise of the Internet and social media, people have become increasingly aware of the alternative discourses of new social movements and radical left-wing political parties that have recently emerged. Within academia, the failure of most orthodox economists to predict the financial crisis has also dealt a blow to the authority of some of its greatest proponents (Lawson 2009). For the first time, TINA—the notion that 'there is no alternative' to liberal democratic capitalism as the best way for humanity to develop—has become suspect and more difficult to sustain.

The Conference Behind This Book

Against this backdrop, Torsten Geelan proposed organising a conference which sought to address the social and political reverberations of the financial crash. He was joined by 12 fellow graduate students, who were to share responsibilities as conference organisers, including his two co-editors. Following the suggestion of Eric Lybeck, author of this book's third chapter, we viewed our task as providing perspectives that were *constructive* as well as critical. This was reflected by the core theme of our conference as well as its main title: *Crisis and Social Change*. The subtitle—*Towards Alternative Horizons*—was the idea of our colleague, Kusha Sefat, which placed an emphasis on exploring alternative social imaginaries.

With the subject for our conference settled, the organising committee next resolved to make the event more than just an *academic* conference. In reviewing the scholarly and popular literature on the financial crisis, we noticed that, despite its impressive volume, richness, and diversity, the voices of non-academics—practitioners, professionals, activists, artists, and others affected by the events of 2007 and beyond—were in short supply. More particularly, such people are seldom given the opportunity to present in academic settings. This is despite an acknowledgement that their perspectives are indispensable to an understanding of the many ways in which the crisis has affected people's lives. Hence, giving non-academics the opportunity to offer their observations and insights to an interested audience became our conference's second distinctive feature. This aim, and our desire to invite constructive solutions to our social problems, was evidenced by our Call for Papers, issued on May 27 2014:

> This conference moves beyond 'crisis' as a category of diagnosis and critique to explore alternative horizons. We are motivated by the generational need to draw upon the legacies of critique, while shifting toward the production of alternative futures. From diagnosis to treatment. From deconstruction to reconstruction. From negation to vision. From crisis to progress. Such is the responsibility of our age, from which positive social change might arise.
>
> We welcome contributions from researchers, activists, artists, and professionals from across the world…

Four months later, on Friday and Saturday of the 26 and 27 September 2014, the University of Cambridge welcomed over 100 guests to its inaugural Graduate Sociology Conference. It comprised 46 presentations by delegates from over 20 countries. The debates were varied, textured, often powerful, and decidedly free of academic pretence. External speakers, many of whom travelled long distances to be with us, included Ted Benton, Donatella della Porta, John Kelly, Greg Philo, and Jane Wills. These were complemented by a number of University of Cambridge academics: Manali Desai, Lawrence King, David Lane, Jeff Miley, and Göran Therborn, who concluded our conference with his talk 'The global socio-political landscape after the North Atlantic financial crisis'.

Social Change in Theory and in Practice

After the conference, we thought to publish a selection of the best contributions as an edited volume. To help ensure that our authors had a shared set of concerns and themes, we asked them to read Erik Olin Wright's *Envisioning Real Utopias* (2010). The book provides a useful framework for exploring emancipatory alternatives to contemporary capitalism. Its central thesis is that to advance egalitarian democratic ideals it is necessary to enhance *social power* vis-à-vis economic and state power. This social form of power is rooted in the voluntary association of people in civil society, and based on their capacity to engage in collective action of various kinds. According to Wright (2010, 274–276), the greatest obstacle to deepening and extending the weight of social power is *social reproduction*: the processes that maintain the underlying structure of social relations and institutions in capitalist society, either *passively* through the mundane routines and activities of everyday life, or *actively* through an array of institutions.

More specifically, he identifies four clusters of mechanisms through which various institutions influence the actions of people, individually and collectively (Wright 2010, 278–290). *Coercion* raises the cost of collective action through the threat or imposition of punishment. This can involve either the state's regulation of associational practices such as strikes and civil disobedience, or non-state forms of repression that are endorsed or tolerated by the state, such as corporate surveillance of activists. As Wright aptly notes, however, repression sometimes fails, undermining the legitimacy of the repressors while breeding solidarity among the repressed. Furthermore, *institutional rules* make some courses of collective action more difficult to pursue than others. By way of illustration, the engagement of social movements with representative democracy through alliances with political parties compels them to play by the rules of electoral politics, which often acts to erode militancy and subdue their aim of radically transforming society and the economy.

Similarly, for Wright *ideology* and *culture* shape the subjectivities of people in ways that contribute to the sustainability of structures of power, inequality, and privilege. An example of capitalist *ideology*, which encapsulates the conscious aspects of subjectivity (e.g. beliefs, ideas, values), is the belief that competitive individualism and the market are good and preferable to collectivist solidarity and state intervention. An example of capitalist *culture*, which refers to the nonconscious aspects of subjectivity (e.g. dispositions, habits, tastes, skills), is the attitude that wealth generation and accumulation is paramount. Perhaps the most crucial aspect of these two processes, observes Wright, concerns beliefs about *what is possible*. For if people believe that there are no alternatives to make things better, and that any attempt to do so would in any case be defeated, then they will be unlikely even to try (2010, 286). Hence, the educational sector and the media are two particularly important battlegrounds for social struggles aimed at expanding people's horizons of possibility.

Finally, within a well-functioning capitalist society, the *material interests* of almost everyone depend to a significant degree on a vibrant and thriving economy, which acts as a constraint on social movements that seek to transform how the economy is organised. However, this close relationship is substantially weakened during a period of crisis, such as the one we are currently experiencing, in which large numbers of people are marginalised from the labour market and living standards are in decline. As such, people are more likely to be receptive to alternatives and willing to act to realise them.

Wright identifies three other limits to social reproduction that create spaces for transformative resistance: the complexity involved in state attempts to regulate the market, the inability of institutions to adapt to a new context, and the unpredictability of socio-economic and political changes (2010, 290–297). In so doing, he offers a rebuff to social theorists such as Foucault who offer little hope for meaningful resistance.

How, then, does social change come about? According to Wright, the large-scale social transformations that we observe throughout history are the result of two kinds of change-generating processes: cumulative unintended by-products of people operating under existing social relations, such as the decision to have fewer children, and the intended efforts of conscious projects of social change by people acting strategically to transform those social relations. This involves actors within social movements, political parties, and non-governmental organisations, in their various forms of collective action. While both processes are crucial, the focus of our contributors is the latter.

Importantly, the two transformative strategies at the heart of their accounts are what Wright terms *interstitial* and *symbiotic*. Interstitial strategies operate in the 'cracks' within the ascendant societal structure of power, in which the logic of that system is not yet fully dominant, giving actors the space to act in ways that are counter to that logic. An example of an interstitial transformative strategy is the cooperative movement, which seeks to build new forms of social empowerment in those niches within capitalist society where its logic is not yet totally stifling. By contrast, symbiotic strategies encompass attempts that *work with* existing institutional forms of social empowerment, such as representative democracy, and seek to extend and deepen them. Crucially, both of these types of strategy for major social change aim at achieving a sustained metamorphosis of existing institutions and power structures, rather than any dramatic rupture.

Having thus outlined the theoretical concerns that guide the analyses of this book, we may now summarise these contributions and explain the rationale for each of the three sections within which they fall: reclaiming universities, revitalising democracy, and recasting politics.

Outline of the Book

Section I. Reclaiming Universities

This section focuses on the university as a site that adopts and inculcates neoliberal ideas and practices, as well as provides a potential site for their resistance. On the one hand, universities are the place where a great deal of young people become politically aware and active. Indeed, university students have frequently been at the forefront of political movements that have led to important social change: most notably, the countercultural protest movements associated with 1968—anti-war marches, the sexual revolution, second-wave feminism, gay liberation, and the struggle for civil rights in the USA. This can be explained partly by the degree of freedom experienced by those attending university. Being away from home for the first time and hence largely free of parental control, while not yet being constrained by the necessity to put food on the table, students thereby enjoy greater opportunities to think, share ideas, and invest their energy and idealism into contesting, and perhaps thereafter reshaping, societal institutions. That the number of university students continues to increase due to the global expansion of higher education suggests that their potential political clout will only continue to grow.

On the other hand, universities have been subject to neoliberal policies. In the UK, this has involved cuts to funding which have forced universities to introduce student fees and compete to maximise enrolment. Moreover, government funding is now allocated according to crude indices of rank and productivity (Sayer 2014); teaching is measured by student satisfaction and employability and research by funding, 'impact', and commercial potential. Put simply, this marketisation of higher education acts as a constraint on the inclination and ability of young people to get involved in political action by burdening them with debt and emphasising employability as the main purpose of education rather than the furthering of human knowledge and the cultivation of critically minded citizens able to participate effectively in the steering of the democratic polity. Moreover, the syllabuses of the most prestigious economics departments, which produce many of society's business elites, are instilling a neoliberal predisposition by giving a substantially disproportionate emphasis on mainstream neoclassical economics at the expense of more critical approaches such as political economy and Keynesian, Institutionalist, and green economics. Thus, we suggest, it is necessary for students, activists, and academics to *reclaim* the way universities currently function.

This first section begins with Mike Finn's contribution, which unveils how the notion of a 'crisis' within higher education has been deployed in UK political discourse to gradually privatise the academic profession. Only by placing this process of marketisation in an historical perspective, he argues, can we effectively critique and challenge this neoliberal agenda. In a similar vein, Eric Lybek points to another long-standing and worrying trend within Western universities: the prioritisation of the research function over its traditional teaching function. Moreover, the contribution shows that alternative visions of higher education face serious obstacles, evident in Lybeck's unsuccessful attempt to become Graduate Union President at the University of Cambridge on a platform to (re)introduce the model of the scholastic guild prevalent centuries ago. Finally, Alice Pearson highlights the importance of broader student mobilisations aimed at reforming the economics curricula by offering compelling ethnographic insight into the struggle at an elite British economics department. The danger, she argues, is that students may reinforce the very thing they are trying to dismantle—the dominant approach to the study and practice of economics—by using the language of free markets and consumer choice.

Section II. Revitalising Democracy

This section focuses on social movements: groups of closely or diffusely organised people striving towards a common goal requiring some form of social change. As touched on earlier, there is a strong synergistic relationship between universities and social movements, with the former providing a fertile source of participants for the latter. After 2008, new youth-driven social movements have emerged around the world such as Occupy, Los Indignados, and 15M to name merely the best-known. Their principal aim has been twofold: to highlight and critique the stark levels of high and rising income inequality observable across all advanced economies and to reveal the limitations of our representative democracies, which have become captive to corporate interests, hence all too often failing to respond to popular opinion. Their response to this situation has been to adopt and promote participatory democratic practices that encourage engagement in the political process through such means as direct action, occupying public space, and the creation of people's assemblies as alternative decision-making forums. In doing so, these self-organised movements are envisioning and prefiguring a more democratic future. These collective efforts to revitalise democracy, however, face considerable barriers in the form of state repression and co-optation.

Section two begins with Olga Zelinska's novel perspective on the Maidan movement in Ukraine which involved as many as a million protestors in near daily demonstrations. Focusing on the deliberations of local people's assemblies that emerged across all the regions of the country as part of this uprising, Zelinska demonstrates the role of utopian thinking in efforts to supplement and supplant existing democratic institutions. Next, Steven Speed offers a riveting account of how a local protest movement in England halted the drilling of a fracking well in Barton Moss, despite mounting government and corporate pressure. Particular attention is devoted to the innovative tactics used by protestors to neutralise the impact of political policing—most notably 'slow walking'. Benjamin Anderson concludes the section by examining how *Adbusters*, the Canadian magazine of alternative culture, inspired the initial occupation of Wall Street and why, when they attempted four years later to recreate this past success, they failed to catalyse a similar movement. As an explanation, the chapter points to the severe limits of individualised and mediated protest. Moreover, it reminds us that while alternative media can help cultivate the radical imagination, the agency of what is mediated is derived from the creative actions of social movements 'on the ground'.

Section III. Recasting Politics

In this final section we focus on the work of critical social theorists. Out of the mass mobilisations organised by new social movements, new left-wing political parties have also emerged and successfully entered the political arena, most notably, Syriza in Greece, Podemos in Spain, and Jeremy Corbyn's Labour Party in the UK. This transition from extra-parliamentary to parliamentary politics involves numerous age-old dilemmas and challenges: the need for a coherent political vision that appeals to a mass public; the tension between horizontally oriented grass-roots activists and representational democracy; and the difficulty of implementing policies aimed at the transformation of the economy and state institutions. What is needed, then, are grounded theoretical reflections that can help guide movements through the process of developing a political form that can force contemporary capitalism towards a more progressive development or lay the foundations for an alternative system altogether. Historically, public intellectuals have fulfilled this role, and it is therefore to them that we now turn to recast politics and breathe new life into the ideas and practices of radicalism, populism, and socialism.

The final section begins with Mike O'Donnell's discussion of the work of C. Wright Mills and Herbert Marcuse in relation to the populist aspects of the 1960s' radical activism. Through a historical comparison with the Occupy movement, he argues that both share a broadly populist character, with each movement's limited impact due partly to an inadequate appreciation of the importance of accessing state power. Indeed, by engaging in a dialogue with Marx, Rune Møller Stahl and Andreas Mulvad help us rediscover parliamentary democracy's radical roots, thereby contesting the myth that it is intrinsically bourgeois. Turning to the case of Greece, Rosa Vasilaki examines the vibrant political activism against austerity and the rise to power of Syriza. She concludes that Syriza's experience in government demonstrates why 'un-systemic' thinking that challenges power itself, once power is seized, is essential for future social struggles. Finally, Charles Masquelier shows how the libertarian-socialist vision of G. D. H. Cole could help renew the socialist imagination, and argues that the expansion of the cooperative sector in the digital age may be paving the way for the large-scale institutionalisation of an alternative economic system.

* * *

But first, in order to set the stage for what follows, we begin with Alex Simpson's journey through the rabbit hole of financial capitalism in the City of London, whose reckless and unregulated speculation contributed to the financial crash. Simpson shows how financial elites interact with the City's topographical, technological, and social environment to actively (re)produce a dominant cultural system of competitive market behaviour.

Works Cited

Campos Lima, Maria da Paz, and António Martin Artiles. 2013. Youth voice(s) in EU countries and social movements in Southern Europe. *Transfer: European Review of Labour and Research* 19 (3): 345–363.

Chung, Heejung, Sonja Bekker, and Hester Houwing. 2012. Young people and the post-recession labour market in the context of Europe 2020. *Transfer: European Review of Labour and Research* 18 (3): 301–317.

Lawson, Tony. 2009. The current economic crisis: Its nature and the course of academic economics. *Cambridge Journal of Economics* 33 (4): 759–777.

Monticelli, Lara, and Matteo Bassoli. 2017. Precarious voices? Types of "political citizens" and repertoires of action among European youth. *Partecipazione e Conflitto* 9 (3): 824–856.

Mudge, Stephanie. 2008. What is neo-liberalism? *Socio-Economic Review* 6 (4): 703–731.

Sayer, Derek. 2014. *Rank hypocrisies: The insult of the REF*. London: SAGE.

Therborn, Goran. 1980. *The ideology of power and the power of ideology*. London: Verso.

Wright, Erik Olin. 2010. *Envisioning real utopias*. London: Verso.

Consecrating the Elite: Culturally Embedding the Financial Market in the City of London

Alex Simpson

To climb the stairs out of Bank tube station is to enter an elite space of financial activity: the City of London. The broader capital's artful vibrancy seems instantly left behind, replaced by a world of suited finance workers, brinkmanship, and a dominant landscape of market wealth. Opposite the exit to the tube station stands the neo-classical grandeur of the 1930s reconstruction of the Bank of England Building, as well as the sixteenth century Royal Exchange, the historic commercial centre of the City of London and now an exclusive shopping arcade. Up above, the ever-expanding wealth of the City is present both physically and symbolically in the burgeoning towers that stand tall, blocking sky. These constructions, such as Norman Foster's 'Gherkin' and Renzo Piano's 'Shard', serve to maintain the City's prominence and, in the case of the latter, mark the City's expansion beyond its traditional geographical boundary. This is a space of enormous wealth, its power *rooted* for all to see. Towering financial institutions. Tailored suits. Exclusive restaurants. Historical landmarks. This is a space which is made by, and operates for, the procurement of money.

A. Simpson (✉)
University of Brighton, Brighton, UK

T. Geelan et al. (eds.), *From Financial Crisis to Social Change*,
https://doi.org/10.1007/978-3-319-70600-9_2

Against a backdrop of increasing market abstraction and internationalisation in capital flows, the City represents an impressive, yet still human-scale and bounded setting in which the global financial system is rooted and enacted (Cetina and Bruegger 2002; MacKenzie 2009). Within this arena of competition and exchange, the abstractions of the market system become reduced, in a solid, tangible sense, to social, physical, and material relations that are played out, in real time, within the institutions and public spaces of the City. At once, the elite dominance of the market's mechanisms, so visibly pressed onto the City's topographical landscape, becomes internalised in a system of what Bourdieu would call 'durable, transposable disposition' (1990, 53). In other words, the very material formation of the City is internalised by the individual agents acting within its parameters to form a distinct and marketable *habitus*. Focusing on the material landscape of the City, in this manner, deepens a collective understanding of the financial market as an intergenerational statement of power, wealth, and ubiquity.

What explains the enduring significance and supremacy of the City? Who are its constituent actors? What is their distinctive way of life? And what is the relation between the City and the bearers of its markets and culture?

Introduction

Crises, economic or otherwise, are the product of change. As French and Leyshon (2010) argue, they signal the demise of past unsustainable conditions—whether or not people recognise it—and the recalibration towards an equilibrium that is more profitable for society as a whole. In this manner, the 2007 financial crisis provided an opportunity to challenge the power of capital and a dominant market order. It should have been a moment in which the far-reaching programme of 'more market' was reversed. Interests, ideas, and ideologies that operated at the heart of the financial services industry had brought the global economy to the brink of collapse; it was a time to re-couple the unshackled market institutions with regulatory controls born of, and sustained by, democratic governance. However, rather than representing a catalyst for change and the re-regulation of the market's runaway influence over social life, the 2007 financial crisis has presented precisely the opposite. The dominant formation of market power continues to impose a 'taken-for-granted way of life' that exists beyond the scope of contestation or critical discussion. Eight years on and the sobering realisation is that the immediate post-crash clamour for 'change' has not spelt the end of the neoliberal maxim of 'more market'. To the contrary, the effects of the crisis—and their *causes*—continue to exert their usual impacts upon inequality and social justice.

Liberal market societies continue to be a source of crises that have defined the twentieth and early twenty-first centuries (Pauly 2011; Stiglitz 2010). Yet the hegemonic dominance of the market order continues to be represented as a 'pure and perfect order' of political and economic 'truth' (Bourdieu 2001). It is in this context that this chapter develops the picture of a dominant financial *doxa*. In short, this *doxa* represents the 'cultural unconsciousness', or what is taken for granted, within a given social context—here the financial world within the City of London. Through engrained norms, values, and the acceptance of a non-contested version of 'truth', the cultural *doxa* leads to a shared perception of a version of 'reality' (Bourdieu 1998; Chopra 2003). In presenting the market as a form of *doxa*, this chapter highlights how the dominant institutions of political economy establish and perpetuate an embedded cultural 'respect' for their inherent logic of market competition. Rather than existing within some form of 'social essence', the market is viewed as a 'coherent idea' that must be 'realised' and 'sustained' by both the state and individual citizen's practice (Foucault 2010). What emerges is a situated and relational version of reality that structures, and is structured by, the impressions on the mind, body, and material environment to [re]produce a dominating set of positive (ennobling) or negative (stigmatising) cultural practices. For Bourdieu (1984), this legitimises cultural practice and imposes the norms and realities of the financial experience. Imposing specific forms of struggle, the deep structure of the field of finance and the dominance of the financial markets represent a tacit, fundamental, and, crucially, enduring order of the social world. This is, as Swartz (1997) argues, much more powerful than the 'invisible hand' that structures action, since it speaks of power relations and the competitive struggle for scarce resources.

This Study

Drawing on a three-tiered ethnographic approach, incorporating in-depth interviews, non-participant observation, and photographic representation, this three-year study sought to access the individual experiences of City life. The principal aim was to establish an overarching picture through which it is possible to explore a culturally embedded system of situated action and meaning-making that shapes meaning, produces practice, and builds social structures. The research focused on gaining access to public sites of social interaction while purposively targeting front office economic actors, including traders, investment bankers, brokers, and sales managers. This largely exploratory research process aimed further to reveal the broad cultural assumptions and practices of a culturally elite social group. Generating an 'atmosphere of place' to frame the cultural activity within the City, the project targeted engrained social practices of day-to-day City life, linking these with the material environment.

Based on the full range of ethnographic material gathered through this study, this chapter is divided into two parts. The first presents an analysis of my detailed ethnographic field-notes, underpinned by an interpretivist philosophy, to present the topographical and material formation of the City of London. I suggest that the extraordinary wealth generated by the financial services industry is etched into the topographical landscape—a physical manifestation of market dominance. The second part draws on interview data to examine the way in which this institutional and material topography enshrines a distinct symbolic vision of success. In particular, I seek to show how competitive market actors endeavour to internalise qualities viewed as characteristic of the 'perfect market'—speed, intelligence, and discipline—in order to attune their social disposition to the field of finance, thereby reproducing the dominant perception of 'market reality'. Together, what emerges is a cultural market framework that is upheld by those who engage in its processes within the City as the dominant fulcrum not only of 'truth' but of 'virtue'.

The strategic action of the financial games at the heart of our subject is organised around the material landscape of the City of London, and played out through a competitive struggle of resistance and domination.

Here, normative predispositions and cultural inclinations impinge on the bodies and actions of individual agents, resulting in an acquired, individual disposition (Bourdieu 1973). These processes form the cultural *habitus* that leads to an 'elective affinity' between agents, enforcing and reproducing an established set of normative cultural assumptions and practices (Bourdieu 1984). Establishing a unity between the minds, bodies, and the market, in the manner of Bourdieu (1996) is established a self-defined 'intellectual nobility' and 'structural elite' that upholds the integrity of the market system through their thoughts and actions. Moreover, this union forms a 'dialectic of consecration and recognition' (Bourdieu 1977, 104) that both selects, and is selected by, a dominant social biography or individual disposition. The framework of the market, and the individual, become entwined as a cohesive whole, reproducing a durable set of expected values and demands, to engender a long-lasting socially and culturally determined collective of values, experiences, and power.

The Physical Construction of an Elite Space

The City of London refers to the historical cluster of financial services industries located within a 1.22 square mile that stretches from the Thames at Victoria Embankment, clockwise up through Fleet Street, the Barbican Centre, then to Liverpool Street in the north-east, and back down to the Tower of London (Shaxson 2011). The home of the UK's financial centre, the City is the largest concentration of banking and financial services industries in the UK (ONS 2012). Along with its tributary, Canary Wharf, the City represents one of the world's most prominent—in fact near-unrivalled—cultural and technological monuments to market ideology (Kynaston 2002). In total, it is estimated that the City of London presides over \$1.9tr foreign exchange turnover each day, a figure which accounts for 37 per cent of global capital flows (City of London 2013). As a social site, the City explicitly carries within it relations of power that establish a cultural axis of inclusion and exclusion (Abu-Lughod 1999; Sack 1993, 1999). Its material and cultural construction project only a limited welcome, equally clear to those for whom it is 'home', as for others merely passing amongst it. The very architectural formation of the City reflects a coming together of power, privilege, and wealth. Beyond this, the entire topographical landscape is rich in symbolic wealth; seen from far beyond the City, it impresses upon its beholders the ubiquity of the market and its evident mechanisms of magic and power. Filtering down to the occupants who work with the speed and the flow of the market in these spaces, they become, in Smithsimon's (2010) terms, embodied defenders of this market exclusivity.

The entire architectural and physical construction of the City is defined—or distinguished—by the collective wealth and success that the financial services industry generates. The iconic buildings of finance dominate the landscape and stand as physical manifestations of the City's position of economic power at the heart of the global marketplace, and of cultural power at the geographic centre of the capital. Beneath these imposing structures, it is hard to escape their long shadows, which loom over a tightly knitted collection of lanes and alleys, creating a sense of enclosure. The symbolic tapestry of market success, framed by these vast temples of steel and glass, provides a coherent structure of 'oneness', 'wholeness', and 'greatness' that evokes the image of the Renaissance cathedral, while serving as a very physical reminder of the non-spiritual and material power of the market. Yet they have their 'spiritual' dimension. Much like the power of the church prior to the Enlightenment, they elicit a dominant and legitimate principle of vision, constructed around a fundamental 'truth' through which an axis of unity is constructed (Bourdieu and Wacquant 1993). Though counter to the axis of the Church that asserted the 'truth' of God, the 'truth' of these structures is asserted through the market institution, in all its global unity, and the perpetual struggle for efficiency. As the material manifestation of financial market dominance, the importance of these physical constructions is a reminder that social reality exists not just within the minds of actors, but is also etched onto the material structure of society (Bourdieu 1980).

For the City workers who pass through the streets on a daily basis, the scale and grandeur of these buildings are a reminder of who delivers. The markers of wealth and power that dominate the landscape are complemented on the ground by more personal inscriptions of status, power, and belonging: the wearing of designer suits, well-pressed shirts, and slick accessories acts as a transformative rite of passage which is required to legitimately participate in the financial marketplace. Thus, the material construction of the City enshrines a dominant and legitimising system of capital, organised around projections of power, authority, and wealth.

Ideology and Culture: The Biography of Success

The rules of this game, played out over time, define how economic agents engage with multiple markets and are structured by the spatial relations and positions people and objects share in the field of finance. This intrinsic tempo of market action produces a legitimised body of knowledge that is implicitly held by all who engage it its processes—and many beyond—to be 'true' and 'right'. As the embodiment of belonging and success (not to mention the counterpoint of failure), economic actors engage in a competitive struggle for domination or recognition by reproducing and upholding the 'sanctity' of market action—which is never questioned. The market, however, serves to reduce the complexities of social life to monetary gain and, in so doing, becomes its own dispositional logic. Positioned as the dominant structure, the formation of the market removes the costs of economic action from the social consciousness of economic agents, positioning itself as a structuring moral authority. As Thomas, a former CEO, explains while speaking of his own experiences in turning a struggling bank around:

> What was happening, particularly in some of the trading environments of banks, was that the reward mechanisms got out of control. It became crazy. You had these pot-headed guys running round and they were all focused on making money because that is what their incentives were, and they lost sight of the impact of what they were doing was [...] They just got out of control [...] you had these obscene scenarios where people were trading companies, asset stripping companies, making vast amount of money along the way and saying, 'That's alright, that is what I was targeted to do, make lots of money'. But look what they did?

What Thomas describes is a situation where incentives and reward mechanisms concerned only specific targets of making money. With no consideration of the wider social and economic impact of this, the result was a loss of 'sight of the impact of what they were doing'. Within this statement is the notion of a legitimised and even incentivised myopic focus upon wealth creation. While the economy produced wealth, and shareholder value grew, the wider social impact of their actions was a mere irrelevance. Here, the formation of market action within financial life shapes the aspirations and outcomes of practice by recognising the virtues of individual greed and private accumulation.

As Thomas highlights, the logic of the market contains its own rationalising discourse that turns the market into a definitive body of knowledge. In this manner, and drawing on Sack (1999), the material and ideological phenomenon of the financial marketplace comes to impinge on social reality in a dialectic of consecration and recognition, establishing a common framework of truth that enshrines and produces its own situated version of reality: a reality of competition that demands a unified application of speed, intelligence, and discipline as agents seek to embody the very essence of financial movement.

The cultural legitimacy of financial market action that is present in the topographical landscape is reflected in the economic agents who uphold its ideology. Suits, watches, handbags, cars, and life-style choices all become a personalised display of financial, market-based exclusivity and belonging. Quentin, a metal broker in his late 20s who has worked in the City for the past five years, explains how the controlling interests of financial life play a crucial part in communicating the emblematic power and privilege of the market system:

> I know what it's like, you get caught up in it when you see the guy next to you has got a better watch than you, you need a better watch. It's all competition, everyone is competitive, you want a better car, you want to tell someone that you've just bought a Lamborghini. It's not even the fact that you like driving it, it's the fact that you want other people to know that you have it. It's like a symbolism of success [...] you're just thinking about making more money than the next guy, I want to make more money than this guy. It's all about being better, it's all about competition.

As Quentin explains, the competitive instinct of financial life becomes inscribed upon the body, in taste and a performative way of being that is played out through the conspicuous consumption of all manner of luxury goods and accessories, from bags to private schools for their children—whose worth in this world is realised from its symbolic display. The value is not inherent in the car, bag, or watch but in the mark of distinction, so that other people 'know that you have it'. This is a marker of not just wealth but market success—mastery of the game. Crucially, the symbols display an individual's position within the field of financial action, as markers of status, power, and belonging. In the way of Bourdieu (1996), the physical manifestations of wealth and status denote not just status and unity, but serve, as for Quentin, as a marker of distinction.

Embedded in the material landscape of the City of London, the financial market system exists as an instrument of both knowledge and communication that, as Bourdieu (1977) argues, produces a 'logical' and 'moral' system of action and integration. Its spatial and cultural organisation engenders social worlds that impinge on the individual's strategic interests to establish a dominant principle of vision, around which an axis of unity is constructed. In this respect, the dominant and legitimate vision—of the financial marketplace—is not just etched onto the topographical landscape but is pressed onto the bodies and lives through the minds of economic actors who engage in a competitive struggle for domination or recognition. The outcome is a unifying habitus of strategies, constraints, and opportunities by reproducing the homologous effects of the social class structure (Bourdieu 1991). It is at this level of analysis where the market of financial life enters the body and, in Bourdieu's (2011) terms, is transformed into an embodied manifestation of cultural capital. Characterised by a competitive struggle for resources, resistance, and domination, the cultural legitimation of capital establishes the set of constraints that govern the setting as well as determine the likelihood of success. Within this, the financial market does not exist as an abstract or ethereal phenomenon but is a construct that is present and brought to life through the consciousness of each individual of financial action. It is through action played out over time, as economic agents each engage with the multiple markets, that the intrinsic tempo of the market emerges as a legitimised body of knowledge and is implicitly held by all who engage it its processes to be 'true' and 'right'.

Through a collective engagement of market practice, the external position of the market as a rationalising discourse becomes more tangible, bestowing the rules of the game and establishing a ruling cultural formation. At the heart of the cultural essence of the market is the logic of competition. In an economic sense, this serves to keep prices down and, more importantly, as an incentive for efficiency since it ensures that no one actor has absolute, monopolistic power (Sloman et al. 2012). However, the performance of 'the competition' stands as an ideological construct that serves to purge the financial market of inefficiencies and to establish an inherent 'force' and 'superiority' of capital accumulation. As a 'natural' discourse, competition is an individualising force that serves to dispel the weak and the inferior while rewarding the strong through profits and continued involvement in the game. Competition also establishes a high degree of insecurity and vulnerability. Up on the eighth floor of a corporate office block on Fleet Street and speaking to me in the comfortable opulence of the conference suit, Yuri, a senior investment banker for a large American firm, outlines the situation as he sees it:

> I have been doing this [job] for fifteen years [and] while I am not unhappy with the job, I know that it doesn't feel right [...] It's a very lonely place. You're constantly on alert. It is like you are going through a jungle with like a gun in your hand, you are constantly on alert for, you know, you could get four hundred pages of information to digest incredibly quickly but there is one paragraph in there that could just kill you. And so you are constantly on alert, [thinking] am I processing enough information quickly? You are constantly concerned that about where you are weak relative to others. And then there is your day job as well, right? Am I getting enough business in? Is my business stable? Is my forward looking good? You know, what other politics is there and how is that playing out? Am I being a nice person? Have I got time to think about all these things, coping strategies? I am going to get setbacks, how am I going to deal with them? So there is that whole spectrum that I find is more of a physical drain than anything else. So when you finish you are just tired. And it's, it's not so much the work, right? It's the environment. It is an incredibly pressurised environment.

The visceral sense of loneliness and isolation within Yuri's account is born of the uniquely competitive nature of financial life. Going through 'the jungle' with a 'gun in your hand' while needing to be 'constantly on alert' for that 'one paragraph' that could 'kill you' instils the extent to which competition serves to divide as much as it can unite. Here, market life transpires as a game of self-preservation. This 'unending trial of competition', however, serves to create a 'better' and 'more efficient' system of exchange, driven by a large body of 'rational and informed' profit maximisers who implicitly adhere to the logic of the market as the principal moral authority. Those who succeed are self-enshrined as a 'separate, sacred group' that ritualises their own exclusivity and adherence to the embedded values of the market (Bourdieu 1996).

To act within the spatial framework of the City is to fine-tune its necessary skills and hone in on and control the rapid fluctuations of the market in the pursuit of profits. The very experience of financial life demands a common internalisation and embodiment of the speed and the flow of the market itself. Played out on a global scale, agents are pitted against those sitting both right next to them and their counterparts in competing organisations in the City of London, New York, and beyond. It is a Darwinian game of natural selection, survival, and economic adaptation that demands speed, intelligence, and discipline. Through this, an affinity emerges between agents, who recognise and reward their sacrificial commitment to the seemingly infinite demands of the market above the more limited demands of the body. Establishing a natural stock of 'difference' and 'superiority', those who can internalise the defining features of financial market action are the only ones that thrive. Conversely, the 'positive Malthusian check' of market competition works to quickly dispense of those who are unable to succeed within this cultural framework.

The speed of market action establishes a particular form of high-stakes individual and institutional struggle, characterised by 'ultra-high low latency engagement' with the financial markets. Each institution arms itself with the technological infrastructure that enables individual agents to react and engage—the 'ultra-high'—in the market mechanism unencumbered by frictions of time (the 'low latency'). The demand for ever greater speed comes to structure the technological and material landscape in a manner that ensures individual market actors can respond that millisecond faster than anyone else.

In the drive to accelerate critical market response, every firm is seeking to deliver data, price discovery, and trade execution at a rate faster than the next. On an individual level the demands are such that agents compete to internalise this speed through their everyday actions and engagement in the market mechanism. With a 'churn and burn' character where traders simply 'take stuff down and sell it', financial market action is experienced as a form of intuition, bringing together the institutional environment, technological landscape, and the market system. The challenge is not just limited to reacting to the market, but internalising its complexities and managing the visceral struggle of intellectual competition. Again, Yuri's earlier quote establishes a vision of intelligence that, as a system of embodied cultural capital, manifests as a weapon that is used against others for the purposes of exclusion and dominance. As Yuri later recounts:

> You will be in a room and people will be competing to talk about an even more convoluted proposition, layering on, putting on layers and layers of complexity and opening up several thought processes. Effectively it is a challenge to others in the room to keep up.

Here the challenge laid down to others is simple: win the intellectual battle for supremacy and control, thereby avoiding punishment for weakness. It is a form of 'natural selection' that rewards those who are 'intellectually endowed' and by which the weak are exploited for their inability to keep up with financial complexities. Commitment and capability become an embodied form of discipline, expressed in the acceptance of the necessary constraints and sacrifices inherent to financial life.

To reconcile the vulnerabilities, insecurities, and personal sacrifices that are the usual product of market competition, Zaloom (2006, 111) argues that economic actors employ what she terms 'discipline', which I use to build on the more conventional kind of discipline already mentioned. In its idealised form, discipline requires economic actors to acknowledge the market as the only authority; its movements represent financial truth and operate as the definitive moral authority (ibid.). Most commonly, discipline is manifested through the recurring maxim, 'your word is your bond'. With operations running back-to-back and at high speed, once a deal is made it becomes tied up into a matrix of other exchanges and market plays. Going back on your word, in this context, is to undermine the integrity of the market mechanism and to bring the whole system of exchange operations into disrepute. As a set of strategies, discipline is in part deployed to ensure that investments are managed with 'unobstructed' perception. As Robin, a senior broker on the money markets, explains:

> [There are a lot of things that you] just can't do. A lot of it is down to that old fashioned gentlemanly conduct, it fits a purpose. Your word is your bond. When you trade, close a trade, you stand by it. Rule number one [...] This is where the military thing factors in. I think the military is very closely in tune with the City because you can't muck about [...] You can't have doubt in the line, your good boys know that along the line. There are guys who get it. True to your word. There are people who get that culture [...] There is an element of discipline that is extremely important.

As Robin expresses, the highly pressurised environment of financial life ensures that failing to back your word on a trade or sale is actively weeded out. This construction of discipline is seen by Robin to uphold a 'gentlemanly' standard of conduct that rejects practices that fail to uphold the integrity of the market. Echoing Zaloom (2006), Robin outlines a set of strategies that acknowledge the market as the only authority while creating a boundary of expected behaviour. Within this, the 'doubt' that Robin mentions risks muddying projections of success or failure by introducing unpredictability unconnected to the inherent fluctuations of the market mechanism.

This sought-after system of speed and discipline comes together through the experience of the speed and the flow of the markets at a *corporeal level*, by which actors are said to 'absorb' its fluctuating movements and rapid shifts. Felt as an 'innate' response that exists within them, several participants talk of the need to back their 'gut instinct', retain 'courage in their convictions', and, most importantly, be 'pro-active' and 'think on their feet'. An inability to keep up with the pace of the market is an imperfection to be exploited. Situated within an enacted market-based reality with its constituent technological and institutional infrastructure, a distinct financial habitus—a fusing of mind and body—is shaped. As Robin illustrates:

> When you come in [to the City] you might [...] not necessarily [be] as sharp as the [next] City bloke, but when you are training as a City guy [you have] got to be sharp. You can't have people, and there are a lot of people who do, namby-pamby around and they get things wrong and it causes car crashes. It is just not good [...] In money markets, you can't have this namby-pamby attitude. People get quick at it and then you get confidence. There is a certain amount of quickness in the City, fast language and conviction. When everyone is smooth and everyone knows and they can trust each other, there are quality individuals and then you get this super-subset of individuals that are very, very sharp, very quick, honour each other with a very strong bond.

The speed of action and sharpness of thought that Robin describes serves to combine and establish close bonds of trust and unity. It is a mutually recognisable union organised around market exchange and manifested in 'confidence', 'quickness', and 'conviction'. Within this system, there is no space for pause or reflection. In the manner of Bourdieu (1977), the framework of the market is seen here to both construct and select an individualised disposition of economic life that is rewarded with a self-defined 'elite status' that serves to separate consecrated 'insiders' from 'commonplace' 'outsiders'. As Robin's statement suggests, when the speed of the market exists through the minds and bodies of economic agents in the field of finance, what emerges is a self-defined 'super-subset of individuals' who are united by their 'sharpness', 'speed', and hence collective 'honour'. Bringing together the integrity of the frictionless market experience, this 'super-subset of individuals' establishes, in the words of Bourdieu (1977, 104), a 'dialectic of consecration and recognition'. In other words, the symbolic valuation of market action consecrates those who have embodied and chosen it, in part, because it has chosen them by recognising and rewarding a particular social identity or individual disposition. Thus, the framework of the market and the individual become entwined, forming a cohesive whole, reproducing the expected values and demands of the field.

Conclusion: A Dominant 'Way of Being'

Within the boundary of the City of London, the symbolic capital of speed, intelligence, and discipline establishes a competitive arena in which economic agents engage in a struggle for distinction. In doing so, competitors contribute to the autonomy and functioning of the field by internalising the symbolic capital of the market system and reifying its product of economic capital. This requires a fundamental *doxa* to be shared by the competitors, a *doxa* that indicates a shared boundary of 'reality' within which the rules of the financial game are seen to be wholly 'true' and essentially 'right'. The financial marketplace is characterised by a spatial and symbolic topography of market prominence and success, elite institutional organisations which are the principal producers of economic and symbolic capital—bound together by the rule of profit. In short, this is a cultural frame characterised by the power and ubiquity of the market mechanism as well as the symbolic tapestry of wealth to establish a legitimising framework of market action.

Within this established field of financial action, the pressures of competitive individualism, shaped by the structural organisation of the market system, serve to dispel the weak and the inferior through the atomised struggle for survival, while rewarding the strong through profits and continued involvement in the game. Those who succeed in this game are self-enshrined as a 'separate, sacred group' that ritualise their own exclusivity and adherence to the embedded values of the market (Bourdieu 1996). As a system of embodied capital, economic agents compete and fine-tune their skills to hone in on and control the rapid fluctuations of the market in the pursuit of profits by embodying the dominant values of market action. Within this, an affinity emerges between agents who recognise and reward their 'sacrificial' commitment to the infinite demands of the markets over the more limited demands of the body. As such, there is a shared sense amongst financial agents of being connected to one another through a collective ability to 'feel the market' as a form of 'rooted essence' to engender an internalised 'way of being'.

Whereas capital, particularly cultural capital, is thought of usually in relation to socially desirable traits (such as intellectual acumen in the university setting or emotional responsiveness in the healthcare system), in the financial field, speed, discipline, and intelligence each manifest through a prism of individualist competition. In this manner, intelligence is turned into a weapon that is used to exploit other actors in the field in the pursuit of profit. Together, speed, discipline, and intelligence are a ruling and embodied system of cultural capital through which these agents of economic life internalise the speed and the flow of the market system. It is, in this manner, a competitive struggle of dominance and distinction that both focuses the mind and enters the body as a constraining set of personal dispositions.

As a social relation of power, the legitimate domination of the market order can be seen to directly impinge on these dispositions of financial life to produce a 'logical' and 'moral' social integration of an 'elite' social group who, collectively, feel the speed and the flow of the market through their everyday practices. This produces a cultural mechanism of enshrinement in which individuals 'become at one' with the market. Impacting on both the mind and the body, the participants of market life reproduce an elite subset of individuals who are marked by their adherence to economic efficiency and competition. It is in this interplay that the City forges the 'elite' biographies of its agents, through their cultural enactment of its markets.

Works Cited

Abu-Lughod, Janet. 1999. *New York, Chicago, Los Angeles: America's global cities.* Minneapolis: University of Minnesota Press.

Bourdieu, Pierre. 1973. Cultural reproduction and social reproduction. In *Knowledge, education and cultural change*, ed. Richard Brown, 71–112. London: Tavistock.

———. 1977. *Outline of a theory of practice.* Cambridge: Cambridge University Press.

———. 1980. *Questions desSociologie*. Paris: Editions de Minuit.

———. 1984. *Distinction: A social critique of the judgement of taste*. London: Routledge.

———. 1990. *The logic of practice*. Stanford: Stanford University Press.

———. 1991. Le champ littéraire. *Actes de la Recherche en Sciences Sociales* 89 (September): 4–46.

———. 1996. *The state nobility: Elite schools in the field of power*. Cambridge: Polity Press.

———. 1998. The essence of neoliberalism. [Online]. *Le Monde Diplomatique [English Edition]*, December. http://mondediplo.com/1998/12/08bourdieu. Accessed 10 Aug 2015.

———. 2001. *Firing back: Against the tyranny of the market*. London: The New Press.

———. 2011. The forms of capital. In *Cultural theory: An introduction*, ed. Imre Szeman and Timothy Kaposy, 81–93. Chichester: Wiley-Blackwell.

Bourdieu, Pierre, and Loic Wacquant. 1993. From ruling class to field power: An interview with Pierre Bourdieu on La noblesse d'Etat. *Theory, Culture and Society* 10 (3): 19–44.

Cetina, Karin, and Urs Bruegger. 2002. Global microstructures: The virtual societies of financial markets. *American Journal of Sociology* 107 (4): 905–950.

Chopra, Rohit. 2003. Neoliberalism as doxa: Bourdieu's theory of the state and the contemporary Indian discourse on globalisation and liberalisation. *Cultural Studies* 17 (3/4): 419–444.

City of London. 2013. *Key Facts*. http://www.cityoflondon.gov.uk/about-the-city/who-we-are/Pages/key-facts.aspx. Accessed 25 Sept 2013.

Foucault, Michel. 2010. *The birth of biopolitics: Lectures at the College de France, 1978–79*. Basingstoke: Palgrave Macmillan.

French, Shaun, and Andrew Leyshon. 2010. 'These f@#king guys': The terrible waste of a good crisis. *Environment and Planning* 42 (11): 2549–2559.

Kynaston, David. 2002. *The City of London volume IV: A club no more 1945–2000*. London: Pimlico.

MacKenzie, Donald. 2009. *Material markets: How economic agents are constructed*. Oxford: Oxford University Press.

ONS. 2012. *Business register and employment survey*. London: Office for National Statistics.

Pauly, Louis. 2011. The political economy of the financial crisis. In *Global political economy*, ed. John Ravenhill, 215–272. Oxford: Oxford University Press.

Sack, Robert. 1993. The power of place and space. *Geographical Review* 83 (3): 326–329.

———. 1999. A sketch of a geographic theory of morality. *Annals of the Associations of American Geographers* 89 (1): 26–44.
Shaxson, Nicholas. 2011. *Treasure islands: Tax havens and the men who stole the world*. London: Vintage Books.
Sloman, John, Alsion Wride, and Dean Garratt. 2012. *Economics*. 8th ed. Harlow: Pearson Education Limited.
Smithsimon, Gregory. 2010. Inside the empire: Ethnography of a global citadel in New York. *Urban Studies* 47 (4): 699–724.
Stiglitz, Joseph. 2010. *Freefall: Free markets and the sinking of the global economy*. London: Penguin Books.
Swartz, David. 1997. *Culture and power: The sociology of Pierre Bourdieu*. Chicago: University of Chicago Press.
Zaloom, Caitlin. 2006. *Out of the pits: Traders and technology from Chicago to London*. Chicago: University of Chicago Press.

Section I

Reclaiming Universities

The Never-Ending Crisis in British Higher Education

Mike Finn

Deconstructing 'Crisis'

The relationship of higher education to crisis is, in the United Kingdom at least, an intimate one. Most recently, the 'crisis in the university'[1]—this time relating to funding—originated from a more existential crisis of Western society, namely the North Atlantic financial crisis which began in 2008. But 'crisis' has a long history as a 'frame' in the discursive politics of British higher education, which at least in part owes something to the peculiarities of post-war British history. The crises of British higher education have varied over time, ranging from a self-declared crisis of moral mission in the immediate post-war era (espoused by figures as diverse as Sir Walter Moberly, T. S. Eliot and Lionel Robbins) (Mullins and Jacobs 2006; Robbins 1966) to a crisis of scientific manpower—most notably evinced in the 1946 Barlow Report (Committee on Scientific Manpower 1946)—to a crisis of places amid rising 'social demand' in the later 1950s

M. Finn (✉)
University of Exeter, Exeter, UK

T. Geelan et al. (eds.), *From Financial Crisis to Social Change*,
https://doi.org/10.1007/978-3-319-70600-9_3

and 1960s, to (continual) crises of funding up to the present (Hillman 2013; Shattock 1994, 2012). There have been many more besides.

The impact of the financial crisis highlights the dynamic remaking of British higher education which is taking place at the time of writing (Finn 2015; McGettigan 2013). As with other Western nations, government orthodoxy in response to the tumultuous events of 2008 was to implement fiscal retrenchment and more-or-less severe expenditure cuts, often characterised as 'austerity' (Blyth 2013; Krugman 2015; Seymour 2014). In the United Kingdom, these took hold most significantly with the arrival of the Conservative-Liberal Democrat coalition government in May 2010, which packaged these measures under the label of 'austerity' (Chivers and Johnson 2015). Prior to the arrival of the Coalition, in late 2009, the previous Labour government under Prime Minister Gordon Brown referred the question of how to fund British higher education (more precisely, higher education in England, Wales and Northern Ireland—Scotland, with its devolved SNP government, eschewed these arrangements) to an independent review led by former BP chief executive Lord Browne of Madingley (Brown 2015). This was the culmination of a series of changes in funding higher education which had begun with the Blair government's reintroduction of student payment of tuition fees in 1998, and in clear continuity with the increased marketisation of British higher education since the Thatcher era. But there was also a particular moment of 'crisis', as Browne noted:

> Public spending constraints in the wake of the economic crisis have also sparked public debate about private contributions to higher education. Finland, Sweden and Denmark have adopted the international trend and recently introduced tuition fees for some programmes. Many countries have seized the opportunity to accelerate other reform policies to improve the capability of their higher education systems to compete internationally. (Browne Review 2010, 17 cited in Brown and Carasso 2013, 4)

Such 'moments of crisis', Stephen Ball argues, allow particular 'intellectuals' the scope to 'play a key role in discursive struggles' (Ball 2013, 7). By intellectuals, Ball means 'policy intellectuals', a group 'privileged' within a particular 'regime of truth', imbued with oracle-like qualities to pronounce on what is 'necessary'. By this reading, Browne—neither an academic nor a politician, but a businessman—is one such intellectual, privileged within a regime of truth that espouses markets first, last and always as the not merely desirable but *necessary* means of delivering policy outcomes. The centrality of 'market fundamentalism' (Stiglitz 2009) to the political economy of the British state following the election of Margaret Thatcher's first government in 1979 has consistently privileged those with private sector business backgrounds (invariably regarded as 'efficient' and superior) to those with supposed 'producer interest' public sector backgrounds (regarded as self-serving and inefficient) in public policy discourse (Raven 1989). The vernacular, 'commonsensical', economics of the New Right, which valorises the consumer and appeals to 'rational', individual self-interest as the ordering principle of the economy, has therefore reoriented higher education away from the 'public university' model in favour of prioritising accreditation for employment and the pursuit of economic growth. This latest 'crisis', which will be discussed in greater detail later, represents (for critics of 'neoliberalism') the culmination of three decades of rightward drift in public policy, both in higher education and beyond.

In this chapter, I wish to propose a somewhat different reading of the contemporary higher education situation, one grounded in an historical perspective. It is different not in that it disagrees substantively with the arguments made by critics of neoliberalism and scholars such as Brown, McGettigan, Ball, and Collini (Collini 2017), but that it seeks to augment them. In short, the story of marketisation since the 1980s, ably told by Brown, is not the full story. Nor is 'neoliberalism', too often deployed as a catch-all which fails to adequately appreciate the national context. On this point, the deterritorialisation implied by analyses of political economy and public policy focusing on neoliberalism has several aspects to it; one is a simple recognition of neoliberals' conviction that as an economic gospel theirs is a universal one, which in an era of globalisation will work well in all places. It is for this reason that scholars—including eminent critics of neoliberalism such as Joseph Stiglitz and David Harvey—frequently group figures such as Ronald Reagan and Margaret Thatcher together, implying that events in the United States, Britain and elsewhere were fundamentally anchored in the same processes (Harvey 2005, 39; Stiglitz 2009, 346). By extension, there is a generalised belief (though not shared by serious analysts of UK university reform, such as Brown and McGettigan) that Britain is moving—in many areas of policy—towards a 'US', 'market' model (Shepherd 2010).

As a scholar first trained in the historical disciplines, with a strong empiricist bent, it is perhaps unsurprising that I should dissent—at least a little—from such an overarching grand narrative and instead offer some special pleading for the vicissitudes of policy development in one particular island. However, it is not only historians who have grown dissatisfied with the all-too-inclusive narratives of neoliberalism, and globalisation, on offer. The political economist Craig Berry recently noted that:

> The globalisation concept can be deemed to have given rise to a relatively distinct and novel 'globalisation discourse' in British politics, defined in a broad sense as political dialogue concerning the nature and effects of globalisation, and including within it appeals to a process of globalisation by political actors as the context of – and rationale for – their actions and decisions. (Berry 2011, 1)

Berry is right. British discourses of globalisation, and its attendant vocabulary (including the meanings associated with terms such as the 'knowledge economy'), are 'distinct and novel'. They are imbued with dissimilar meanings to such discourses in the United States or continental Europe, even as they use the same language. These are anchored in the British historical experience, in particular, the experience of post-war Britain, which was intimately connected to developments elsewhere in the world but which was also constructed domestically in terms of its relationship to the rest of the world from a vantage point (imperial decline) and with an 'empiricist idiom' specific to itself (Edgerton 2006, 11, 226). It is important, as both scholars and activists, to understand more clearly the specifics of the British situation.

In the spirit of this volume's focus on moving towards alternative horizons, this chapter seeks to perform three main tasks as part of its contribution. Firstly, it aims to offer a new perspective on British higher education, through grounding contemporary critique in a theoretically informed analysis of the post-war period, allowing for a richer interpretation of the present crisis. Secondly, it seeks to make a small contribution to the development of scholarship on neoliberalism, not by rejecting a concept which has huge explanatory value, but by augmenting it through the case study of one area of public policy in one nation-state. Finally, it aspires to show how by engaging with historical analyses of policy development it is possible for the activist to both avoid the rhetorical traps of 'golden ageism' and effectively construct alternatives for the future. In terms of method, it seeks to highlight several ostensible (and rhetorical) moments of 'crisis' in the discursive politics of higher education. It is not possible (nor is it desirable) in this essay to write a history of higher education in post-war Britain. Histories are available elsewhere (Shattock 2012; Tight 2009). Instead, the aim is to use the lens of crisis to tease out the continuities and the changes within British higher education which will both enable us to see the context of contemporary debates over British higher education more clearly, and in a small way gain a more nuanced perspective on the political economy of the British state more generally. Only once we have grasped the historical complexities which situate our present crisis, can we hope to move beyond it.

Crises Past

The Second World War concluded with British higher education ostensibly in crisis, both imagined and real. The war years had impacted significantly on the universities, both in terms of physical damage to their buildings and facilities and the departure of many of their staff and students for service in the government apparatus and the military machine. In terms of the purpose of the university, there were at least two discursively constructed 'crises' taking place simultaneously; for some academics, chief among them the chairman of the University Grants Committee, Sir Walter Moberly, the crisis lay in the appropriate role of the university in a society embattled by totalitarianism and the atom bomb. Moberly, a devout Christian, penned a polemic in 1949 whilst still serving on the UGC, entitled *The Crisis in the University*. For Moberly, the war demonstrated both the devastating power of modern science represented by the development of atomic weaponry and strategic bombing, and the evil of totalitarian ideology in the form of fascism (Moberly 1949, 15–29).

Moberly's argument stressed the role of the university in promoting an appropriate ethical response on the part of British society, arguing that the Western university tradition had been threatened by the culpability of the German universities in both the rise and sustenance of the Nazi regime. 'The old gods [have been] dethroned' thundered Moberly, arguing that moral relativism in universities, fostered in great part by the specialisation and technocratic nature of undergraduate education, led to otherwise intelligent minds embracing the abomination of totalitarianism (Moberly 1949, 16). Moberly's was a particular, Christian, standpoint. But it was echoed by the socialist principal of the University College of North Staffordshire, later known as Keele University, A. D. Lindsay (Mountford 1972). Lindsay—with allies including R. H. Tawney—helped push through the proposal for Britain's first post-war university foundation through the UGC with Moberly as chair (Mountford 1972). Lindsay had served on an Allied-sponsored commission for the reconstruction of German universities, and had been horrified at some of the attitudes he encountered in discussions with German academics (Phillips 1980, 97).

The spectre of the bomb and the legacy of war fascinated academics searching for a curriculum for the university in post-war society. Lionel Robbins, the most prominent spokesperson for British higher education following the publication of his famous Report in 1963 (Committee on Higher Education 1963), consistently emphasised the need to educate students for 'a free society'. At a conference in Göttingen in 1964 (a year after the publication of his famous report), he stated that:

> As university teachers, we are naturally expected to provide acquaintance with particular branches of knowledge and training in the exercise of various intellectual skills. But we are expected to do more than that…to cultivate intellectual and moral habits suitable for adult membership of a civilized society. It is this last duty which raises problems…We are the universities of free societies; and nothing could be more alien to the spirit of such societies than that we should again become the instruments for the inculcation of particular dogmas or creeds. (Robbins 1966, 14)

In expressing such sentiments, Robbins echoed Moberly's views of 15 years earlier; it was such thinking which at least in part animated discussions about university residence in the 1950s and which influenced the development of the new universities in the later 1950s and the course of the 1960s. The obsession with Oxbridge and the benchmarking of all subsequent 'ideas of the university' against the two ancient English universities have obscured the significance of the post-war moment, a time when Britain began the journey to mass higher education and did so against a background of a particularly vital academic debate about the role of the university in society. On curricula, Robbins' views were clear:

> There is one creed the free society cannot repudiate without decreeing its own abdication – the creed of freedom itself. And this I submit is the answer to our problem [...] We must emphasize the common element in civilizations, rather than the minor variations. We must teach at all times the impersonality of knowledge and the transcendence of values. We must dwell always on the universal element in the human spirit. Above all, we should set our forces against the intrusion into science and learning of the anti-social forces of nationalism. Under the influence of *a misguided historicism*, our universities have not been guiltless of fostering such fissiparous tendencies. We need – Britons, Frenchmen, Germans, all of us – to return to the outlook and values of the *Aufklarungzeit*, to that Enlightenment which stressed the unity of humanity, rather than its differences. (Robbins 1966, 14, 16)

How to do this—how to develop a form of higher education aimed at fostering active citizenship and emphasising a common humanity—had been a central concern of those academics involved in the development of new university foundations in the course of the 1950s and 1960s. They were, as John Fulton later noted (1964, 11–12), indebted to A. D. Lindsay's experience at Keele in the 1940s, and there was a continuity in attempts to develop 'education for a free society' by 'drawing a new map of learning' (Briggs 1964).

At this point, academics were still able to translate such 'experiments' into institutional form; higher education was still an elite system, and academics were the key policymakers within the higher education framework, staffing as they did both the universities themselves and the Treasury committee committed to funding them. But the second crisis in the university at war's end reflected a transition taking place which would marginalise them. In 1946, the previously mentioned Barlow Committee on *Scientific Manpower* reported. Against a background of wartime advances in science and a belief that Britain lacked the resources of other major powers, it adopted a vernacular form of human capital theory in addressing the nation's problems:

> We do not think that it is necessary to preface our report by stating at length the case for developing our scientific resources. Never before has the importance of science been more widely recognised or so many hopes of future progress and welfare founded upon the scientist. By way of introduction, therefore, we confine ourselves to pointing out that least of all nations can Great Britain afford to neglect whatever benefits the scientists can confer upon her. If we are to maintain our position in the world and restore and improve our standard of living, we have no alternative but to strive for that scientific achievement without which our trade will wither, our Colonial Empire will remain undeveloped and our lives and freedom will be at the mercy of a potential aggressor. (Committee on Scientific Manpower 1946, 3)

Geopolitical power projection—what David Edgerton has described as the maintenance of a 'sharply differentiated third place' in world affairs—still animated the British state, and these concerns were at the heart of government thinking on the universities (Edgerton 2006, 1). The Barlow Report called for the doubling of graduates in science within ten years, and the foundation of a new university (which became Keele). Though the crisis in scientific manpower was a post-war issue, it did not abate, instead becoming a permanent crisis—or insecurity—about the adequacy of British human capital. In the mid-1950s, the debacle at Suez and the *Sputnik* crisis both played their part in British self-examination on the subject of scientific and technological education. The White Paper *Technical Education* was published by the Ministry of Education in the same year as the Suez Crisis, and the paper was (again) uncompromising in its views of Britain's needs:

> From the U.S.A., Russia and Western Europe comes the challenge to look to our system of technical education to see whether it bears comparison with what is being done abroad…it is clear enough that all these countries

> are making an immense effort to train more scientific and technical manpower and that we are in danger of being left behind. (Ministry of Education 1956, 4)

This White Paper made provision for Colleges of Advanced Technology under the stewardship of the Ministry of Education, separated from the universities and more amenable to government direction, awarding the 'degree equivalent' qualification of the Diploma of Technology. The Robbins Report of 1963, often regarded as the foundation document of the public university in the era of British mass higher education, contained similar rhetoric to the 1956 White Paper:

> [...] the growing realisation of this country's economic dependence upon the education of its population has led to much questioning of the adequacy of present arrangements. Unless higher education is speedily reformed, it is argued, there is little hope of this densely populated island maintaining an adequate position in the fiercely competitive world of the future. (Committee on Higher Education 1963, 5)

The following year Harold Wilson won a majority for the Labour Party at least in part due to his promise to reforge Britain in the 'white heat of the technological revolution', and with a manifesto commitment to expand higher education to serve this purpose (Labour Party 1964). A rhetorical arms race on higher education—anchored in ideas about Britain's place in the world—had begun and would not cease. As for Britain, so too for higher education—in permanent crisis and struggle against foreign competition. Wilson's government has been the subject of much controversy, with critics arguing forcefully that despite vanity projects such as Concorde and the establishment of the Ministry of Technology, they failed to 'reforge Britain' as promised (Francis 2013). But the commitment to higher education was real and continuous. In 1965, the Secretary of State for Education and Science, Anthony Crosland, proposed the creation of a 'public sector' of higher education in the form of polytechnics, institutions of higher education which would grant degrees under the supervision of the Council of National Academic Awards (CNAA) and with a clearly vocational bent. In his infamous 'Woolwich speech' (as it became known), Crosland articulated criticisms of the universities that are today part of ministerial vernacular. In Dennis Dean's words:

> He clearly believed that, for too long, the older universities had pursued their own ends and had created barriers to educational and social advance. The creation of a new Polytechnic sector, Crosland hoped, would force older universities to reconsider out-moded practices in selection and teaching and stimulate educational advance. (Dean 1998, 79)

As in 1966, so too 50 years later, a minister with responsibility for the universities blamed them for their supposed intransigence and lack of responsiveness to national economic needs (Department for Business, Innovation and Skills 2016). In 2016, the rhetoric would be about 'challenger institutions' (Department for Business, Innovation and Skills 2016, 6), in 1966 it was about polytechnics. And even in the 1946 Cabinet debate on the same sentiments had been voiced by the Lord President of the Council (the then-Science Minister), Herbert Morrison:

> I am not sure whether as a Government we have yet faced the full implications of the unprecedented demands which will be made on the Universities if our country is to get from them the men and women it needs for the purposes and of the quality it requires. Teachers, administrators, economists, scientists, doctors, to take but a few examples, will be wanted in vastly increased numbers…But what assurance do we have that the Universities will deliver the goods? (Morrison 1946, 1)

In 1946, the response was to change the UGC's terms of reference (Tapper 2007, 26). In 1956, it was to found Colleges of Advanced Technology. In 1966, it was to found polytechnics. In 2016, it was to promote 'challenger institutions'. This was a story of continuity, rather than change, of rhetoric and a process which predated neoliberalism, and was anchored in the post-war crisis of the British state and its place in the world, a crisis which is still to abate.

Neoliberalism did, however, from the 1970s have an impact on higher education policy in the United Kingdom and farther afield. Following the 'oil shock' of 1973, British universities faced a series of funding crises, which culminated in the 'Cardiff affair' of the mid-1980s when a college of the federal University of Wales reached near-bankruptcy (though its critics alleged considerable mismanagement) (Smith and Cunningham 2003, 29). This paralleled the intellectual development and subsequent political success of Thatcherism, which was rhetorically tough on largesse from the public purse (Green 1999). With the British state now gripped in two 'crises', namely the permanent crisis of globalisation and the more ephemeral, yet profound, crisis of the public finances, neoliberalism—with its drive towards marketisation—sought to secure the needs of the state even as it displaced the burden of meeting them. This was truly the measure of the 'free economy and the strong state' approach which Andrew Gamble described as characteristic of Thatcherism (Gamble 1988).

The crisis of the public finances was used to move universities in the direction of greater financial 'discipline', a process only heightened with the Blair government's moves to introduce tuition fees after Labour's election victory in 1997. The minister for higher education, Margaret Hodge, highlighted the extent to which neoliberal values permeated Labour's approach to higher education when, in November 2002, she asked whether the 'dustman should subsidise the doctor' (Finn 2002). This was higher education framed in terms of return to the individual, not society, not anchored in a view of cultural exchange and citizenship as Robbins had argued for. But the continuities were there too; in 2003 the Secretary of State for Education and Skills, Charles Clarke, justified the government's decision to raise fees further (in defiance of a manifesto pledge) in its White Paper:

> [...] the world is already changing faster than it has ever done before, and the pace of change will continue to accelerate. Our national ability to master that process of change and not be ground down by it depends critically upon our universities. Our future success depends upon mobilizing even more effectively the imagination, creativity, skills and talents of all our people. (Department for Education and Skills 2003, 2)

This was rhetoric characteristic of the post-war period, characteristic of the perennial crisis of British power. It would recur in the Browne Review in 2010, and in the White Paper of the Conservative government of

2016. In this last, *Success as a Knowledge Economy*, the minister for universities Jo Johnson phrased it thus:

> If we are to continue to succeed as a knowledge economy, however, we cannot stand still, nor take for granted our universities' enviable global reputation and position at the top of league tables. We must ensure that the system is also fulfilling its potential. (Department for Business, Innovation and Skills 2016, 4)

The crises of Britain's universities in the past, and the present, are only intelligible in terms of the state's wider ambitions and political economy. Notwithstanding the rise of the New Right and the advent of neoliberalism, the state's priorities in higher education—anchored in a particular notion of crisis—have been more consistent than critics have been willing to admit.

Conclusions: An Inheritance Worth Forgetting?

For activists, the search for a usable past in relation to higher education is a vital concern. Critics of contemporary university reform, including the Campaign for the Public University (of which this author is a member), frequently refer back to the supposed halcyon era of the Robbins Report and post-war expansion as *the* appropriate model of mass higher education. Through the vignettes of crisis adduced above, however, the aim of this chapter has been to offer a rather different perspective. For contemporary critics of reform, the issue has been the purposes to which the university has been put since the 1980s, notably in terms of the redefinition of the university mission, the remaking of students into consumers and the privatisation of higher education in order to develop a quasi-market. For this author, writing both as an historian and as an activist, the issue is rather different.

Britain's universities, as David Edgerton (2006) recognised, were always children of the 'warfare state'. This was a state which sought (aggressively) to maintain global power in an era of imperial decline, and which has continued to seek that world role up to the present. As such, in the 1940s and subsequently, as Edgerton (following E. P. Thompson) notes, the language of the British state was the language of political economy, and higher education was thus constructed within a strategy which saw domestic and foreign policy as inextricably linked (Edgerton 2006, 11). Academics, as Salter and Tapper noted, wielded huge influence in shaping the expansion of higher education in the 1940s, 1950s and 1960s (Salter and Tapper 1994), but it did not take place because academics and intellectuals felt the need to grow a 'clerisy', secure a 'free society' or, in Robbins' words, emphasise the 'common elements' in civilisations (Robbins 196, 16). It took place because successive British governments took the view that higher education was essential for national survival through the development of trained human capital and scientific and technological research. The grip of the academic elite on the levers of university policy-making was strong, but it was not unassailable, and it was not the case that state direction of university objectives began in the 1980s as some, such as Roger Brown, have argued. In the 1950s there were already complaints on the UGC as to the extent of state and NATO funding for military research within universities (Hale 1957), and the role of military training organisations grew within university campuses in the post-war decades. The Royal Navy founded its University Royal Naval Unit system, to parallel the Army's Officer Training Corps and the Royal Air Force's University Air Squadrons, in the 1960s, with the first unit—Aberdeen—founded four years after the publication of the Robbins Report (Currie 1999).

But to look at the directly 'military' aspects of university education is to miss the point of Edgerton's (convincing) warfare state thesis—universities were expanded (and in Edgerton's words, 'masculinised' and 'scientised') in the immediate post-war decades due to the state's conviction that the production of more graduates (and in particular more graduate scientists and technologists) was essential to the economic competitiveness of the country, which was one aspect of the permanent war the British state found itself in. These concerns—and the language used to articulate them—predated contemporary globalisation discourse and neoliberalism. Even in the much-vaunted age of supposed economic nationalism, the fear of global competition drove British policy and played a key role in the evolution of Britain's nascent 'mass' higher education system.

This reflects both the character of the British state's ambitions, but also the character of the state itself. The British polity is not the same as that in the United States or its nearer neighbours in Europe, whatever similarities in process it may evince. The British state, though at risk of disintegration due to nationalist tensions, is a unitary state with tremendous power vested in the executive (Finn and Seldon 2013). Infamously, the former Conservative education secretary and minister for universities Lord Hailsham termed it in the 1970s 'an elective dictatorship' (Lord Hailsham 1976). With no codified constitution, no entrenched Bill of Rights and no separation of powers, there were and remain few brakes on a government with a good majority,[2] whether this is a single-party government or a coalition (as the events surrounding the Browne Review showed). None of this is 'news', but it is often missed by those analysing the history of higher education in Britain, who instead offer a mythology of higher education expansion, where a benign state expanded higher education as a social good within the context of a social democratic political consensus. This state was then 'captured' by neoliberal political economy through the means of the electoral success of the New Right.

But if the task of history is to 'rescue the past from the condescension of the present' for the mutual benefit of both (to add a little to E. P. Thompson), then it is worth recalling the words of one critic of the form of university expansion as it took place in the supposed 'golden age' of the 1960s. David Adelstein, a young radical associated with the *New Left Review*, wrote a series of thoughtful comments on the Robbins Report in a Penguin Special published during the aftermath of the 'student revolt' of 1968. It is worth quoting from him at some length (the emphases are mine):

> The Report did not attempt to reach its recommendations on the basis of the needs of the economy (perhaps because it didn't know how), but based them purely on estimates of the numbers of qualifying sixth formers – the so-called 'pool of ability'. This is not to say that an economic case was not made for expansion. It was, but only in the general sense that higher education helps the economy and that in order to maintain our place in relation to other countries it was necessary to expand student numbers. In this sense the Robbins Report was 'student oriented' – it catered for apparent student demand. In so far as it based its case on the *inherent value of*

> *expansion* rather than *economic demands, the Report represents possibly the last 'liberal' document* that a government will produce for some time...The Robbins Report attempted to direct *old liberal notions into a new techno-cratic programme.* (Adelstein 1969, 67)

Robbins, as Adelstein saw, marked the end of an era, not a beginning. It was an attempt to square the circle between the academic 'crisis' of the mission of the university, the 'crisis' of 'social demand' and the more general strategic crisis of the British state. Adelstein was prophetic in his words on 'old liberal notions'; the emphasis on technocracy, already embedded in 'policy texts', would only grow in strength, and in turn be succeeded by a discursive vocabulary associated with globalisation and the knowledge economy. Academics would still be privileged within the new 'regime of truth', but they would increasingly be academics like John Vaizey rather than Lionel Robbins, economists who advocated the link between education and economic growth rather than—despite Robbins' professional background as a member of the LSE's Economics Department—philosophers attempting to foster active citizenship. The state's ambitions in relation to higher education remained remarkably consistent, but the ability of liberal academics to mediate these ambitions declined. In 1946, in the immediate aftermath of the Barlow Report, the Labour government considered placing universities directly under the control of the Ministry of Education (Wilkinson 1946, 1–2). A little under two decades later, this came to pass. The shibboleth of 'academic freedom' was just that—a shibboleth.

Fifty years later, academics had seen their tenure abolished by statute (in 1988), and were heavily regulated through the state-driven Research Excellence Framework (REF) the Teaching Excellence Framework (TEF) and the forthcoming Knowledge Excellence Framework (KEF), not to mention the Office for Students (OfS). The *Prevent* 'counter-extremism' duty on universities imposed considerable restrictions on academic discussion (Adams 2016). The state had never been so influential, nor universities so subordinate in modern times, notwithstanding the shift of the financial burden from the state to the student in the form of fees. As this essay has shown however, whilst many of these individual changes owe much to neoliberal political economy and the 'market fundamentalism' it espouses, the 'origins of the present crisis' (to shamelessly appropriate Perry Anderson (Anderson 1964)) lie not in the emergence of the New Right and neoliberalism, but decades earlier with growing aggrandisement on the part of the state in developing higher education. If, in fact, at base the state is the problem—rather than the mechanisms the state uses (such as marketisation)—then any alternative horizon for higher education must be anchored in a repudiation of the state's mandate to determine the shape of the university in contemporary Britain.

The free universities movement has recognised this and begun a process of academic self-ownership on the part of both students and academics. But it is only a beginning. Developing a coherent response to the subordinated university of today requires a fundamental revision of vernacular history in respect of the post-war university. It was never the creature of a benign state, expanded for the public good. The state is not a benign political entity, regardless of which party is in power.[3] The subordination of the universities did not begin with market fundamentalism; it was 'present at the creation' of mass higher education and grew ever stronger. Addressing this, developing a new horizon of higher education, will require facing this hard truth about an overly idealised past.

Notes

1. The phrase is Sir Walter Moberly's (which referred to something quite different, as we shall see) (Moberly 1949).
2. Notwithstanding the centripetal tendencies of devolution (Bogdanor 2009).
3. For anarchist critiques of the state's role in education, see Ward (1996) and Suissa (2010).

Works Cited

[Browne Review]. 2010. *Independent review of higher education funding and student finance, securing a sustainable future for higher education*. London: The Stationery Office.

Adams, Richard. 2016. Anti-terror laws risk "chilling effect" on freedom of speech – Oxford college head. *Guardian*, February 7.

Adelstein, David. 1969. Roots of the present crisis. In *Student power: Problems, diagnosis, action*, ed. R. Blackburn and A. Cockburn. Harmondsworth: Penguin.

Anderson, Perry. 1964. Origins of the present crisis. *New Left Review*, 1/23.

Ball, Stephen J. 2013. *The education debate*. 2nd ed. Bristol: Policy Press.

Berry, Craig. 2011. *Globalisation and ideology in Britain: Neoliberalism, free trade and the global economy*. 1st ed. Manchester: Manchester University Press.

Blyth, Mark. 2013. *Austerity: The history of a dangerous idea*. Oxford: Oxford University Press.

Bogdanor, Vernon. 2009. *The new British constitution*. 1st ed. Oxford: Hart.

Briggs, Asa. 1964. Drawing a new map of learning. In *The idea of a new university: An experiment in Sussex*, ed. David Daiches. London: Andre Deutsch.

Brown, Roger. 2015. Education beyond the Gove Legacy: The case of higher education. In *The Gove Legacy: Education in Britain after the coalition*, ed. Mike Finn, 75–86. London: Palgrave.

Collini, Stefan. 2017. *Speaking of universities*. London: Verso.

Committee on Higher Education [Robbins Report]. 1963. *Higher education: Report*. Cmnd. 2154. London: HMSO.

Committee on Scientific Manpower [Barlow Report]. 1946. *Scientific Manpower*. Cmnd. 6284. London: HMSO.

Currie, Jennifer. 1999. Why choose a life on the ocean wave? *Times Higher Education*, August 6.

Dean, Dennis. 1998. Circular 10/65 Revisited: The labour government and the "comprehensive revolution" in 1964–1965. *Paedagogica Historica* 34 (1): 63–91. https://doi.org/10.1080/0030923980340103.

Department for Business, Innovation and Skills (BIS). 2016. *Success as a knowledge economy: Teaching excellence, social mobility and student choice*. Cmnd. 9258. London: TSO.

Department for Education and Skills (DfES). 2003. *The future of higher education*. Cmnd. 5735. London: HMSO.

Edgerton, David. 2006. *Warfare state*. 1st ed. Cambridge: Cambridge University Press.

Finn, Mike. 2002. The new elite. *Guardian*, November 27.

———. 2015. Education beyond the Gove legacy: The case of higher education (2) – Ideology in action. In *The Gove Legacy: Education in Britain after the coalition*, ed. Mike Finn, 87–100. London: Palgrave.

Finn, Mike, and Anthony Seldon. 2013. Constitutional reform since 1997: The historians' perspective. In *The British constitution: Continuity and change*, ed. Matt Qvortrup. Oxford: Hart.

Fulton, John. 1964. New universities in perspective. In *The idea of a new university: An experiment in Sussex*, ed. David Daiches, 1112. London: Andre Deutsch. in Sussex (London, 1966).

Gamble, Andrew. 1988. *The free economy and the strong state*. 1st ed. Basingstoke: Macmillan.

Green, E.H.H. 1999. Thatcherism: An historical perspective. *Transactions of the Royal Historical Society* 9: 17–42. https://doi.org/10.2307/3679391.

Hailsham, Lord. 1976. Elective dictatorship: The Richard Dimbleby Lecture 1976. *The Listener*, October 21.

Hale, Sir Edward. 1957. Letter to R. N. Quirk, Lord President's Committee, December 10. National Archives [NA] CAB 21/4627.

Harvey, David. 2005. *A brief history of neoliberalism*. Oxford: Oxford University Press.

Hillman, Nicholas. 2013. From grants for all to loans for all: Undergraduate finance from the implementation of the Anderson Report (1962) to the implementation of the Browne Report (2012). *Contemporary British History* 27 (3): 249–270. https://doi.org/10.1080/13619462.2013.783418.

Johnson, Paul, and Daniel Chivers. 2015. The coalition and the economy. In *The coalition effect, 2010–2015*, ed. Anthony Seldon and Mike Finn, 159–193. Cambridge: Cambridge University Press.

Krugman, Paul. 2015. The case for cuts was a lie: Why does Britain still believe it? *Guardian*, May 10.

Labour Party. 1964. *Let's go with labour for the new Britain: The labour party's manifesto for the 1964 general election*. 1st ed. London: Labour Party.

McGettigan, Andrew. 2013. *The great university gamble: Money, markets and the future of higher education*. London: Pluto Press.

Ministry of Education. 1956. *Technical education*. Cmnd. 9703. London: HMSO.

Moberly, W.H. 1949. *The crisis in the university*. 1st ed. London: SCM Press.

Morrison, Herbert. 1946. Government and the universities: A memorandum by the Lord President of the Council. June 29. National Archives PREM/8/478 [L.P. (46) 160].

Mountford, James Frederick. 1972. *Keele, an historical critique*. 1st ed. London: Routledge & Kegan Paul.

Mullins, Phil, and Struan Jacobs. 2006. T.S. Eliot's idea of the clerisy, and its discussion by Karl Mannheim and Michael Polanyi in the context of J.H. Oldham's Moot. *Journal of Classical Sociology* 6 (2): 147–156. https://doi.org/10.1177/1468795x06064852.

Phillips, David. 1980. Lindsay and the German universities: An Oxford contribution to the post-war reform debate. *Oxford Review of Education* 6 (1): 91–105. https://doi.org/10.1080/0305498800060107.

Raven, James. 1989. British history and the enterprise culture. *Past and Present* 123 (1): 178–204. https://doi.org/10.1093/past/123.1.178.

Robbins, Lionel. 1966. *The university in the modern world.* 1st ed. Macmillan.

Salter, Brian, and Ted Tapper. 1994. *The state and higher education.* Abingdon: Routledge.

Seymour, Richard. 2014. *Against austerity: How we can fix the crisis they made.* 1st ed. London: Pluto Press.

Shattock, Michael. 1994. *The UGC and the management of British universities.* 1st ed. Buckingham: Open University Press.

———. 2012. *Making policy in British higher education, 1945–2011.* 1st ed. Maidenhead: Open University Press.

Shepherd, Jessica. 2010. UK universities likely to follow US model, says leading vice-chancellor. *Guardian*, October 8.

Smith, Brian, and Vanessa Cunningham. 2003. Crisis at Cardiff. In *Managing crisis*, ed. David Warner and David Palfreyman. Maidenhead: Open University Press.

Stiglitz, Joseph. 2009. Moving beyond market fundamentalism to a more balanced economy. *Annals of Public and Cooperative Economics* 80 (3): 345–360. https://doi.org/10.1111/j.1467-8292.2009.00389.x.

Suissa, Judith. 2010. *Anarchism and education: A philosophical perspective.* 1st ed. Oakland: PM.

Tapper, Ted. 2007. *The governance of British higher education: The struggle for policy control.* Dordrecht: Springer.

Tight, Malcolm. 2009. *The development of higher education in the United Kingdom since 1945.* 1st ed. Maidenhead: Open University Press.

Wilkinson, Ellen. 1946. Government and the universities: Memorandum to the Lord President of the Council's Committee. July 9. National Archives: PREM/8/478 [L.P. (46) 174].

The Coming Crisis of Academic Authority

Eric R. Lybeck

In 1970, Alvin Gouldner penned a book titled *The Coming Crisis of Western Sociology* in which he observed that the radical 1960s student movement had slipped out of sync with the conservative structural-functionalist paradigm represented by Talcott Parsons (Gouldner 1970). More recently, John Levi Martin has noted the 'passing crisis of Western sociology', saying that 'even the most sour doomsayer cannot in good conscience point to any signs that there is a deep theoretical rupture or confusion in academic sociology as it currently stands, nor is there reason to suspect crisis looming in the near future' (Martin 2003, 1).

In many ways, the title of this chapter, borrowed from Gouldner's indictment of postwar positivism, should more appropriately be drawn from Martin. We are presently humming our way through a crisis of academic authority across the Western world. In the UK, the coalition government continues to liquidate the historic value of the nation's globally esteemed higher education sector. Lovely Only recently, Pearson College, a for-profit subsidiary of Pearson Publishing, passed the Quality Assurance

E. R. Lybeck (✉)
University of Exeter, Exeter, UK

T. Geelan et al. (eds.), *From Financial Crisis to Social Change*,
https://doi.org/10.1007/978-3-319-70600-9_4

Agency (QAA) review to access public student loans, a key stage on its route to attaining full degree-awarding powers (Morgan 2014). As Andrew McGettigan has so effectively documented, a flotilla of policy adjustments at the Department of Business, Innovation and Skills has opened the trough to low-cost providers as part of the government strategy to meet the domestic and international demand for university degrees (McGettigan 2013). Meanwhile, the Russell Group seeks to break away from the pack of former polytechnics to consolidate their position at the top of the heap. In their imagination, universities, administrators, and ministers are reproducing the competitive conditions of the thriving American university system. The recently published government Green Paper, *Fulfilling Our Potential*, deepens the penetration of these market forces and calcifies existing university hierarchies (Department for Business, Innovation and Skills 2015).

And yet, the American tertiary education 'market' does not work like this at all. For-profits, for example, are not low-rent bottom feeders setting up shop in abandoned office blocks. Rather, to provide two particularly egregious cases, the University of Phoenix and Corinthian College exploit the high tuition available to veterans and other recipients of subsidised federal loans. Neither do the majority of the 4400 institutions of higher education thrive in the privileged Ivy League. Most occupy that vague, multi-functional middle ground—the one the UK is presently liquidating.

As Fig. 1 implies, in only 15 years, the UK shifted from a public system of tertiary education to an American system funded by privatised student loans. To understand the dynamics propelling this transformation of higher education, we can refer to Fig. 2, which provides a model of the three sources of academic authority within American higher education. As the UK opens itself to competition, without reconstructing this structural environment it opens itself up to 'Americanisation'.

According to Andrew Abbott, the structure of the American academy has remained remarkably stable for over a century due to a dually institutionalised 'basket structure' consisting of departments and disciplines organised in national associations (Abbott 2001, 126–129). A suite of core disciplines are reproduced isomorphically according to the broad categories of undergraduate college majors mirrored in divisions amongst

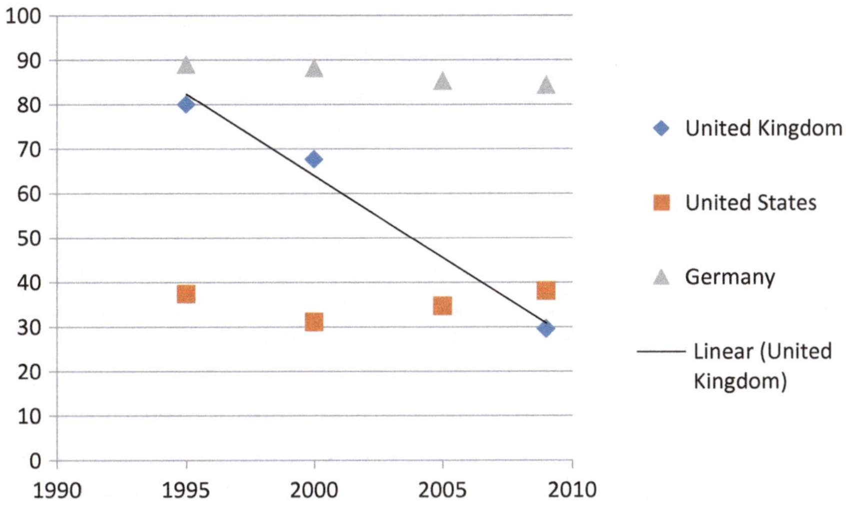

Fig. 1 Share of public expenditure on tertiary education (% of total education spending) (Source: (OECD 2012))

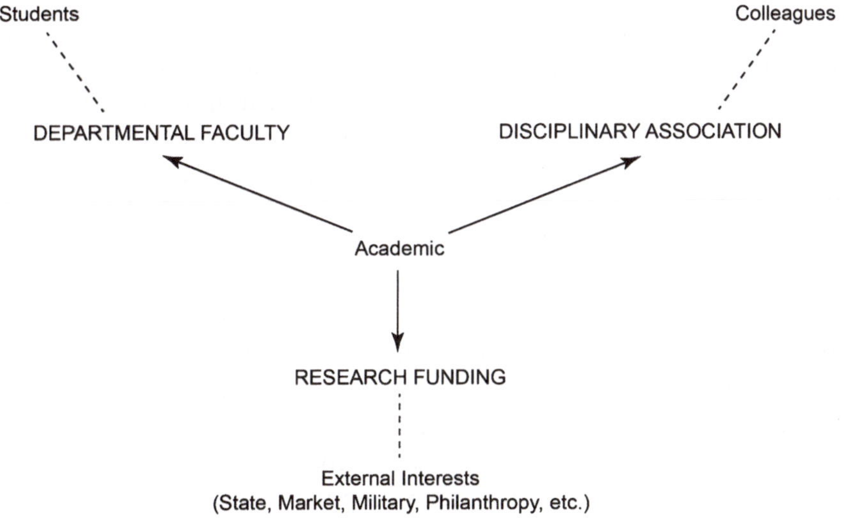

Fig. 2 Sources of academic authority

major journals, conferences, and advocacy groups. Academics preserve reputations in each—department and discipline—thereby obtaining a diffuse, de-centred authority. I have added to Abbott's dual basket structure external funding sources—state, business, philanthropy, military, and so on—which deliver resources, often entering through the cipher of 'interdisciplinarity' (Lamont 2010; Fleck 2011).

According to scholars of the 'triple-helix', a government-university-industry complex stimulates technological innovation according to a coherent pattern that effectively socialises the costs of research and development within the university (Block and Keller 2009; Etzkowitz and Leydesdorff 1996, 1998). The profits, however, tend to go to patent-holding companies—industrial firms, private equity, or start-ups run by entrepreneurial scientists themselves. A changed notion of science as economic engine began in the 1970s, following the promotion of university-industry partnerships, favourable developments in patent law, and successful cases of entrepreneurship in biotechnology (Berman 2011, 3). This shift began when the State assumed the ideology of innovation in which science and technological research produce economic growth and wealth creation.

As a secular trend, the triple-helix pattern emphasising technical research over teaching undermines the humanistic disciplines, as recent reports from Stanford, Harvard, and Princeton indicate (Lewin 2013; Nussbaum 2010). In the UK, Terry Eagleton recently despaired that the humanities have been cordoned off within academia since Margaret Thatcher, becoming 'servants of the status quo' (Eagleton 2014). The implication is that neoliberalism causes the death of the humanities and academic critique. Yet, while these external pressures are real, my own research suggests the roots of the problem lie much closer to home, in the authority structure of the academic profession itself.

Recall Fig. 2, in which academics vie for recognition from departments and disciplines: in the former, the 'clients' are students (more precisely, their parents seeking to reproduce inherited privileges). Departments, however, outsource this reputational work to administrators, who promote institutions in numerically classified rankings published by Times Higher Education, QS, and so forth. For all their methodological differences, these academic billboard charts ultimately revolve around research output and reputation. Reputational stability is ensured by surveys completed by alumni, typically members of the business, government, professional, and academic elite. These are disinclined to undermine the reputation of the schools by which their identity and status privileges are borne. We need no further example than the case of Princeton Law School being selected as the sixth best in America, despite the fact that Princeton has not had a Law School since 1852! (Hoffman 1998).

But reputation is certainly not everything—minimally weighted, in fact—since due to a twist of fate, research output amounts to as much as 60 per cent within these rank orders. Social researchers of higher education during the 1960s and 1970s found it impossible to numerically measure the qualitative value of teaching provision across the incredibly diverse American tertiary-education sector (Geiger 1985). As a stand-in for *teaching*, these researchers simply doubled the weight of *research*, based on the assumption that the best researchers *are* the best teachers, wanting the best students, who enrol in the best schools. Locating the best students is an easy (if Darwinian) calculation derived from rejection rate figures—and lo and behold a correlation obtained between rejection rates and research prestige.[1] Statistical assumptions proved; the research rank has since stood in for both research itself and as the *indirect* measure of teaching quality. Of course, administrators, academics, newspapers, parents, and students—*everyone*—have forgotten this statistical rationale so that now, in the race to move up the ranks, the dependent variable 'research impact' has become an end in itself. Pumping out publications translates directly to a rise in rank, regardless of the underlying teaching provision.

We are now in the position to observe the contours of a processual trend: the increasing prominence of the *research* function of the university. This puts pressure on the academic to secure more external grants, while publishing more and more within their discipline's top journals. In other words: away from the department and toward the disciplinary associations—which are located primarily in America. These become effective gatekeepers—lowering the drawbridge for trusted colleagues or graduate students socialised in the elite departments and embedded in the central professional network.

Added to this, as Abbott explains, there is a general phenomenon of 'professional regression' common to any professional workplace. The elite of any profession gains internal status recognition by distancing themselves from practical work—in this case, teaching (Abbott 1981). The elite centre thereby maintains an air of 'purity' as they engage in logical abstraction and research for its own sake. University rankings reward these pedants by declaring them the best teachers in the world. This does not mean that Ivy League students do not receive high quality education, but that training is likely delivered by elite graduate students massaging their PhDs for ten years, or via teaching 'buy-outs' built into research grants, funding temporary untenured lectureships. Teaching becomes a 'semi-profession' *within* the academic profession increasingly evaluated in terms of research alone (Etzioni 1969). For the prestigious research scholar interested in broad problem-portable knowledge, there are few trade-offs. External research grants fund adjuncts or graduate students, while providing administrators and reputation rags the numbers they need. And, since even these grants are determined by interdisciplinary review panels consisting of academics occupying similar roles and positions—albeit differing in subject expertise—'fair' distribution is ensured across the respective disciplines.

In other words, the academic profession's internal mode of establishing reputation amongst itself is reproduced by governments and other external actors seeking to quantify and reinforce existing hierarchical reputational advantage across the sector. They do not care why Harvard and Cambridge are the best, they simply repeat back whatever criteria we academics affirm. If that means the highest rank goes to the department with 27 per cent of its faculty consisting of absent honorary directors of research (as was the case in Cambridge's Department of Sociology at the time of writing), so be it. Once this reputational game is in play, the rewards accumulate to research-oriented scholars who can translate their esoteric knowledge into the exoteric interdisciplinary terms for funding committees (Baldamus 2010). It is worth distinguishing, however, between the humanities and social sciences vs. the natural sciences in terms of the effectiveness of interdisciplinary study. The former are not organised around similar sorts of objects: English is organised around texts in the English language, anthropology around the ethnographic method, political science around relationships of power, and economics around an action theory of rational utility maximisation (Abbott 2001, 140). The latter, natural sciences, do have aligned 'axes of cohesion' insofar as the levels of analysis between physics, chemistry, organic chemistry, up to, say, experimental psychology, reflect hierarchical ontological levels of material reality. Interdisciplinary research between physicists and geologists addresses different analytic levels of the *same* objects. These findings tend toward verifiable conclusions, predictions, and technologies, unlike humanistic interdisciplinary kitchens cooking mutually allergenic food for thought. In submitting to the external reward incentives of research councils, the humanities generate massive redundancy, as Abbott describes, 'creating a wildly duplicative system it allows many people (in different problem areas) to get credit for the same "discoveries"'(Abbott 2001, 135 f21). Judith Butler is imported into multiple disciplines, encouraging the proliferation of Butlerian scholars whether or not this contributes to better research or cumulative advancement of Butler's insights.

This would amount only to a regrettable waste of resources, were it not for the fact that the humanities professors remain teachers. In filling these disciplines with every 'new' and 'innovative' approach, by gathering the best publicists rather than the best teachers, the humanities come to be filled with scholars serving impressionable students a diet of identity politics repackaged as 'intersectionality', while every social problem is explained as a product of the great Satan, neoliberalism. This amounts to a radical detemporalisation of the human condition. As David Inglis has described, in the case of sociology, we are transfixed with the theories of Giddens, Bauman, Castells, Beck, and Latour, which reproduce the self-understanding of the contemporary social order—as unprecedented, liquid, reflexive, hyper, and so on (Inglis 2014). Scholars purporting to understand the social order learn next to nothing about the historical origins of our contemporary circumstances, and are thus unprepared to do anything to substantively change them.

But, of course, sociology is a social science, not a humanity—or so we tell ourselves. In fact, sociologists consistently delude themselves to think they explain the world via a scientific method. In fact, contemporary academic sociologists are indistinguishable from humanistic academics and cultural critics who encourage *others* to think before they act. These 'others' tend to be 18–22-year-olds. Unlike economists, political scientists, or military psychologists, sociologists rarely address *powerful* actors; and their obsession with 'science' serves primarily as a self-delusion of 'physics envy'. The result is an epistemological confusion in which the *actual* significance of science and technology in modern society is conflated with social scientific understanding itself. This implies that one's correct analysis *matters* more than it actually does in terms of practical effects.

This inflated self-worth is socialised in students who learn to address common-sense observations with quantitative methods that assume a mode of linear causal reasoning only a *mad* scientist would accept; the remainder attend 'qualitative methods' courses consisting of a nominalist philosophical critique of their colleagues' quantitative research, treated as alternately stupid, totalistic, capitalist, fetishistic, *and* constructed. Each affirms the students' immature solipsism: that their identity is a valorable construct of overlapping social networks or the product of hierarchies of privileges conferred by race, class, gender, and sexuality. Graduates can efficiently demystify the world, but are utterly void of realistic alternatives to a world composed of social constructions, agential materiality, and intersectional identities. Without historical consciousness these are meaningless buzzwords.

The legacy of the shift toward research away from teaching instructs students to seek out injustices in published representations of society rather than the historical conditions which have reproduced human civilisation for thousands of years. Discursive representations are deemed 'unfair' if certain populations or 'voices' are excluded, but concerns for the actual historical conditions and trends which led to that exclusion are not fully engaged with. Lessons become courses in how to identify offensive speech on twitter, rather than how to understand and wield power effectively.

Were the academic profession seriously interested in addressing issues of social mobility, or the 'neoliberal' 'managerialism' under pressures of 'Americanisation', it would recommit to its primary mission as an institution of higher learning. For universities are not social equality machines, they are a self-regulating guild to preserve the quality of conferred degrees. This requires interpersonal attention between teachers and students across long gestation periods. Low-cost private providers should not get degree-granting powers, not because they exploit the poor, but because they are 'sham universities'. The public university should be universal and free because we need the authority to kick lazy students out and deliver honest grades without the additional guilt relating to a student's loan portfolio. Administration should avoid inefficient external audits because they distract the faculty from performing their core duty as teachers of future teachers.

To recover the authority of higher learning acquired over years of intensive study, we should not look to the generic buildings smothering the Greenbelt in Northwest Cambridge—'paid for' with a £350 million bond to accommodate ever more natural scientists. That may be the future of an industrial research park branded with the Cambridge Crest. For us, the university must be reconstructed from the abandoned spirit of the old Cambridge estate, which lies dormant more often than it is used. Where have all the teachers gone? They're off at a conference. An editorial board meeting. Field work. Picking up the next honorarium. Meanwhile their students are compelled to learn to live-tweet their dissertation just in case that academic job doesn't pan out. If you listen closely enough, you can hear the crisis of academic authority passing the lot of them by.

Epilogue

A few months after first drafting this chapter, I determined to do something to redress some of the problems identified as the 'passing crisis of academic authority'. The crisis can be summarised as being the retention of academic rights, without corresponding responsibility for those in their care, particularly students. This is reflected especially in the ascent of the research function of the university at the expense of the teaching function. This not only affects the quality of teaching as such, but equally turns academics into supplicants serving at the pleasure of external powers, especially governments and market interests.

I argued previously that academics have a responsibility not only to criticise but to construct and reconstruct institutions which encourage social change through the education of publics (Lybeck 2011). These publics may or may not exist, and likely need to be created. I further resisted the tendency within critical scholarship to 'reach out' to distant others before redressing injustices and contradictions that lie closer to home: that is, within the academic profession.

As noted above, the bifurcation of the profession into elite researchers and itinerant teachers produces a range of effects which destabilise, delegitimise, and discourage capable academics from obtaining stable and secure employment in universities. Having worked for years at Cambridge within school councils on postgraduate concerns I was struck that no one seemed to have in view the needs of the academic profession as a whole. Policies were never developed from utopian, or even reformist ideals, but were entirely reactive. Despite the 'informality' and non-binding nature of the government's white and green papers, university administrators and faculties bent over backwards to accommodate and adjust *the language* of what they are doing to accommodate the 'new' order. In a Wittgensteinian game, meeting after meeting involved the renaming of the *status quo ante* as 'innovation', 'impact', 'excellence', 'open access', or whatever the most recent buzzword of the day was.

This is no shock to any student of bureaucratic inertia and is not a problem unique to academia. But it became apparent that no substantive change redressing the bifurcation of the academic profession could come from such a set of practices. I determined that what would be necessary, as unlikely as it would be, would be recommitment to the *values* of the universities as *guilds*. I was nearing the end of my PhD and decided that my research into universities might have 'impact' if I ran for graduate union president. Knowing that Cambridge has a unique, central position within both the UK and global higher education system, construction of a new form of graduate students' guild could have the effect of transforming the university system in general. The plan was ambitious, but rooted in what would actually be necessary to transform the system and redress the passing crisis.

The idea was relatively simple: use the graduate union and university to construct an insurance scheme that redistributed the risk of unemployment, especially at the stage early career academics face in between graduate school and their first secure position. This would require recognition that postgraduate students, particularly PhDs, are junior members of the profession and not 'students' per se. If postgraduates contributed to an insurance scheme during their studies, this could then be matched by universities, grants, and, importantly, professors themselves—who, as noted above, have considerably greater income than either their past or future counterparts. Such insurance would bind the profession together in a relational web, while removing the existential crisis that besets the postdoctoral applicant at the end of study. There does not have to be a cliff at the end of postgraduate scholarship, the severity of which is ultimately inhumane. Early career teaching positions could be negotiated and renegotiated with a greater level of job security.

How is this different from a union offering unemployment insurance? What I envisaged was rooted in the fact that guilds were professional bodies committed to maintaining *quality*. In this sense, acceptance into the guild (the university) would recover a certain level of seriousness that is evacuating the modern university. For example, there is a pernicious trend within the top universities in the UK and elsewhere by which degrees—particularly postgraduate degrees—are offered to the highest bidders. Often these 'students' hail from international contexts that are unscrutinised, as the 2011 LSE/Gaddafi case revealed (Baehr 2011). Meanwhile, vast resources are spent to widen participation and access to undergraduate students—in a fanciful effort to redress the UK class structure via university admissions forms—and yet no attention is drawn to the social class of postgraduates, either domestically or abroad. Inflation of degrees worldwide means that bachelor's and now master's degrees are insufficient to distinguish job applicants, making the PhD an increasingly generic degree rather than a conferral of the privilege to teach within an academic setting. The academic guild would recover the responsibility the university has relinquished in terms of identifying, insuring, and supporting postgraduate students who are actually committed to working in the academic profession. A shared commitment to quality would recover the value and esteem of advanced degrees.

If the guild model were successful in Cambridge, the institution would ideally be reproduced across universities resulting in a network of young academics involved in scholarship in the roundest sense possible. In time, a new generation of committed academics would replace the existing generation of rent-seeking professors and administrators content to collect fees from students, who, unlike their elders, have to pay back fees and loans for the rest of their lives (unless they are born wealthy). With sufficient coverage across the UK, and perhaps worldwide, the guild might in time have a substantial asset portfolio and could then function as a consumer credit union. The 'real utopian' model here is the United Services Automobile Association (USAA) which began as an auto insurance company for American servicemen and women, eventually expanding to provide a range of financial services for veterans and active military personnel. Unlike commercial banks there is no incentive to, for example, hide nasty terms and conditions in fine print. As a financial union of equal members, the USAA works because the members' needs come first. If one considers the population of the global academic profession as a similarly large group of potential members, the distribution of risk and insurance would be considerable, indeed. Equally, such a credit union could encourage responsible and ethical investments, retirement pensions, and even purchase of the student loan portfolio from the government. This would mean presently indebted students could own their own debt liabilities. Repayments would go back into the academic guild itself, turning what has been an individualisation of the costs of higher education into a recollectivised investment in the future of the academic profession.

Certainly the notion was, and is, a utopian pie-in-the-sky idea; but one which, it struck me, could actually transform the current crisis of academic authority. I had hoped to present my idea to the graduate student population and then work for a year developing the institutional framework as president of the graduate union. In the end, as is well documented in the Cambridge student press, the election was a thoroughgoing disaster. Debates were cancelled, votes were miscounted, and constitutional complaints were ignored. In the end, the billowing gales of the crisis were too strong. The alternative horizon was, at that time, not given the air to be heard. Perhaps the publication of this epilogue, which stands as a description of the kernel of an idea, might mean that, in time, the seed may gain roots. One day, a robust academic guild may grow and change the passing course of the crisis of academic authority.

Notes

1. The statistical logic underpinning the idea that rejection rates identifying the best students presupposes that the better the university, the more students apply, and the more students who apply, the more will be rejected, thereby leaving only the 'cream of the crop'.

Works Cited

Abbott, Andrew. 1981. Status and status strain in the professions. *American Journal of Sociology* 86 (4): 819–835.

———. 2001. *Chaos of disciplines*. Chicago: University of Chicago Press.

Baehr, Peter. 2011. Purity and danger in the modern university. *Society* 48 (4): 297–300.

Baldamus, Wilhelm. 2010. The sociology of Wilhelm Baldamus: Paradox and inference. Edited by M. Erickson and C. Turner. Basingstoke/Abingdon: Ashgate Publishing, Ltd.

Berman, Elizabeth Popp. 2011. *Creating the market university: How academic science became an economic engine*. Princeton: Princeton University Press.

Block, Fred, and Matthew R. Keller. 2009. Where do innovations come from? Transformations in the US economy, 1970–2006. *Socio-Economic Review* 7 (3): 459–483.

Department for Business, Innovation and Skills. 2015. *Fulfilling our potential: Teaching excellence, social mobility and student choice*. London: Department for Business, Innovation and Skills.

Eagleton, Terry. 2014. The death of universities. *The Guardian*, December 17. http://www.theguardian.com/commentisfree/2010/dec/17/death-universities-malaise-tuition-fees. Accessed 24 Apr 2017.

Etzioni, Amitai. 1969. *The semi-professions and their organization: Teachers, nurses, social workers*. New York: Free Press.

Etzkowitz, Henry, and Loet Leydesdorff. 1996. A triple helix of academic-industry-government relations: Development models beyond "capitalism versus socialism". *Current Science* 70 (8): 690–693.

———. 1998. The endless transition: A "triple helix" of university-industry-government relations. *Minerva* 36 (3): 203–208.

Fleck, Christian. 2011. *A transatlantic history of the social sciences: Robber Barons, the Third Reich and the invention of empirical social research*. London: Bloomsbury Academic.

Geiger, Roger L. 1985. Hierarchy and diversity in American research universities. In *The university research system: The public policies of the scientists*, ed. Björn Wittrock and Aant Elzinga, 53–74. Stockholm: Almqvist & Wiksell.

Gouldner, Alvin W. 1970. *The coming crisis of Western sociology*. New York: Basic Books.

Hoffman, Jan. 1998. Judge not, law schools demand of a magazine that ranks them. *New York Times*, February 19.

Inglis, David. 2014. What is worth defending in sociology today? Presentism, historical vision and the uses of sociology. *Cultural Sociology* 8 (1): 99–118.

Lamont, Michèle. 2010. *How professors think*. Cambridge: Harvard University Press.

Lewin, Tamar. 2013. As interest fades in the humanities, colleges worry. *The New York Times*, October 30. Retrieved 2 November 2013 (http://www.nytimes.com/2013/10/31/education/as-interest-fades-in-the-humanities-colleges-worry.html).

Lybeck, E.R. 2011. For pragmatic public sociology: Theory and practice after the pragmatic turn. *Current Perspectives in Social Theory* 29: 169–185.

Martin, John Levi. 2003. What is field theory? *American Journal of Sociology* 109 (1): 1–49.

McGettigan, Andrew. 2013. *The great university gamble: Money, markets and the future of higher education*. London: Pluto Press.

Morgan, John. 2014. Students at Pearson College get green light for SLC funds. *Times Higher Education*, August 21. http://www.timeshighereducation.co.uk/news/students-at-pearson-college-get-green-light-for-slc-funds/2015273.article. Accessed 24 Apr 2017.

Nussbaum, Martha C. 2010. *Not for profit: Why democracy needs the humanities*. Princeton: Princeton University Press.

OECD. 2012. *Education at a glance 2012: OECD indicators*. http://www.oecd.org/edu/eag2012.htm. Accessed 24 Apr 2017.

Consuming Education

Alice Pearson

The financial crisis of 2008 catalysed major shifts in universities in the UK, both in the content of education and in the way they are evaluated. The legitimising capacity of the economic crisis was seized by the 2010 governing coalition in the UK, who adopted a platform of austerity, bringing in a wide array of public spending cuts and privatising measures under the rubric of deficit reduction. Following the increase in the percentage of British students attending university and the introduction of tuition fees in the prior decade, in 2012 the government tripled undergraduate tuition fees to £9000 per year.[1] Meanwhile, a movement emerged on campuses whereby students sought to challenge austerity policies by undermining the neoclassical orthodoxy of their degrees that many in the movement felt had been used to legitimise such cuts to public spending and increases in privatisation.

As such, this chapter will address two responses to the financial crisis within universities: from the policymakers reforming university structures and from the students attempting to reform their economics

A. Pearson (✉)
University of Cambridge, Cambridge, UK

T. Geelan et al. (eds.), *From Financial Crisis to Social Change*,
https://doi.org/10.1007/978-3-319-70600-9_5

syllabi. It will do so based on interviews and participant observation in conferences, organisational meetings and public events of the emerging economics student movement.

Firstly, it will address government attempts to reframe tertiary education in terms of dual education and employment markets. These markets are linked through a process whereby students act as consumers who purchase degrees and in doing so transform themselves into commodities available to employers. The policies proposed to facilitate this process include the introduction of a Teaching Excellence Framework (TEF) for assessing university desirability. The TEF uses metrics linked to employer and student perceptions, which determine the value of education according to demand for its consumption on both education and employment markets, rather than processes of its production. The chapter will then go on to outline a parallel shift amongst university students who are challenging the dominance of orthodox economics in their degrees, many of whom were supportive of the proposed TEF, and who sometimes mobilise platforms of consumer sovereignty in pursuing their demands.

The chapter will explore the tensions that emerge when confronting logics of economic rationality and the market[2] in the content of economics education while simultaneously drawing on these logics in the way education is valued. It will argue that logics of the rational economic consumer have become orthodoxy, an orthodoxy that links the ethnographic terms deployed by students of 'neoliberalism' and 'neoclassical' economics. On one level, many students in the movement link their aversion to 'neoclassical' economics to the notion that it legitimises 'neoliberal' policies, in particular recent austerity cuts and a concomitant application of market-based consumer logics to public services. Yet on another, many such students utilise such consumer logics in education in order to challenge the dominance of 'neoclassical' economics on the syllabus. The chapter will trace the potential paradoxes entailed in the relationship between the content of the student demands and the forms by which they articulate them, particularly as concerns consumer logics.

Orthodox Political Economy of Education

The tripling of fees in the UK was a rapid increase, but such attempts to subject education to market logics are not isolated. In the UK, they began during the Thatcher period and accelerated significantly under Tony Blair with the initial introduction of top-up fees (Wright 2015). Elsewhere, university education has been framed similarly by market logics in a global 'knowledge economy' (Shore 2010; Wright 2015; Wright and Rabo 2010). Academics have documented the proliferation of market mechanisms in the universities that house them through the interrelated phenomena of rapidly increasing levels of student debt, the outsourcing and informalisation of teaching, privatisation of facilities, the economic instrumentalisation of research design and funding, and the concomitant devaluation of the arts and humanities (Nussbaum 2010; Shore 2010; Shore and Davidson 2014; Wright 2015).

They have argued that these policy shifts are reshaping the conduct of the actors who pass through universities by 'instilling new beliefs, affects and desires in students, faculty and administrators' (Hyatt et al. 2015). Specifically, it is suggested that such changes contribute to the inculcation of the subjects embroiled in them as rationally calculating individuals, who in the case of students seek to evaluate education according to economic criteria (Hyatt et al. 2015; Shore 2010). The use of language is central to this exercise of reframing, where the 'vocabulary of customer, consumer, choice, markets and self-interest moulds both our conception of ourselves and our understanding of and relationship to the world' (Massey 2013, 5). In the case of universities, consumer logics are spreading along with market infrastructures.

In the UK context, such discourses are increasingly deployed in efforts to reform tertiary education. This emerging linguistic register was evident in a 2015 Green Paper and 2016 White Paper that outlined reforms to university regulation, funding and assessment. The press release for the first report ran with the title 'Student choice at the heart of new higher education reforms' (BIS 2015b) and this language of consumer demand ran through the document itself, with the third most common phrase as 'what students want' and the second as 'value for money' (NUS 2015, cf.

Collini 2016): linking choice to a particular financialised form of cost-benefit analysis. The implication of combined shifts in UK universities towards demand-orientated policies and increasing fees is that students should purchase an education according to the consumer logics of a competitive market, by applying a utilitarian equation of efficient allocation to decipher where to buy their degree. The provision of education should therefore be determined by the sovereignty of the consumer. These shifts suggest a particular form of evaluation whereby education is to be exchanged as a commodity on a market, rather than as a right to be claimed or a gift from the state with a possible corresponding social debt.

However, the key consumers in the future of education are not framed as students but as employers. The most common phrase in the document is 'what employers want' appearing a total of 35 times (BIS 2015a; NUS 2015), and the product it seeks to market to employers is the students themselves. In order to do this, students must create themselves as a commodity for the employment market, so the student-as-consumer produces the student-to-be-consumed. Thus, central to the success of this conception of universities is the ability of students to enact a 'transformation of consumers into commodities' (Bauman 2007, 12). Bauman described this process as a shift in subjectivity undertaken to attain sovereignty as a subject in certain societal arrangements and argued that it required actors to premise the authority of their demands both on their own actions as consumers and their ability to transform themselves through their consumption choices into a marketable product. Thus, he argues that in such conditions:

> [N]o one can become a subject without first turning into a commodity, and no one can keep his or her subjectness secure without perpetually resuscitating, resurrecting and replenishing the capacities expected and required of a sellable commodity. The 'subjectivity' of the 'subject', and most of what that subjectivity enables the subject to scheme, is focused on an unending effort to itself become, and remain, a sellable commodity. (2007, 12)

While the absolutist tone of Bauman's assertion is questionable, the analysis seems highly pertinent for the students who are called upon to intertwine two types of markets in the site of universities, those of education and those of employment. Under this conception, the future of universities is determined by interlinked education and employment markets, with the student as consumer-cum-commodity as the agent expected to connect them.

The introduction of such consumer logics into universities has been accompanied by an 'audit culture' generating measures of 'accountability' and 'performance' to assist in ranking the available options for consumption (Power 1997; Strathern 2000; Shore 2010; Shore and Wright 1999). Shore and Wright argue that this 'new regime of managerialism in British higher education confuses "transparency" with the Benthamite principles of panopticon visibility and "inspectability"' (1999, 566), while the emphasis on measurement instead encourages academics to generate fabrications for the purposes of ratings games (Shore 2010, 27). The recent UK proposals continue the proliferation of assessments by outlining further measures for students and employers to rank their consumption preferences.

Most notably, the recent policy proposals include a Teaching Excellence Framework (TEF) in the image of the already existing Research Excellence Framework (REF). While the move may be a somewhat predictable answer to those who critique the primacy of research over teaching in the evaluation of academic output (cf: Lybeck this volume), it is surprising given the widely perceived flaws within the REF itself. These include the significant expense of both time and money, which even the Green Paper itself highlighted in a call to 'address the "industries" that some institutions create around the REF and the people who promote and encourage these behaviours' (BIS 2015a, cf. Collini 2016), implying that the introduction of such assessments serves to divert away from rather than support the practices perceived internal to the value of academia, in this case research. This suggests that the REF does not actually serve as a suitable measure for monitoring research quality, and there is little indication that the structure of the TEF will do any more to decipher the quality of teaching.

On the contrary, it actually appears that the TEF will be significantly less successful at measuring quality than previous rankings, due to the proposed metrics. The criterion it outlines for assessing teaching does not directly relate to pedagogical practices in the classroom, rather to their exchange value on education and employment markets. The three core metrics include graduate incomes alongside student perception and completion rates. While the latter two of these metrics may illuminate student satisfaction with institutions, it is not clear that they will necessarily do so by assessing the standard of teaching itself, so much as a fulfilment of prior expectations. Meanwhile, the use of graduate incomes aligns with a conception of education as an instrumental good with the goal of marketable graduates. The weakness of graduate earnings as a measure of teaching quality was highlighted in interim reports by the Parliamentary Committee advising on the TEF design, where it was argued that 'there are so many factors affecting future employment it seems to us difficult if not impossible to make a meaningful linkage to teaching quality' (BIS 2016, 10). Using a metric of graduate income will potentially have the impact of reinforcing the very dynamics that the TEF was supposed to destabilise: instead of challenging existing perceptions of university quality that in turn result in certain students attaining higher earning jobs, they will take these higher earnings as evidence of a university's teaching standards.

Each of these metrics overlooks the processes of production known to generate successful teaching practices, such as wages and the stability of teaching contracts. Such employment conditions are actually being rapidly eroded by the casualisation and outsourcing of university teaching labour at the same time as the expectations placed on output are increasing (cf:Shore 2010). Moreover, performance in the TEF has recently been linked to increases in fees in accordance with inflation, implementing a form of valuation according to consumer perception. Rather than on the processes of producing education, the metrics of the TEF focus on perceptions of consumers, both students and employers.

This assessment also shifts focus from knowledge that academics want to produce onto the knowledge that business and governments want to consume. This shift of focus from knowledge production to consumption calls for a parallel move in sociological analysis. While attention has been fruitfully ploughed into knowledge production (e.g. Bourdieu 1988; Gramsci 1972; Foucault 1972) and reproduction (e.g. Bourdieu 1984; Bourdieu and Passeron 1990), less has been paid to the consumption of knowledge (although cf. Baudrillard 1994; Collini 2016). Yet, recent moves by the UK government place student choice and consumer demand at the centre of the generation of knowledge, and this shift remains theoretically under-examined.

Two significant theoretical analyses of the emerging modes of valuing education elucidate this dynamic by positing a relationship to frameworks in neoclassical economics. Freire (1970) critiqued a banking model where education is considered deposits in the student. Meanwhile, Foucault et al. (2008) described the logic of education as an investment in human capital enacted by the agent of *homo economicus* deployed by neoclassical economists. Both of these analyses are premised on a neoclassical Human Capital model, which conceives of education as enabling accumulation of capital by students: consumption thus affects an alteration in the interior substance of those who invest in it.

However, another model which is taught simultaneously and often more frequently on current economics syllabi perhaps has more resonance with current dynamics in the evaluation of education. The Job Market Signalling model, proposed by Spence (1973), argues that education has no intrinsic value but rather is a signal to employers that students are have "higher productive capacities" by virtue of having undertaken the expense of attending university. This expense is measured predominantly in effort, and as this effort is considered higher for less able students, the model argues that they are less likely to undertake a degree. In this model, university education itself is not perceived to hold any intrinsic value nor to add to students any knowledge or skills, it is merely a signifier of being a more capable worker: education is actually wasteful, as it entails an expense without any direct increase in productivity. This resonates strongly with both Baudrillard's notion of the empty signifier, consumption undertaken to create associations with brands rather than to affect any intrinsic change. It also resonates with a TEF whose metrics are based on consumer perceptions rather than productive processes.

The Human Capital model and the Job Market Signalling model compete for dominance in economics as explanatory mechanisms for understanding the value of education. Both have strong resonance with recent shifts in government policy towards valuing education instrumentally as a means to improving employment prospects. However, the primacy of employer perceptions in the TEF metrics suggests that it is the pre-existing signifiers of different universities, as opposed to the productive processes of education itself, which is being asserted in recent government policy. It is challenges to such neoclassical frameworks in economics that the next section will explore.

Heterodox Education of Political Economy

The financial meltdown of 2008 precipitated another crisis, one of legitimacy. The authority of economists was undermined by their failure to predict the crash before it happened, and the legitimacy of tertiary economics education was destabilised by its failure to address the crisis as it unfolded. In universities across the UK, as well as many other countries across the world, a broad student movement gained momentum with the primary goal of changing the economics syllabus. Many branches of the movement had already been operating in the decade prior to 2008, so as one of the organisers suggested: 'it's not that Rethinking Economics is a response to the crisis, it's just that the crisis puts such a sharp relief between what's in that classroom space where you're told this is how it works and the outside space where you see it's not working like that.'

Members of the movement argue that current economics teaching is dominated by a framework premised on a certain atomistic set of assumptions, notably including the rationality of the representative agent *homo economicus*, and extrapolated with extensive mathematical modelling (Eliassen et al. 2015; ISIPE 2014; PCES 2014). This mainstream emerged in the marginal revolution of the late nineteenth century, precipitated by economists' admiration for the models of Newtonian physics (Mirowski 1989; Mitchell 1998), which brought into being Lionel Robbins' definition of economics as 'the science of human behaviour as a relationship between ends and scarce means which have mutually exclusive uses' (1935). The agent enacting this relationship was *homo economicus*, and economics became the study of the processes of this rational utility-maximising self-interested individual, with the atom of the representative agent lending itself to modelling through mathematics. As opposed to the earlier focus of political economy on historical productive processes, economics became the analysis 'of the internal rationality, the strategic programming of individuals' activity' (Foucault et al. 2008, 223), or as one member of the Rethinking Economics movement put it, 'the science of choice'. This focus on choice in the content of economics teaching is currently mirrored in the audit mechanisms and markets constructed to exchange this education.

This mainstream is often called 'neoclassical' by members of the movement, though the concept of 'neoclassical' economics, similar to that of 'neoliberalism', is elusive and contested both within academia (cf. Lawson 2013) and within the student movement itself, with one organiser noting that 'what we're railing against is economics as taught to undergraduates, and neoclassical economics happens to be just a good label to describe that entire group of theories'. While there is debate as to whether neoclassical economics is primarily composed of the theoretical adherence to the representative agent or its methodological faith in mathematics (cf. Lawson 2005), both of these are underpinned by a formalist atomistic ontology that critics argue is unsuitable for capturing the enactment and organisation of social relations (Lawson 1997, 2005, 2009; Eliassen et al. 2015). Microeconomics became the foundation of this mainstream built upon the pillars of the representative consumer and the representative firm. It is from this that we find the student-consumer and university-firm as the foundational units of the education market, and thus there is a strong link between the frames of mainstream economics and the rhetoric of recent policies in UK universities.

By contrast, heterodox economics is an assemblage of different schools, defined as a group primarily by what they are not. Collectively, they oppose the insistence upon mathematical modelling in the formalist-deductive framework of the economic orthodoxy (Lawson 2005, 493). They often undertake analyses that are not confined to the atomistic ontology of the representative agent writ large, such as those primarily concerning institutions or class, and include schools as diverse as Marxists, neo-Keynesians and Environmentalist Economists. Due to the hiring practices of departments and ranking of mainstream economics journals, they have largely been excluded, even purged, from many economics departments over the past few decades and those who remain report struggling for institutional recognition (Fourcade et al. 2015; Lebaron 2001; Mirowski 2013).

There is also another dimension to the notion of what constitutes neoclassical economics, which draws on perceived links between the discourses of orthodox economics and what are considered neoliberal reforms such as the construction of a university marketplace upon logics of the consumer. These links relate to 'neoliberalism' both in its conception as a proliferation of market policies (cf. Harvey 2005) and as utilitarian economising logics (cf. Foucault et al. 2008). The latter of these links was made several decades ago by Foucault a series of lectures given at the Collège de France in 1979–80, when he defined the emerging condition of neoliberalism as the deployment of rationales such as those put forward by prominent Chicago School economist Gary Becker of *homo economicus* as a mode of intelligibility to sites such as education and kinship relations. Others argue that the neoclassical school is an orthodoxy that lends legitimacy to a certain political order, namely that associated with a set of neoliberal market policies since the Thatcher-Reagan era of the 1980s (Harvey 2005; Mirowski 2013). Together, these contribute to the cultivation of certain types of subjects who are encouraged to act as economically calculating agents within education markets (Hyatt et al. 2015).

Many within the Rethinking Economics movement hold similar analyses, arguing that the dominance of mainstream economics has contributed to an acceptance of recent austerity policies, and the motivation of some members is to undermine austerity through challenging the syllabus. Following the financial crisis, these students are creating a frontier in economics education to challenge the spread of austerity policies and enable what they see as broader policy possibilities for the future. One organiser, Richard,[3] said that for him this was 'part of a bigger fight', one of tackling the inevitability that arises from the sense that there is no alternative to current policies:

> I see [neoclassical economics] as political, as associated with neoliberalism… it's a kind of pervasive discourse, a pervasive set of 'these are the kind of things we will discuss, these are the kind of policy solutions which we all know to be the right policy solutions'.

For some of those who hold this conception, the problem with orthodox economics is not just whether it is an accurate reflection of an external reality but also the influence it has in shaping (or at least legitimising) that reality: the problem is what the discipline does, as much as what it does not.[4] In this critique, the problem with economics is not its failure to represent action in the real world but its success at producing it, in ways that are considered undesirable. The contention with orthodox economics becomes another arena for a broader socio-political project of opposing neoliberal policies and the subjectivities they promote. These different conceptions of neoclassical economics influence the student movement that is seeking to challenge the existing syllabus, with different notions of the problem intertwining with different proposals for the solution.

As such, the emerging student movement is dynamic and diverse. Broadly, the proclaimed goals of the variety of student groups include the diversification of methods and theoretical approaches, the elucidation of the historical and political contexts in which models were developed to facilitate critical reflection, and the expansion of the dialectical relationship between theory and 'real world' examples (Eliassen et al. 2015; ISIPE 2014; PCES 2014). As a movement encompassing students across a variety of campuses both nationally and worldwide, it has neither a singular orientation to the mainstream that it seeks to destabilise, nor of the paradigm it wishes to replace it with. There are multiple groups who are complex and intertwined, and often act on many dimensions at once.

Their names are indicative of what such dimensions may seek to address. Specifically, some of the groups' names invoke a crisis of representation as precipitated by the events of 2008, with the titles of the Real World and Post-Crash societies suggesting that current economics teaching is divorced from an observable economy and falsified by recent events, positing a divide between an external 'reality' and the existing internal 'representation'. Organisers argue that this generates a 'sense of cognitive dissonance', which the movement seeks to address. Others such as the Open Economics Forum reference the democratisation of education beyond the bounds of the university (or at least its individual departments). Again, this suggests the dissolution of boundary at the edge of an institution, but rather than a divide of reality and representation this time it highlights the border's separation of people: between an elite of certified economists and a outsiders unable to access this arena. By opening up a forum beyond the (at least linguistic) bounds of a student 'society', it seeks to erode the division between those who have purchased their education to become certifiable students and those who have not. Finally, Societies for Economic Pluralism suggest yet another focus, again one of democratisation but this time of the paradigms taught more than the people who have access to teaching. The organisations are complex and interlinked, and names by no means indicate coherent or singular projects of individual groups. However, they are indicative of some of the alternative approaches that have arisen and the different dimensions of the contention with the existing status quo.

What is at stake in these conceptions is the relationship to the existing mainstream. Some oppose what they consider the existing neoclassical orthodoxy, while others seek to include the neoclassical school in a pluralist set of options. While the pluralist project seeks to include alternate schools alongside neoclassical economics in a pragmatic array of analytical approaches, the heterodox project is a set of separate paradigms that aligns itself in opposition to the existing orthodoxy. This relationship has several strands. One of them is a matter of epistemology, through the conception of what economics can and ought to be, which affects the content of the movement's demands. Yet the orientation of this relationship to the neoclassical school is also reflected in the form that the student movement takes, of both how it organises itself in relation to the status quo and how it seeks to change it. This chapter is primarily concerned with the latter of these dynamics, of how the perception of what needs to be changed relates to the strategy of how to change it.

In particular, it is concerned with the implications of the position that some members of the student movement oppose neoclassical economics due to its perceived links with a neoliberal political project. Some members of the movement who hold this view sometimes share links with other student movements that have accelerated after the crisis, particularly those calling for free education. They see the struggle they are embarking on within the classrooms as deeply intertwined with the context in which those classrooms are situated: who can access them, how they are funded and what the impact is of the knowledge they produce. In doing so, they seek to address the form of education as well as its content, by linking resistance to the pro free-market syllabus to the resistance of the marketisation of the degrees that the syllabi constitute.

Heterodox Political Economy of Education?

This presents those involved in the movement with a potential paradox, of how to relate claims over the content and the form of education, that is both the knowledge that is taught and the way this teaching is evaluated, and this shapes how the movement makes their demands. Students can either base demands to change the syllabus on their sovereignty as consumers, thus reinforcing free-market logics in education while perhaps seeking to undermine them on the syllabus itself, or opt for other strategies which seek to oppose free-market logics in both the content of degrees and the ways in which these degrees are circulated.

As mentioned above, the motivations of many of those joining the movement have a political dimension: they are opposed to austerity, and believe that more critical and diverse economics teaching can raise awareness of alternative economic policies. However, when it comes to austerity measures enacted on campus, some students are more resigned to the introduction of such policies, such as the increase in fees. Richard, who was quoted above expressing that he joined the movement in part to oppose to what he called 'neoliberalism' and a certain set of policies termed austerity, observed that mention of fees was 'like a version of Godwin's Law for university related discussions', implying that students regularly adopted the rhetoric of consumers to claim sovereignty. He explained that fees 'are sort of becoming the new normal' and adopted a tone of inevitability that they were here to stay. Richard actually was not opposed to fees himself, as he felt they were potentially a good way to fund universities if they were introduced 'progressively'. Many members of the movement are ambiguous or supportive of the introduction of fees, and consider education as a good which already is, or even should be, circulating on the market.

The awareness that there are other ways to fund education than through students' fees suggests that Shore was perhaps pre-emptive in arguing that 'many neo-liberal norms and assumptions (including the idea of "user-pays", higher education as a personal investment and the inevitability and desirability of free markets) have become hegemonic or "doxa"' (Shore 2010, 19). Ongoing discussion of the need for fees suggests that they are not 'doxa' yet; however, the predominance of considering fees the most legitimate source of university income and the resignation of those who do not hold this view suggest that the market has at least taken the hold as orthodoxy in terms of how to evaluate education in the UK. While students are attempting to challenge the orthodoxy of the free market in the content of their degrees, some have simultaneously become resigned to orthodoxy of the market in the ways such degrees are exchanged.

Moreover, the movement at times even reinforces this orthodoxy by deploying consumer logics itself when pursing its demands. This tension is visible in discussion over strategy. In his keynote speech at the London Rethinking Economics Conference in June 2014, an economist and vocal critic of the 'free market' argued to students in the brimming lecture theatre that 'the economics movement is built on the idea of consumer sovereignty'. He urged the theatre, 'Please use the economic theory your lecturers have taught you, and demand a change in syllabus'. This thinker has been critical of the expansion of free-market logics in the provision of goods and services, a position that aligns the views of many students in the movement. As such, he added a disclaimer to his call to the students: 'but it doesn't work for me because I don't believe in consumer sovereignty'. In doing so, he highlights the tension between students mobilising on a free-market platform that they are simultaneously trying to undermine.

Some members of Rethinking Economics deployed the notion of student demand in their strong support of the idea of an aforementioned Teaching Excellence Framework. Many thought the measure would highlight what they considered low teaching standards on many economics courses in comparison to more engagement with students and a greater focus on critical pedagogical models in other social sciences (cf. CSEP 2014; PCES 2014). However, while the TEF they envisaged would use measures of teaching quality that would challenge the dominance of economists over other social scientists (cf. Fourcade et al. 2015; Lebaron 2006), the metrics of graduate income actually used are actually likely to have the opposite effect, as economics majors tend to have higher earnings in comparison with graduates in other social sciences. This grants the authority to employers to decipher the quality of degrees. Thus, contrary to expectations, the measurement is likely to sustain existing advantages of some subjects over others.

Moreover, similar to the framing of the BIS Green Paper in terms of 'what employers want', the movement for changing the syllabus often cites employer dissatisfaction with skills of current economics graduates as a main impetus for change. The Cambridge Society for Economic Pluralism (CSEP 2014) stated that the one of the three primary concerns arising from a student survey they conducted in 2014 as a need for 'a greater focus on career skills' (CSEP 2014). This drive has been met from employers themselves. The Bank of England's Chief Economist Andy Haldane wrote the forward to a report by the Manchester Post-Crash Economics Society, stating that '[e]mployers of economists, like the Bank of England, stand to benefit from such an evolution in the economics curriculum' (PCES 2014, 6). The Bank also hosted a conference in early 2012 entitled 'Are Economics graduates fit for purpose?', the broad consensus of which was that they were not. The 'purpose' proposed for graduates is to fulfil the desires of employers, and students use this reference point of becoming 'fit for purpose' as an aspiration which they can call upon stakeholders to help them achieve, both employers and the policy-makers who are moulding tertiary education according to 'what employers want'.[5]

In doing so, students draw on discourses of both the education and employment markets in mobilising for change, and have supported efforts to link the two through measures such as the TEF. They mobilise the logic of consumer sovereignty in two distinct ways: both as their own sovereignty as consumers purchasing an education, and through the sovereignty of employers who demand the availability of attractive graduates. The demand of these two groups of consumers rests upon the tenet that students are able to undertake a transformation during their time at university to graduates who are 'fit for purpose'. This is reminiscent of Bauman's notion of the consumer-cum-commodity referenced above, whereby the validity of the demands of subjects rests upon their ability as to act as consumers who in turn reform themselves as commodities.

The notion that the platform of consumer sovereignty is necessary for the movement's success is questionable. Many within it are dubious of mobilising this position, with some rejecting it outright and others utilising it only in instrumental strategic terms. Ultimately, many members feel this tension is unresolved. As one organiser put it: 'the idea of students as consumers has particular resonance with economics and I think students as consumers works well as a rhetorical device because it's economics… but I also have a nagging sense we should be wary of linking our right to good education to the fact that we're paying for it'. Clearly these questions are unlikely to be resolved in ways that are cohesive and homogenous, and nor necessarily should they: the form that Rethinking Economics seeks to take is in many ways as pluralist as its content, with authority distributed horizontally in fluid and shifting assemblages of activists, which some note to be an 'anarchic structure'. However, the emerging strategy by which the movement addresses economic orthodoxy in education will also shape its relationship to orthodox education policy. Whether the movement tackles the sources of austerity on campuses as well as what many consider the theoretical frameworks that legitimise austerity elsewhere remains to be seen.

Ultimately, it seems that in deploying consumer logics many members do not necessarily intend to undertake a transformation into the consumer-cum-commodity, but merely wish to present the appearance of prioritising their desirability to employers as a means of legitimising their concerns. Yet in doing so they also legitimise the platform that policy changes in education encourage them to occupy, that of the consumer concerned with their own attractiveness on the employment market, and so the position has performative impacts of reinforcing the existing orthodoxy. This represents a form of Erik Olin Wright's 'symbiotic metamorphosis' with their 'contradictory character' (2010, 305) of 'both expanding social power and strengthening aspects of the system' (*ibid*). Whether this contradiction undermines the movement depends of course on its aims: whether the goal is just to change the content of economics education, or whether ultimately to change the modes by which goods and services, including this education, are evaluated and circulated. For those who are opposed to free-market logics in orthodox economics, either in terms of its dependency on them in the abstract or its application in policies, this position appears somewhat paradoxical: deploying the logic of the market in order to contest the dissemination of the logic of the market. It remains to be seen to what degree the movement will take a heterodox approach to the political economy of education, as well as to the education of political economy.

Notes

1. While this move was framed by the logic of austerity, it actually resulted in a significant increase in short-term government debt, with sell-off of loans likely to result in long-term losses due to the reevaluation of payback rates (McGettigan 2013).
2. Within this chapter 'neoliberalism' and 'neoclassical economics' are treated as ethnographic categories. The links between 'neoclassical economics', 'neoliberalism' and 'the market' also draw on understandings of interlocutors, and are not meant to suggest that schools of heterodox economics, including Austrians, do not also draw on the concept of markets. However, the chapter does suggest that a particular form of atomistic formalism that utilises the representative agents of consumer and firm is foundational to mainstream economics.
3. Names have been changed for purposes of anonymity.
4. For discussions of the performative relationship between economics and the economy, see Callon (1998) and MacKenzie (2007).
5. For links between student and employer demands, see Eliassen et al. (2015) and PCES (2014).

Works Cited

Baudrillard, Jean. 1994. *Simulacra and simulation*. Ann Arbor: University of Michigan Press.

Bauman, Zygmunt. 2007. *Consuming life*. Cambridge: Polity Press.

BIS. 2015a. *Fulfilling our potential: Teaching excellence, social mobility and student choice*. https://www.gov.uk/government/uploads/system/uploads/attachment_

data/file/474227/BIS-15-623-fulfilling-our-potential-teaching-excellence-social-mobility-and-student-choice.pdf. Accessed 24 Apr 2017.

———. 2015b. *Press release: Student choice at the heart of new higher education reforms*. https://www.gov.uk/government/news/student-choice-at-the-heart-of-new-higher-education-reforms. Accessed 24 Apr 2017.

———. 2016. *The teaching excellence framework: Assessing quality in higher education*. http://www.publications.parliament.uk/pa/cm201516/cmselect/cmbis/572/572.pdf. Accessed 24 Apr 2017.

Bourdieu, Pierre. 1984. *Distinction: A social critique of the judgement of taste*. London: Routledge.

———. 1988. *Homo academicus*. Stanford: Stanford University Press.

Bourdieu, Pierre, and Jean-Claude Passeron. 1990. *Reproduction in education, society and culture*. London: Sage.

Callon, Michel. 1998. *The laws of the markets*. Oxford/Malden: Blackwell Publishers.

Collini, Stefan. 2016. Who are the spongers now? *London Review of Books* 38 (2): 33–37.

CSEP. 2014. *CSEP survey of economics students: Is it time for change at Cambridge?* http://www.cambridgepluralism.org/uploads/1/7/4/9/17499733/report_v14_w.appendix.pdf. Accessed 24 Apr 2017.

Eliassen, Raman, Jostein Løhr Hauge, and Ivan Rajić. 2015. *Fit for a fix: Why the economics curriculum needs a pluralist revamp*. https://www.jiscmail.ac.uk/cgi-bin/webadmin?A3=ind1510&L=HETECON&E=BASE64&P=1574821&B=--Message-Boundary-5594&T=Application%2FOctet-stream;%20name=%22Fit%20for%20a%20fix%20(English%20version).pdf%22&N=Fit%20for%20a%20fix%20(English%20version).pdf&attachment=q&XSS=3. Accessed 24 Apr 2017.

Foucault, Michel. 1972. *The archaeology of knowledge*. New York: Pantheon Books.

Foucault, Michel, Graham Burchell, and Arnold Davidson. 2008. *The birth of biopolitics*. Basingstoke: Palgrave Macmillan.

Fourcade, Marion, Etienne Ollion, and Yann Algan. 2015. The superiority of economists. *Journal of Economic Perspectives* 29 (1): 89–114.

Freire, Paulo. 1970. *Pedagogy of the oppressed*. New York: Herder and Herder.

Gramsci, Antonio. 1972. *Selections from the prison notebooks of Antonio Gramsci*, ed. Quintin Hoare and Geoffrey Nowell-Smith. New York: International Publishers.

Harvey, David. 2005. *A brief history of Neoliberalism*. Oxford: Oxford University Press.

Hyatt, Susan Brin, Boone W. Shear, and Susan Wright. 2015. *Learning under neoliberalism: Ethnographies of governance in higher education*. New York: Berghahn Books.

ISIPE. 2014. *International student initiative for pluralism in economics*. http://www.isipe.net. Accessed 24 Apr.

Lawson, Tony. 1997. *Economics and reality*. London: Routledge.

———. 2005. The nature of heterodox economics. *Cambridge Journal of Economics* 30 (4): 483–505.

———. 2009. The current economic crisis: Its nature and the course of academic economics. *Cambridge Journal of Economics* 33 (4): 759–777.

———. 2013. What is this 'school' called neoclassical economics? *Cambridge Journal of Economics* 37 (5): 947–983.

Lebaron, Frédéric. 2001. Economists and the economic order: The field of economists and the field of power in France. *European Societies* 3 (1): 91–110.

———. 2006. "Nobel" economists as public intellectuals. *International Journal of Contemporary Sociology* 43 (1): 88–101.

MacKenzie, Donald. 2007. *An engine, not a camera*. Cambridge: MIT Press.

Massey, Doreen. 2013. Vocabularies of the economy. In *After neoliberalism? The Kilburn manifesto*, ed. Stuart Hall, Doreen Massey, and Michael Rustin, 3–17. London: Lawrence and Wishart.

McGettigan, Andrew. 2013. *The great university gamble: Money, markets and the future of higher education*. London: Pluto Press.

Mirowski, Philip. 1989. *More heat than light*. Cambridge: Cambridge University Press.

———. 2013. *Never let a serious crisis go to waste*. London: Verso.

Mitchell, Timothy. 1998. Fixing the economy. *Cultural Studies* 12 (1): 82–101.

NUS. 2015. *The higher education green paper in a nutshell*. http://www.nus.org.uk/en/news/the-higher-education-green-paper-in-a-nutshell/. Accessed 24 Apr 2017.

Nussbaum, Martha C. 2010. *Not for profit: Why democracy needs the humanities*. Princeton: Princeton University Press.

PCES. 2014. *Economics, education and unlearning: Economics education at the University of Manchester*. Manchester: The Post-Crash Economics Society.

Power, Michael. 1997. *The audit society: Rituals of verification*. Oxford: Oxford University Press.

Robbins, Lionel Charles Robbins. 1935. *An essay on the nature and significance of economic science*. 2nd ed. London: Macmillan.

Shore, Cris. 2010. Beyond the multiversity: Neoliberalism and the rise of the schizophrenic university. *Social Anthropology* 18 (1): 15–29.

Shore, Cris, and Miri Davidson. 2014. Beyond collusion and resistance: Academic management relations within the neoliberal university. *Learning and Teaching* 7 (1): 12–28.

Shore, Cris, and Susan Wright. 1999. Audit culture and anthropology: Neoliberalism in British higher education. *The Journal of the Royal Anthropological Institute* 5 (4): 557–575.

Spence, Michael. 1973. Job market signaling. *The Quarterly Journal of Economics* 87 (3): 355.

Strathern, Marilyn. 2000. *Audit cultures*. London/New York: Routledge.

Wright, Erik Olin. 2010. *Envisioning real utopias*. London: Verso.

Wright, Susan. 2015. Anthropology and the "imaginators" of future European universities. *Focaal* 2015 (71): 6–17.

Wright, Susan, and Annika Rabo. 2010. Introduction: Anthropologies of university reform. *Social Anthropology* 18 (1): 1–14.

Section II

Revitalising Democracy

Local Maidan Across Ukraine: Democratic Aspirations in the Revolution of Dignity

Olga Zelinska

Introduction: What Is Maidan?

From 21 November 2013, Ukraine was convulsed by three months of near-daily demonstrations, of a scale and intensity unprecedented in the recent history of Europe. The epitome of what political scientists call 'contentious politics'[1]—used to refer to popular anti-government uprisings deploying socially disruptive tactics—in the end, the protests generated much more than mere contention. They effected social transformations. By March 2014, Ukrainian President Viktor Yanukovych had been ousted, having fled to Russia. Yet celebrations were short lived. Shortly thereafter followed Russia's military invasion and annexation of the Ukrainian Autonomous Republic of Crimea, fuelling a bloody conflict in eastern Ukraine that continues to this day.

These momentous episodes of civil unrest, involving as many as a million participants, who took to the streets of villages, towns, and cities

O. Zelinska (✉)
Graduate School for Social Research, Warsaw, Poland

T. Geelan et al. (eds.), *From Financial Crisis to Social Change*,
https://doi.org/10.1007/978-3-319-70600-9_6

across Ukraine, would come to be known as simply 'Maidan' (or 'Maidans'), meaning 'square'—after the site of the first major protests, Kyiv's Maidan Nezalezhnosti, or 'Independence Square'—as well as 'Euromaidan', after their initial goal of greater EU-Ukraine integration. Whatever their label, in the months and years that followed they would come to symbolise the struggle against outrageous human rights violations, committed by a corrupt and repressive regime. For that reason, Maidan has received a third designation: the Revolution of Dignity.

The proximate cause of Maidan may be traced to November 2013 and the Ukrainian government's sudden and unexpected refusal to sign the Ukraine-European Union Association Agreement, a treaty that would have brought Ukraine economically and politically closer to the EU. In response to the government's decision, a small group of NGO activists and students occupied Kyiv's 'Maidan Square'. Within three months of that November protest, the small camp of tents housing the relatively fringe supporters of European integration had metamorphosed into a nationwide social movement whose demands had correspondingly broadened to encompass an end to government human rights violations, a change of the political regime, and an end to endemic corruption. A series of escalations between protestors and law enforcement culminated, in February 2014, with a raid by armed police officers on Maidan in Kiev, who opened fire, killing over a hundred protestors.

The majority of Maidan's participants demonstrated in the capital city of Kyiv—as many as 800,000 on some estimates—though Maidans also took place in smaller cities, towns, and villages across Ukraine. Aside from civil unrest, their principal products were a variety of 'resolutions' and other documents outlining particular claims, in the form of proposals and demands for social change, directed towards local, national, and global institutions of governance and, in some cases, to the individuals running them. The focus of this chapter is on the nature of these claims and their connection to the movement's medium- and longer-term success in the struggle for democracy. I suggest that a substantial part of these claims amount to utopian visions for a future Ukraine—alternative horizons that open up the possibility of a new, democratically reinvigorated nation.

But first of all: What was the historical and political context in which the Maidan protests (thereafter 'Maidans', following the shorthand common in Ukraine) erupted? Who were the protestors? How did they seek to assert their democratic aspirations? And finally, to what extent did they succeed?

Maidan: Historical and Political Context

The salient characteristic of the political regime inherited by President Viktor Yanukovych from 2010 onwards was its authoritarianism. This tendency had led to the widespread public—and international—perception of endemic government corruption, one-person control over the three branches of power (the executive, legislature, and judiciary), disempowerment of local governments, lack of mechanisms for public participation, and a general distrust in politics and public institutions. One could scarcely imagine conditions less congenial to democracy.

A few months after Yanukovych's election as President of Ukraine in 2010, the Constitutional Court declared that the transfer in 2004 to a parliamentary system of governance was illegal. This returned to the office of the President the full powers it enjoyed before the transfer (The Verkhovna Rada of Ukraine 2010). Within a year, Yanukovych had established full control over all three branches of power, and over local governments (Myseliuk 2010). The move from democracy to dictatorship had all but been confirmed.

Following the financial crisis of 2008, access to investment capital became more difficult for Ukrainian enterprises, leading to economic stagnation. Given that major business interests, including Ukraine's oligarchy, had moved ever closer to the Presidency (Valevskyi 2014), the government's economic plan did not entail increasing taxation on big business. But nor did it implement a programme of austerity to cut state expenditures. As such, its closing of the budget gap depended on its tax increases upon small- and medium-size businesses.

In 2011, Yuiya Tymoshenko, a popular opposition leader, was sentenced by the courts to seven years in prison and banned from holding public office (Ukrainska pravda 2011). That same year, the Parliament voted to revise the electoral law for the 2012 elections, prohibiting the participation of party blocks (coalitions), while raising the vote threshold to avoid both a united opposition and the arrival of newcomers. Consequently, after the 2012 parliamentary elections, the Party of Regions faction (209 MPs) and loyal Communist faction (32 MPs) grew in influence as the opposition dwindled (Tymoshenko's 'Batkivshchyna', 99 MPs; Klitschko's UDAR, 42 MPs; and Tyahnybok's Svoboda, 37 MPs) (RBC-Ukraine 2012)—such that it had little chance of influencing national policymaking and constituted no real threat to the rule of the President and his party (Oleksiyenko and Pototskyy 2013). By 2013, the regime, which had now reached the height of its power, could fairly be characterised, at best, as embodying 'soft authoritarianism'. Certainly, there was no democracy.

Reinforcing this view, the pro-presidential Party of Regions was reported to have 'operated as a political machine throughout the country' (Roberts and Fisun 2014, 6). Civil servants at both national and local levels were forced to enter the party (or else leave their office) and to coordinate all future decisions with the party leadership. The Presidential Administration became the de facto fourth branch of power that, through appointing and dismissing officials, 'manually' intervened in the activities of the executive and exerted strong influence over the legislature and judiciary. The predictable effect of this was a substantially diminished role of representative institutions at all levels of government, and a decline in effective governance in the regions, where local state administrations and self-governments had continually faced difficulties in sharing resources and powers. Thus, local government became further disempowered.

The Constitution of Ukraine foresees two systems of power in the regions: local state administrations—local offices of the executive, with the head appointed by the President—and local self-government, representative bodies of the local communities, with the head chosen from directly elected members of the local council (The Verkhovna Rada of Ukraine 1996). The 1999 Law of Ukraine on Local State Administration prescribed that the functions of local self-governments were delegated to state administrations. Local governments were supported with financial resources allocated by Kyiv. This mechanism was introduced back in the

1990s by President Leonid Kuchma, who sought to centralise the state and manage the flow of taxes through the national treasury (Roberts and Fisun 2014). As such, there were built-in tensions regarding delegated functions and allocated resources, creating confusion that diminished the efficiency of policymaking and implementation (Honcharuk and Prokopenko 2011). Within this system, citizens could influence the local affairs only through direct elections of local self-governments (often compromised by election fraud). But the local self-governments, essentially, remained deprived of their powers, which migrated to state administrations, which are subordinate to the President (Committee of the Regions of the EU 2011).

Moreover, Ukraine's highly centralised state apparatus, essentially controlled by a single political and financial 'family', made public participation in policymaking at both national and local levels difficult (Zelinska 2014). This was not meant to be. The right of Ukrainians to participate in the management of state affairs was guaranteed by Article 38 of the Constitution (The Verkhovna Rada of Ukraine 1996). Different laws and government regulations developed a range of mechanisms for such participation, including open addresses, information queries, surveys, hearings, expert study, and monitoring of state actions (Jizha and Radchenko 2012). In 2004, public participation was also institutionalised in the form of public councils. These are oversight bodies that operate at all levels of administration: the national government, local state authorities, and self-governments (Buzdugan 2012). Yet the democratic promise of these councils remained unfulfilled. With their advisory function often limited to ill-defined 'public pressure', they were widely considered a weak check on executive power (Yermilova 2013). Both national and local governments created obedient public councils out of loyal NGOs and used public participation as leverage in lobbying. The very idea of a handful of 'compromised' organisations speaking on behalf of a wider local or professional community was also frequently decried (Zakharov 2009).

As a result of all these developments, by 2013 the public had little confidence in state institutions. A survey conducted in August 2013 found that in terms of institutional trust, 69% did not trust the President, 77% did not trust Parliament, and 71% did not trust the Government.

Moreover, 70% had no confidence in the police, 72% had no confidence in the courts, and 64% had no confidence in the prosecutor general. The level of distrust in political parties reached similar levels: 69%. The champions of trust were the church, in which 70% of respondents declared confidence; the media (58%), local self-governments (42%), and NGOs (38%).[2]

This was the political context when, in 2013, the President and Parliament were preparing to sign the Association Agreement with the EU,[3] expected to be presented at the Vilnius Summit in November that year. A week before signing the Agreement, the government terminated the plan. And it is this that triggered Maidan.

Why did this seemingly technical decision initiate a nationwide social movement? Preliminary investigations suggest that this agreement meant much more than the direction of foreign policy or potential economic benefits. Rather, Ukrainians belong to those nations for whom the broader meaning of Europe encompasses notions of vision and 'faith' rather than rules and regulations (Yermolenko 2014). It follows that an association with Europe would be perceived at the level of the senses, not the mind—as 'the light at the end of the tunnel'. Others see things rather differently. Campos (2013), for example, typifies one class of competing explanation in stressing the *rational calculus* underpinning the pro-European attitude. On this view, Europe was an 'institutional anchor' that could halt Ukraine's slide into non-democratic government. For these commentators, the government's reversal on European integration therefore signified an alarming move towards authoritarianism.

Who Were the Maidan Protestors?

Despite suggestions in the Western and Russian media that ultranationalist elements played a leading role in the protests (Luhn 2014; Steinberg 2014), a systematic analysis of Maidan participants (Democratic Initiatives Foundation 2014b; Onuch 2014; Onuch and Sasse 2016; Shekhovtsov 2014), their protest rhetoric (Centre for Society Research 2014; Onuch and Sasse 2014; Zelinska 2015), and their oral histories

(Kovtunovych and Pryvalko 2015) found substantial diversity in protestors' ideological identity.

Studies suggest that between 17% and 20% of Ukraine's population participated in the protests, or supported the protestors, with Maidan supporters coming from all regions of Ukraine.[4] The highest rates of participation in the Kyiv protests are recorded for those from central Ukraine (9.5% of respondents), while western Ukraine had the highest proportion of those who protested at home (26.2%), or helped protestors with money, food, or clothing (29.5% of respondents). Declared levels of engagement among respondents in the east and south were much lower, at <2% and <1%, respectively. Support for Maidan also varied according to age. While 25.7% of the youngest age cohort (18–29) declared support, this number gradually decreases as respondents age, with just 11.4% of respondents over 70 declaring support. With respect to level of education, 29.4% of respondents with a higher education qualification supported the protest. This support declined in tandem with each decrease in the level of education, with just 7.3% of those with an incomplete middle school education declaring support. Finally, there were slight differences between the genders: 23.8% of male respondents and 17.8% of female respondents declared support for Maidan (Democratic Initiatives Foundation 2014b).

Evidence also indicates that the composition of Maidan's participants changed throughout the three-month protest.[5] While Kyivites comprised almost 50% of Kyiv Maidan participants in December 2013, by February 2014 their share had decreased to 12%. Throughout the protests, the great majority of protestors (varying between 70% and 92%) did not belong to any organisation, and travelled to Kyiv on their own initiative. Interestingly, though, while in December only 9% of protestors were members of political parties, NGOs, or civil society organisations, by February this had risen to 30%. Female participation was subject not to growth but attrition, possibly corresponding to the increased threat of government repression: in December, Maidan participation by gender was 57% male to 43% female, with the latter falling to 12% by February. Similarly, the average Maidan protestor in December was younger and better educated than in February (in December, 40% belonged to the 19–29 age cohort, and 63% had a university degree, while in February, 56% were aged 30–54, and only 43% held a tertiary degree) (Democratic Initiatives Foundation 2014a).

We know that in 2013–2014, virtually all protestors' claims-making[6] revolved around the Maidan. In the international press, Maidan became synonymous with the protests at the eponymous Kyiv square (The Economist 2013; Walker and Grytsenko 2013). However, while Kyiv was host to the main protest, residents of the Ukrainian east and west played their part. During the winter, people in cities and towns gathered for Sunday rallies called *viches*,[7] or popular assemblies, and directed claims towards local and national governments, planned further actions, coordinated activities with other cities, and sent delegates—along with money, food, and warm clothes—to the movement's centre in Kyiv.

The assemblies issued their own resolutions to both local and national government. They included political claims, grievances, demands, and declarations of support or opposition in relation to various issues. These documents provide a rich source of primary data on protestors' dreams, hopes, and aspirations. These grassroots ideas, developed by the local Maidans, did much to enrich the entire Maidan movement, as well as raise questions about what is politically possible, thereby opening up a space for imagining alternative futures (Fournier 2003, 181).

Utopian Visions

As Langman (2013, 516) suggests, research on social movements needs to re-discover an important aspect of the phenomenon, one critical not only to their achievement of social change, but their very existence, and without which recruitment would be made very difficult. This aspect is their 'utopian visions'. These are expressed in the claims of the protestors and are perhaps most directly expressed in their demands ('We want X'). According to Langman, the role of vision in social movements is in need of rethinking, and at the very least, the utopian visions that were always at their heart, which give their members hope and drive them forward, should be brought back in.

In his analysis of 'real' utopias, Wright (2010, 14–16) suggests that any such social alternative can be elaborated upon and evaluated in terms of three criteria: desirability, viability, and achievability. For an envisioned future to be *desirable* it must simply posit a better version of the world than presently pertains (however 'better' might be defined). Second, in being *viable* they should actually bring about in a sustainable and robust way their intended consequences. Finally, depending on external conditions, and most importantly, people's beliefs in the possibility of their implementation, these ideas must stand at least a minor chance of being achieved.

I base my analysis on Alexander's (2001, 580) definition of utopia—though I also use 'vision' to mean the same—as a normatively desirable model of a fundamentally different social order that regulates both social thinking and social action. Indeed, as we shall see, those involved in Maidans have been engaged in both lived and imagined utopias. Participants' reflections reveal their fascination with a new and more progressive social order, a 'model of a New Ukraine', which for many resulted from, or is promised by, the Kyiv Maidan.[8] Yet Maidan may also be seen as a microcosm, a mini-society all of its own—a community whose participants are united by a shared ethic or set of norms, including deliberative self-government, mutual respect, probity, and a readiness to help. That ethic was reflected in a popular joke of the time: during clashes with police, the first rows of protestors may be heard to say 'excuse me!' (Sviatnenko and Vinogradov 2014). Practising 'activism-as-democracy' (Blee 2012, 4), Maidan created a space in civic life for ideas and actions that existed nowhere else and helped people envision how Ukraine could be transformed for the better.

Thus, having outlined the recent historical and political context of Maidan, and provided a broad-brush portrait of its participants, I now present an analysis of these (local) protestors resolutions, as a means of apprehending their utopian visions and democratic aspirations for a future Ukraine. The remainder of this chapter is divided into two parts. First, I present an analysis of the collection of resolutions issued by the local *viches* in 57 cities and towns across Ukraine. In so doing, I expand analytic attention beyond the usual focus of the Kyiv Maidan, hence providing space for *vox populi*, the expression of local Maidans' grassroots aspirations. Second, I investigate the three most salient visions for further societal transformation and the deepening of democracy, developed by local Maidans, and elaborate on their viability and achievability. This adds to the debate on post-Maidan reformation in Ukraine. Throughout, I have been concerned to understand the story behind these utopian visions, which is, really, the story of Maidan.

Analysing Vox Populi: My Data

My analysis is of resolutions issued by local Maidan protestors that were adopted between 24 November 2013, the day of the first mass rally in Kiev following the government's U-turn on the Ukraine-European Union Association Agreement (Democratic Initiatives Foundation 2013b), and 22 February 2014, on which a new national government was elected, the day after President Yanukovych fled the capital (Democratic Initiatives Foundation 2014c). A qualitatively new period of contention begins on 1 March when the Federal Assembly of the Russian Federation sanctioned the invasion of the Crimean peninsula, paving the way for its annexation (Ukrainska pravda 2014). The week from 22 February to 1 March was the protestors' most active period of claims-making. Key national-level demands—for instance, the resignation of top government officials—were met, with Russian troops yet to step onto Ukrainian soil. Thus, the earliest document in the compendium of resolutions analysed for this chapter dates to 24 November 2013, and the latest to 27 February 2014.

In total, 101 resolutions were collected—92 texts and 9 videos—the most comprehensive dataset on Maidan claims-making[9]. These originate from 57 localities (pinpointed in Appendix 1) in 20 Ukrainian regions in the east and west. This enabled analysis of what types of changes were desired, as articulated by participants of numerous local protests, across Ukraine's regions. Resisting the temptation to give further attention to the already well-studied demands of the Kyiv Maidan (see Onuch and Sasse 2016), I focus solely on local protests, including seven collective resolutions which comprised important informal initiatives that aimed at the horizontal coordination of local Maidan efforts.[10] These assemblies' primary goals were to develop a common agenda for the Maidan movement in general, and to support local Maidans by providing guidelines on protest 'best practice' as well as in specific policy areas. For example, while the Kharkiv Forum (January 2014) issued one joint resolution, the Odesa Forum (February 2014) presented four documents containing claims in different spheres, the product of forum participants dividing into working groups according to the expertise of each delegate. The documents issued by these assemblies should therefore be both representative of the local communities which delegated their participants, and focused on the reform agenda for Ukraine.

Importantly, all local Maidan resolutions were developed by local *viches* (general assemblies of the local population), which practise deliberative democracy. It is perhaps unsurprising, therefore, that they often sought to extend this model of decision-making, which they already practised, to the national government. Particularly striking is how, as the protest events unfolded and new political opportunity structures[11] emerged, these alternative visions differed in their 'radicalism' vis-à-vis the political institutions and procedures of the status quo. In what follows, I discuss what this rich collection of resolutions reveals about the demands and visions of the Maidan protestors and, following Wright, assess their viability and achievability. In doing so, I illustrate the complexities of enacting alternatives to the status quo.

In Search of a Deeper Democracy: Utopian Visions of Local Maidans

Vision 1. A Return to 'People's Rule'

At the earlier stages of the Maidan movement, in reaction to a decline in the ability of the 'ordinary citizen' to participate in political decision-making, the protestors sought a fundamental redistribution of political power. At the same time, they wished to stay within the existing legal framework and invoked the constitutional principle that declared the people to be the only source of power in Ukraine (The Verkhovna Rada of Ukraine 1996). The protestors saw the 'restoration of real people's rule',[12] originally guaranteed by the Constitution, as the logical outcome of their collective action, their mission.[13] This democratic form of power-sharing became perhaps the dominant frame by which the content of their utopian visions were shaped.

From this most general of utopian goals, we can already begin to perceive some of the mechanisms thought necessary to achieve it. At the beginning, suggestions were quite conventional and did not call for any real *alternatives* to the present concentration of power, beyond greater citizen participation in local and national affairs. However, in the wake of protestors' ferocious subjugation at the hands of president-controlled authorities, local Maidans demanded greater alterations to the existing institutional order. These included liquidation—by means of the new law on self-governance—of the 'vertical' power structures in the regions and state administrations, in addition to a major transfer of powers to local communities, with a view to enacting 'people's rule'.[14]

Further, all key administrative appointments at the local level (the protestors did not specify which positions) had to be approved by the local 'lustration commission',[15] composed of local Maidan activists,[16] or otherwise the general assembly—the local *viche.*[17] In order to put pressure on local self-governments, the community planned weekly public hearings to table possible solutions to the perceived political and economic crises gripping the country.[18] Notably, the public hearing is a rare practice in Ukrainian governance. Initiated solely by the national or local authorities, it has traditionally occupied an advisory role only, so one may see a certain novelty in its being wielded as a tool of political pressure.

Local residents were also expected, according to Maidan demands, to gain control over local budgets[19]—and national ones.[20] At that time, both local and national budgets were considered 'regulatory documents', which allow for citizens to register feedback on their content—though authorities' decision to heed or ignore such feedback is entirely at their discretion. The result is that the power of 'the people' to influence budgets is limited to their election of this politician over that, on the basis of candidates' broader political agenda. Granting to citizens direct control over budgets was therefore another novelty proposed by the Maidan activists.

Finally, activists were dissatisfied with what they saw as a dearth of truly consequential mechanisms for 'people's rule' beyond elections and advisory public councils. But believing constitutional rights to be the supreme 'legality', protestors were confident that this would soon be rectified. In this attitude of self-assurance, they demanded that the Maidan headquarters, as well as all self-government authorities, pursue this vision of a genuine people's governance.[21]

Vision 2. Creating Alternative Institutions: The People's Council (Narodna Rada)

Developing the idea of restoring the 'people's rule', local protest groups promoted the creation of alternative—and *de jure* illegal—political institutions. On 19 January 2014, the Kyiv Maidan registered a majority vote for a new supreme legislative body, the 'People's Council' (Narodna Rada) that would replace the existing regime-dependent legislature, the Supreme Council of Ukraine (Verkhovna Rada) (Independent News Bureau 2014a). The proposed model was based on a vertical power structure with the regions as its foundations. The Ukrainian media reported that Councils based on the same model were established in 19 Ukrainian regions (Independent News Bureau 2014b). They operated, however, under a different mandate to the proposed national *Narodna Rada*. In the regions, where local councils were controlled by the opposition, People's Councils were announced as an alternative to the 'corrupt' local councils. Oblasts—the term for Ukraine's primary administrative regions, of which there are 24—that were controlled by the pro-presidential forces, created 'Radas' as 'advisory public councils', which, before the victory of Maidan, were perceived as transitory institutions (Dvoretska 2014).

Local Maidans championed the People's Council as a necessary guardian of the spirit of the Constitution, and the rights and freedoms of the citizens—a curb on the executive excesses characteristic of the previous regime.[22] They saw these parallel power structures as real—and realistic—alternatives consonant with their broader vision to construct, from the bottom up, a more just and democratic Ukrainian Republic.[23] A further innovation, made possible by Maidan pledges to support opposition-led projects, was a kind of 'political contract', in effect to remind citizens' representatives to make good on their own electoral pledges made before assuming office.[24] Maidan activists hoped that, in time, the regional Radas would eventually replace the existing apparatus, and incorporate members from the previously abolished local councils, and public activists, the latter to operate without party affiliation, but instead expressly on behalf of the public.[25]

Despite championing an illegal institution (in proposing a reconfiguration of the three branches of power), local activists stressed that they acted within legal boundaries, and announced their support of the People's Council and the creation of Regional Councils. In accordance with their core belief that the people are the only source of power in Ukraine,[26] the new supreme legislative body was perceived as a viable project. This might be thought remarkable, not least because the degree to which the People's Council differs from the existing Supreme Council of Ukraine remains unclear.

Vision 3. Direct Democracy

The third and final vision for social change foresaw a transformation of Ukraine's philosophy of governance. The Maidan activists wanted the existing representative model to be overhauled in line with direct democracy principles, which would allow citizens to play a more active and hands-on role in political decision-making. Direct democracy would be instituted at the local level—in protestor's streets, neighbourhoods, and towns. Thereafter, the norms of direct democracy would be (voluntarily) introduced in the form of legal codes by the existing legislative bodies.[27]

Local Maidan resolutions provide some details regarding the implementation of direct democracy. For example: the creation of grassroots people's bodies such as street and neighbourhood committees.[28] Regular local referendums on city management were another instrument that was identified; these should be held on issues of local importance, including the removal of elected officials from office.[29] Finally, local *viches* were to be continued, though with the new ascribed (and superior) status of a self-government body wherein all community residents, through deliberation and direct democracy, could decide on local issues.[30]

Although this vision of direct democracy suggested a new philosophy of governance and corresponding institutional changes, it did not entail the transformation of all existing power structures, especially those of central government. This contributed to the belief among local Maidans that it could be achieved, because it involved cooperation with the existing local self-governments, an optimism doubtless reinforced by the resonance of this 'local' innovation with local residents. It is important to recognise an attempt to connect lived and imagined utopian practices: local *viches* sought to continue their existence post-Maidan with an enhanced status as permanent decision-making bodies.

Some Conclusions

The Ukrainian Maidan may be seen to have stirred a number of positive—and swift—changes. Chief among these was the ousting of Viktor Yanukovych and his authoritarian regime. Further, the movement united actors diverse in status, ideology, and languages and created a broad coalition of activists, the political opposition, local self-governments, NGOs, and churches—which doubtless contributed to its success. At the same time, this broad social movement stayed leaderless and decentralised. Hundreds of Maidans across the country gave it a far-reaching success, one sustained by local provision of manpower, money, clothes, and food to the centre. No less important is their provision of fora which invigorated democratic deliberation. Remembering the bitter experience of 2004's Orange Revolution, which against popular expectations did not lead to substantial social change, the activists in 2014 adopted a different aim: 'to change the system, and not just the faces, of government'. In service of this goal, the local Maidan protestors produced three salient visions for a better future to broaden and deepen democracy in Ukraine.

Their initial vision of regaining 'people's power' was planned as a series of minor legal steps within the constraints of existing frameworks of law that would, if successful, empower citizens to have a real impact in decision-making. It was, perhaps, the most desirable: activists were able to advance specific and thoroughgoing improvements in the areas with which they were familiar. By contrast, the proposal to replace old legislature with new appears not to have been deliberated in the regions or enriched by local innovations. The direct democracy concept, too, remained underdeveloped and hence institutionally 'thin'—a mere framework of practice or set of general principles—and was not supported with sufficiently systematic strategies of collaboration with the existing political structures.

The vision of enhanced public control mechanisms was strongly supported by activists, especially members of NGOs, which at that time enjoyed wide public confidence. They hence stood a good chance of successful implementation. The necessary institutional building blocks—public hearings, public budget oversight, and public councils—already existed but required an overhaul (e.g., for councils to be endowed with veto powers rather than be accorded a solely advisory role). The proposal to create an alternative People's Council, despite having the support of the opposition parties, would have been unconstitutional. Proponents of local-level direct democracy also came soon to realise that this project depended for its success upon negotiating with elected local self-governments. These institutions, without assurances for their continued supremacy, could seldom be expected to support an initiative that entailed substantial curtailment of their power.

The viability of the local Maidan's utopian visions may also be hampered by the fact that there was no genuine impetus to create a strong political force to push forward the desired changes—without which it is difficult to replace the old political elites and change the system 'from within'. Although some activists ran for office in the following parliamentary and local elections, or entered the government intent to push for reforms, these were few and far between. While at the national level, two Kyiv Maidans—one embodying the 'public', comprising NGOs and students, the other 'politics', formed by opposition political parties—eventually merged to pursue common goals, local Maidan activists tended to distance themselves from 'established politicians' and the existing political channels they sought to supplant.

Would any of these visions lead to activists' hoped-for deepening of Ukrainian democracy? In keeping with the Maidan's characteristic optimism, I think it is reasonable to venture an affirmative response—in all three cases. For all visions contained an immediate and perceptible shift to greater public engagement in policymaking—through participation in working groups, lustration commissions, public councils, permanent committees, referendums, and legislative assemblies. Instances of what may be termed revolutionary euphoria produce a readiness to contribute to the furtherance of such visions. That said, would not the re-instantiation of 'people's power' require, at the very least, a considerable investment in the tailoring of new legislative norms, and a reinvention of the 'checks and balances' that are the sine qua non for any such institution to function? With respect to the People's Council, that could only succeed with the firm support of the general population. Direct democracy mechanisms, moreover, would require the constant input of local residents, which may be more difficult to garner in less revolutionary times. What is surer is that only further research could settle our question of whether the activists envisioned ways of overcoming the usual barriers to any major reform: institutional deadlocks, overburdened and overlong decision-making, political crises, and conflicts of interest within institutions.

In any case, it must be admitted that the prospects of implementing protestors' visions have been dampened severely by developments that were, as is typical in politics, entirely unforeseen—or perhaps unforeseeable. For all their powers of creativity and vision, the protagonists of Maidan have run up against a destructive reality: an annexed Crimea and war in the east. When it became clear that Ukraine's armed forces were unable to contain the conflict, the Maidan activists joined hastily formed volunteer battalions of the National Guard (Shurkhalo 2014). Similarly, many of Maidan's volunteer groups and organisations have redirected their energies to support the Ukrainian army, thereby halting indefinitely their struggle for social change (Kravets et al. 2016).

Appendix 1

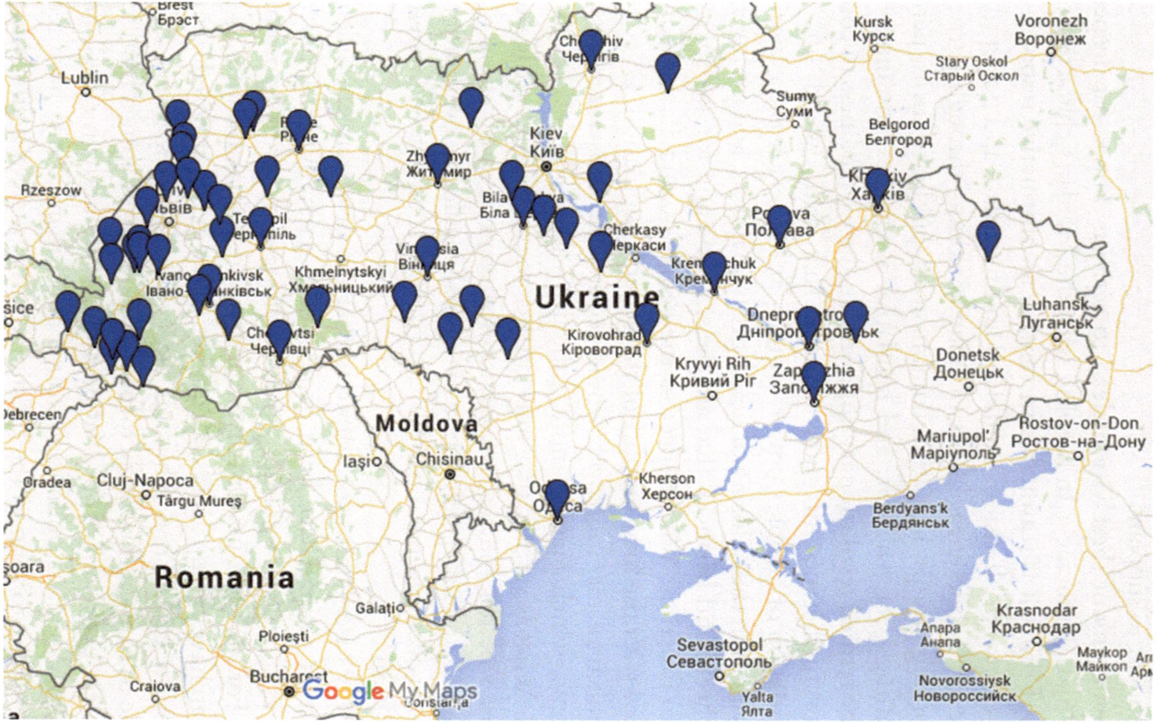

Localities in which local Maidans adopted the resolutions

Notes

1. In this analysis I treat Maidan as contentious politics, defined as public and collective claims making by a connected network of people and groups, where government is the object of claims or is the third party in these claims, following the works of Tilly, Tarrow and McAdam (McAdam et al. 2007; Tilly and Tarrow 2007).
2. This survey was conducted by the Democracy Initiatives Foundation and Razumkov Centre. It surveyed 2010 respondents aged 18+ in all regions of Ukraine (Democratic Initiatives Foundation 2013a).
3. Ukraine-EU Association Agreement is a treaty establishing cooperation in the spheres of economic policy, legislation, and regulation across the broad range of issues, including visa-free regime, information exchange in the area of justice, and modernisation of Ukraine's energy infrastructure. By signing the agreement, Ukraine committed to economic, judicial, and financial reforms to converge its policies and legislation to those of the EU. Ukraine committed to gradually conform to EU technical, consumer, and environmental standards. In return, the European Union agreed to provide Ukraine with political and financial support, access to knowledge, and preferential access to EU markets. The agreement was seen as a logical result of more than two decades of Ukraine-EU cooperation, and considered mutually beneficial. Ukraine was hoping to attract external investments, coupled with better trade, leading to subsequent increase in life standards of its citizens.
4. This survey was conducted by the Democracy Initiatives Foundation and Kiev International Sociology Institute in all Ukrainian regions but Crimea. With 2025 respondents, it found that 20% of Ukrainians either travelled to Kyiv Maidan, protested in their city/town, or supported the protestors with money/food/clothing (Democratic initiatives Foundation 2014b). The analysis of Gatskova and Gatskov (2016), based on the data coming from the survey by Institute of Sociology, Ukraine's National Academy of Sciences, suggests 17% of Ukrainians were either involved directly or supporting the protests.
5. The figures that followed were drawn from a survey of Kyiv Maidan participants conducted by the Democratic Initiatives Foundation in three rounds—on 7 December 2013 (1037 respondents), 20 December 2013 (515 respondents), and 3 February 2014 (502 respondents).

6. While claims-making in general refers to the process of articulating someone else's interests, and necessarily includes two actors (a claimant and addressee) and an action (e.g. demanding or protesting), within contentious politics it has referred to the conscious articulation of political demands in the public sphere, leaving private claims making aside (Lindekilde 2013).
7. Viche as an institute for public participation was practised in the times of Kyivan Rus, the thirteenth-century kingdom which emerged on the territory of modern Ukraine (Tretiak 2014).
8. See Snyder and Zhurzhenko 2014; Kovtunovych and Pryvalko 2015.
9. These documents were collected from April 2014 to February 2015 by both reaching out to participants of the assemblies and manually searching the Internet using complex search algorithms in Google and YouTube. Most of the resolutions come from local media, but also from local authorities, NGOs, political parties, individual social media channels and blogs.
10. These were adopted by local Maidans' representatives at: all-Ukrainian Euro-Maidan Forum in Krarkiv (1 resolution), all-Ukrainian Euro-Maidan Forum in Odesa (4 resolutions), Joint resolution of Lviv region Maidans (1 resolution) and all-Crimean Euro-Maidan Assembly (1 resolution).
11. The 'political opportunity structure' concept holds that exogenous factors enhance or inhibit prospects for mobilisation, claim-making, strategic choices, and movement outcomes (Meyer and Minkoff 2004).
12. Resolution adopted by Lutsk local Maidan on 29 December 2013.
13. Resolution adopted by All-Ukrainian Forum of Euro-Maidans in Kharkiv on 12 January 2014.
14. Resolution adopted by Vinnytsia local Maidan on 3 January 2014.
15. Lustration is a term used in Ukraine which refers to the cleansing of power or a purge. It gained widespread usage in the 1990s in connection with eliminating Soviet nomenklatura from the ruling class of the new independent state. During Maidan, it was given a new meaning—to purge the corrupt, non-professional, and discredited supporters of President Yanukovych's regime, especially those who gave the 'illegal' orders to disperse peaceful protests.
16. Resolution adopted by Kryzhopil local Maidan, Vinnytsia region, on 25 February 2014.
17. Resolution, adopted by Izyaslav local Maidan, Khmelnytskyi region, on 26 February 2014.

18. Resolution adopted by Irshava local Maidan, Zakarpattya region, on 29 November 2013.
19. Resolution adopted by Lutsk local Maidan on 29 December 2013.
20. Resolution adopted by Kharkiv local Maidan on 18 January 2014.
21. Resolution adopted by Drohobych local Maidan, Lviv region, on 11 December 2013. They also hoped that the quality of policies could be improved by assembling consultant groups and implementing further public control over state institutions and local self-governments (Resolution adopted by Izyaslav local Maidan, Khmelnytskyi region, on 26 February 2014).
22. Resolution adopted by Kremenets local Maidan, Ternopil region, on 26 January 2014.
23. Joint resolution of Lviv region Maidans adopted on 1 February 2014.
24. Resolution adopted by Vinnytsia local Maidan on 3 January 2014.
25. Resolution, establishing Narodna Rada as 'advisory council' adopted by Uzhgorod local Maidan on 2 February 2014.
26. Resolution adopted by Odesa local Maidan on 28 January 2014.
27. Resolution adopted by Odesa local Maidan on 28 January 2014.
28. Resolution adopted by Pereyaslav-Khmelnytskyi local Maidan, Kyiv region, on 1 February 2014.
29. Resolution adopted by Kharkiv local Maidan on 18 January 2014.
30. Resolution adopted by Bila Tserkva local Maidan, Kyiv region, on 4 December 2013.

Works Cited

Alexander, Jeffrey. 2001. Robust utopias and civil repairs. *International Sociology* 16 (4): 579–591.

Blee, Kathleen. 2012. *Democracy in the making*. New York: Oxford University Press.

Buzdugan, Yaroslava. 2012. Legal principles of NGOs' participation in public oversight. *Viche* 12. [In Ukrainian].

Campos, Nauro. 2013. What drives protests in Ukraine? This time it is institutions. *VOX, CEPR's Policy Portal*, December 22. http://www.voxeu.org/article/what-drives-protests-ukraine. Accessed 24 Apr 2017.

Centre for Society Research. 2014. *Protests, victories and repressions in Ukraine: Monitoring results of 2013*. http://cslr.org.ua/wp-content/uploads/2014/05/

CSR_-_Protests_in_2013_-_29_Apr_2014.pdf. Accessed 24 Apr 2017. [In Ukrainian].

Committee of the Regions of the EU. 2011. *Local and regional government in Ukraine and the development of cooperation between Ukraine and the EU*. http://cor.europa.eu/en/documentation/studies/Documents/local-regional-government-ukraine.pdf. Accessed 24 Apr 2017.

Democratic Initiatives Foundation. 2013a. *Public confidence in the social and state institutions*. http://infolight.org.ua/charts/riven-doviri-gromadyan-do-socialnih-ta-derzhavnih-institutiv. Accessed 24 Apr 2017. [In Ukrainian].

———. 2013b. Refusal from euro-integration: What next?. *Focus on Ukraine*, November 18–24. http://www.dif.org.ua/en/publications/focus_on_ukraine/zupink-dali_.htm. Accessed 24 Apr 2017.

———. 2014a. *From the Maidan-Camp to Maidan-Sich: What has changed?* http://www.dif.org.ua/ua/polls/2014_polls/vid-maidanu-taboru-do-maidan.htm. Accessed 24 Apr 2017. [In Ukrainian].

———. 2014b. *Maidan anniversary: Public opinion poll and expert interviews*. http://www.dif.org.ua/en/polls/2014_polls/hethrtjhrrhthrtt.htm. Accessed 24 Apr 2017. [In Ukrainian].

———. 2014c. Three months of a Ukrainian revolution: Is this the last straw for Yanukovych?. *Focus on Ukraine*, February 17–23. http://www.dif.org.ua/en/publications/focus_on_ukraine/trhi-janukovicha.htm. Accessed 24 Apr 2017.

Dvoretska, Liliya. 2014. *Power to the people: People's councils created in 19 of Ukraine's regions*. http://nbnews.com.ua/ua/tema/112351/. Accessed 24 Apr 2017. [In Ukrainian].

Fournier, Valerie. 2003. Utopianism and grassroots alternatives. In *Viable utopian ideas: Shaping a better world*, ed. Arthur B. Shostak, 181–189. New York: M.E. Sharpe.

Gatskova, Kseniia, and Maxim Gatskov. 2016. Third sector in Ukraine: Civic engagement before and after the "Euromaidan". *Voluntas* 27: 673–694.

Honcharuk, Nataliya, and Leonid Prokopenko. 2011. The interaction of national government bodies and local self-government: Legal and functional aspects. *Public Administration: Theory and Practice* 3 (7): 31–38. [In Ukrainian].

Independent News Bureau. 2014a. *The opposition decided to create an alternative government (full text of the Viche Resolution)*. http://nbnews.com.ua/ua/news/110898/. Accessed 24 Apr 2017. [In Ukrainian].

———. 2014b. *The opposition MPs have created the People's Council of Ukraine*. http://nbnews.com.ua/ua/news/111250/. Accessed 24 Apr 2017. [In Ukrainian].

Jizha, Mykola, and Oleksandr Radchenko. 2012. *Public control in the system of public administration as an effective tool of the examination of state-managerial decisions.* http://www.kbuapa.kharkov.ua/e-book/putp/2012-4/doc/2/02.pdf. Accessed 24 Apr 2017. [In Ukrainian].

Kovtunovych, Tetyana, and Tetyana Pryvalko. 2015. *Maidan in the first person: 45 stories of the revolution of dignity*. Kiev: K.I.S. [In Ukrainian].

Kravets, Roman, Khomei Oksana, Pasichnyk Andriy, and Valeriya Lopatina. 2016. Grew up in Maidan: Volunteer initiatives two years after Maidan. *Ukrainska Pravda*, February 8. http://life.pravda.com.ua/society/2016/02/6/207741/. Accessed 24 Apr 2017. [In Ukrainian].

Langman, Lauren. 2013. Occupy: A new social movement. *Current Sociology* 3 (4): 510–524.

Lindekilde, Lasse. 2013. Claims-making. In *The Wiley-Blackwell encyclopedia of social and political movements*, ed. David A. Snow, Donatella della Porta, Bert Klandermans, and Doug McAdam. http://onlinelibrary.wiley.com/doi/10.1002/9780470674871.wbespm027/pdf. Accessed 24 Apr 2017.

Luhn, Alec. 2014. The Ukrainian nationalism at the heart of 'Euromaidan.' *The Nation*, January 21. http://www.thenation.com/article/ukrainian-nationalism-heart-euromaidan/. Accessed 24 Apr 2017.

McAdam, Doug, Sidney Tarrow, and Charles Tilly. 2007. Comparative perspectives on contentious politics. In *Comparative politics: Rationality, culture, and structure*, ed. Mark Irving Lichbach and Alan S. Zuckerman, 260. Cambridge: Cambridge University Press. http://socialsciences.cornell.edu/wp-content/uploads/2013/06/McAdamTarrowTilly07.pdf. Accessed 24 Apr 2017.

Meyer, David S., and Debra C. Minkoff. 2004. Conceptualizing political opportunity. *Social Forces* 82 (4): 1457–1492.

Myseliuk, Andriy. 2010. Ten differences between the systems of Yanukovych and of Kuchma. *Ukrainska Pravda*, July 16. http://www.pravda.com.ua/articles/2010/07/16/5226836/. Accessed 24 Apr 2017. [In Ukrainian].

Oleksiyenko, Oles, and Svyatoslav Pototskyy. 2013. "Soft authoritarianism": Yanukovych's regime has chosen the tactics of creeping power usurpation. *Tyzhden*, April 11. http://tyzhden.ua/Politics/77088. Accessed 24 Apr 2017. [In Ukrainian].

Onuch, Olga. 2014. Who were the protesters? *Journal of Democracy* 25 (3): 44–51.

Onuch, Olga, and Gwendolyn Sasse. 2014. What does Ukraine's #Euromaidan teach us about protest? *The Monkey Cage*, February 27. http://www.washingtonpost.com/blogs/monkey-cage/wp/2014/02/27/what-does-ukraines-euromaidan-teach-us-about-protest/. Accessed 24 Apr 2017.

———. 2016. The Maidan in movement: Diversity and the cycles of protest. *Europe-Asia Studies* 68 (4): 556–587.

RBC-Ukraine. 2012. Parliamentary factions of the Verkhovna Rada of seventh convocation. *RBC Daily*, December 13. http://www.rbc.ua/ukr/analytics/fraktsiya-kommunisticheskoy-partii-ukrainy-13122012114400. Accessed 24 Apr 2017. [In Ukrainian].

Roberts, Sean, and Oleksandr Fisun. 2014. *Local governance and decentralization assessment: Implications of proposed reforms in Ukraine*. USAID. https://www.usaid.gov/sites/default/files/documents/1863/LOCAL%20GOVERNANCE%20ASSESSMENT%20FINAL.pdf. Accessed 24 Apr 2017.

Shekhovtsov, Anton. 2014. What the West should know about Maidan's ultra-right element. *Krytyka*, February 1. http://krytyka.com/ua/solutions/opinions/shcho-zakhodu-potribno-znaty-pro-kraynikh-pravykh-na-evromaydani. Accessed 24 Apr 2017. [In Ukrainian].

Shurkhalo, Dmytro. 2014. Volunteer battalions—Between war and politics. *Radio Svoboda*, August 15. http://www.radiosvoboda.org/a/26531775.html. Accessed 24 Apr 2017. [In Ukrainian].

Snyder, Timothy, and Tatiana Zhurzhenko. 2014. Diaries and memoirs of the Maidan: Ukraine from November 2013 to February 2014. *Eurozine*, June 27. http://www.eurozine.com/diaries-and-memoirs-of-the-maidan/. Accessed 24 Apr 2017.

Steinberg, Stefan. 2014. Three dead in clash between Ukrainian regime and right-wing protesters. *World Socialist Web Site*. Retrieved from https://www.wsws.org/en/articles/2014/01/23/ukra-j23.html. Accessed 24 Apr 2017.

Sviatnenko, Sviatoslav, and Benfold Vinogradov. 2014. Euromaidan values from a comparative perspective. *Social, Health, and Communication Studies Journal* 1 (1): 41–61.

The Economist. 2013. Ukraine's protests: A new revolution on Maidan Square. *The Economist*, December 7. http://www.economist.com/news/europe/21591217-hasukrainians-defiance-presidents-european-policy-split-country-new-revolution. Accessed 24 Apr 2017.

The Verkhovna Rada of Ukraine. 1996. *The constitution of Ukraine*. http://zakon2.rada.gov.ua/laws/show/254%D0%BA/96-%D0%B2%D1%80. Accessed 24 Apr 2017. [In Ukrainian].

———. 2010. *The ruling of the constitutional court of Ukraine*. http://zakon2.rada.gov.ua/laws/show/v020p710-10. Accessed 24 Apr 2017. [In Ukrainian].

Tilly, Charles, and Sydney Tarrow. 2007. *Contentious politics*. London: Paradigm Publishers.

Tretiak, Svitlana. 2014. Viche as one of the civil society institutions of modern Ukraine. *Scientific Bulletin of the International University of Humanities*, Jurisprudence (9–1): 56–58. [In Ukrainian].

Ukrainska Pravda. 2011. Court sentence for Tymoshenko: 7 years and 1.5 billion. *Ukrainska Pravda*, October 11. http://www.pravda.com.ua/articles/2011/10/11/6654964/. Accessed 24 Apr 2017. [In Ukrainian].

———. 2014. Putin declared war on Ukraine. *Ukrainska Pravda*, March 1. http://www.pravda.com.ua/articles/2014/03/1/7016683/. Accessed 24 April 2017. [In Ukrainian].

Valevskyi, Oleksiy. 2014. The political crisis of 2010–2013 and the objectives of the new model of public policy. *Scientific Proceedings* 6 (74): 135–144. [In Ukrainian].

Walker, Shaun, and Oksana Grytsenko. 2013. Ukraine protesters return en masse to central Kiev for pro-EU campaign. *The Guardian*, December 15. http://www.theguardian.com/world/2013/dec/15/ukraine-protesters-return-central-kiev-eu-campaign. Accessed 24 Apr 2017.

Wright, Erik Olin. 2010. *Envisioning real utopias*. London: Verso.

Yermilova, Hanna. 2013. Public control in public procurement. *Financial Control*: 24–25. [In Ukrainian].

Yermolenko, Volodymyr. 2014. Dreams of Europe. *Eurozine*, February 6. http://www.eurozine.com/dreams-of-europe/. Accessed 24 Apr 2017.

Zakharov, Yevhen. 2009. *Public control and human rights*. Kharkiv Human Rights Protection Group. http://www.khpg.org/index.php?id=1261552395. Accessed 24 Apr 2017. [In Ukrainian].

Zelinska, Olga. 2014. The prospects of public control in Ukraine. *Open Society Foundation*, NGO. http://osf.org.ua/data/blog_dwnl/Civil_participat_Zelin_artcle.pdf. Accessed 24 Apr 2017. [In Ukrainian].

———. 2015. Who were the protestors and what did they want? Contentious politics of local Maidan across Ukraine, 2013–2014. *Demokratizatsiya: The Journal of Post-Soviet Democratization* 23 (4): 379–400.

Opportunity in Crisis: Alternative Media and Subaltern Resistance

Benjamin Anderson

It all started with an e-mail. On 13 July 2011, *Adbusters,* the Canadian magazine of alternative culture, suggested to its subscribers that a peaceful occupation of Wall Street be staged, later that year on 17 September (Fleming 2011). The call sparked the imagination of countless activists and activist groups around the world, eventually culminating in the transnational movement we now call *Occupy* (White 2016). This massive mobilisation was remarkable for its unification under a single banner—the "99 percent"—of a range of disparate groups, fighting for many causes.

To propose that we might find opportunities for egalitarian social change in times of despair, disorientation, and debility might strike some as idealistic. However, our various crises—environmental, humanitarian, economic—are generating deep schisms in the global order, which have the potential to awaken a dormant global class of the oppressed. Indeed, the UK student movement, *Occupy*, and the Toronto G20 protests reflect the emergence of a new consciousness open to non-hierarchical

B. Anderson (✉)
Simon Fraser University, Burnaby, BC, Canada

T. Geelan et al. (eds.), *From Financial Crisis to Social Change*,
https://doi.org/10.1007/978-3-319-70600-9_7

methods of organisation, strategies of autonomous self-organisation, and a (social) media-based approach to outreach and recruitment (Castells 2012; Fuchs 2014b; Srnicek and Williams 2015).

This chapter explores the role of alternative media in igniting the radical imagination and fuelling political struggle. Specifically, it examines how *Adbusters* inspired the initial occupation of Wall Street and why, when they attempted four years later to recreate this past success, they failed to catalyse a similar movement. Thus, I provide a counterpoint to the champions of the revolutionary potential of networked communication: that while alternative media have indeed provided important sites for critical thought and expression, and have been successful in extending local struggles to broader, even global, contexts, the true agent of social change remains the social movement and its creative actions "on the ground."

In the section that follows I begin by elaborating briefly upon the idea that tensions in the social reproduction of the status quo grant opportunities for critique and resistance. I then turn my attention to the role played by alternative media in the circulation of local and global struggles and in the development of radical imaginaries. Next, I examine the case of the "Billion People March," whose aim to bring a billion protesters to the streets of the world's cities via a revitalisation and unification of social protest movements worldwide ended up generating only small crowds and attracting very limited media attention. Finally, I suggest that the lesson to be learnt from this failure is that a reinvigorated push towards social justice cannot depend solely on a mediated and individualised manner of protest but must recognise that the realisation of alternative social orders depends on the age-old method of on-the-ground activism.

Social Reproduction

Social systems are characterised by a constant tension between the legitimacy of state institutions and the demands of the citizenry. The social order in general and capitalism in particular are dependent for their survival on the consent of the broader population—insofar as our buy-in to those systems is enough to deter us from revolt. If, at any time, the social system neglects to provide the population with what it has come to expect, it runs the risk of social resistance, even overthrow, because any system of social organisation depends for its existence, in the present and future, upon its *reproduction*. In other words, when a system is in crisis, its social reproduction becomes imperilled (Wright 2010).

In his early work on crisis in advanced capitalist societies, Jürgen Habermas (1973) lays out a conception of crises in which structural incompatibilities within society generate systemic instability. "Crises in social systems," Habermas explains, "are not produced through accidental changes in the environment, but through structurally inherent system-imperatives that are incompatible and cannot be hierarchically integrated" (1973, 2). In liberal capitalist societies, these crises arise due to the tensions between social cohesion and the market system. Specifically, the great social inequalities produced by a market-based economy work against social cohesion. For Habermas, a public consciousness arises during such periods of systemic crisis, which contributes to conflicts through which radical social change can be realised. In each moment of systemic tension, the potential exists for the envisioning of alternative modes of social organisation and collective subjectivity. While Habermas's "legitimation crises" are rare, our present moment may be described as just such a crisis.

The Radical Imagination

Many scholars have noted the resurgence of interest in radical theory in times of economic hardship (Fuchs 2014a; Wright 2010). This should not surprise us. In times of crisis, the contradictions of neoliberal capitalism are brought into the light, creating the conditions for renewed questioning of the system. As Christian Fuchs (2014a, 12) explains:

> Due to the rising income gap between the rich and the poor, widespread precarious labour and the new global capitalist crisis, neoliberalism is no longer seen as common sense. The dark side of capitalism, with its rising levels of class conflict, is now recognised worldwide.

This recognition is therefore a crucial strategic moment for anyone dedicated to egalitarian social change. When the naturalised "truths" reinforced through the apparatuses of social reproduction are suddenly exposed to critique, the entrenched belief that "there is no alternative" also dissolves.

The importance of the belief, whether conscious or subconscious, that other futures are possible cannot be overstated. As Wright (2010, 286) argues:

> Of the various aspects of ideology and belief formation that bear on the problem of social reproduction and potential challenges to structures of power and privilege, perhaps the most important are beliefs about *what is possible.*

Thus resistance begins when we dare to imagine alternatives, that is, to borrow a term from Slavoj Žižek, when we choose to "dream dangerously." In his essay on the 2011 global cycle of protests, Žižek (2012) probes both their causes and effects. For Žižek, these instances of resistance entailed simultaneously the rejection of the status quo, and the assertion of alternative horizons of possibility. Occupy, in particular, represents a case study in the rejection of the institutions of contemporary capitalism, and a *reimagining of social relations* that expresses a rejection of the ascendant bourgeois political order. Here the protests may further be viewed as functioning as a kind of laboratory where new forms of social organisation can be tested, where imagination can be put into practice. And when the occupation ends and the protesters return home, the findings of these experiments go with them. Thereafter, these lessons can be applied in new social movements, with different impetuses, and different goals of social change.

But from where does the initial radical impulse come? In a world where creativity is enclosed by the imperatives of cognitive capitalism, the imagination is increasingly informed by the instrumental logic of the market. In his recent collection of essays on the radical imagination, the Canadian cultural theorist Max Haiven (2014, 245) tracks the development of this phenomenon, arguing that "…capitalism has dissolved into society and social relationships themselves and seeks to shape the way people make community, networks, and even their own subjectivity." Dire as this sounds, Haiven finds hope in the post-crisis circulation of struggles, seeing them not only as social laboratories, à la Žižek, but as sites of inspiration and engines of creativity. They awaken within our collective imagination a connection to the history of struggle—what Benjamin (1968) calls "the angel of the past." "The common imagination," explains Haiven "is a reservoir of radical ideas and inspirations we share with the past and to which we contribute" (2014, 253). For Benjamin and Haiven alike, the cumulative power of past struggles serves as a reminder of our collective agency, one that has the potential to propel us into new projects of resistance and actualisation. In other words, political protests, past or present, remind us that we do not have to accept the reality presented to us; we, like our predecessors, have the capacity to rebel.

Alternative Media and Social Movements

The emergence of this realisation and subsequent political protest relies heavily upon a medium of dissemination. As DeLuca and Peeples's (2002) study of the Seattle World Trade Organization protests illustrates, there is a complex relationship between broadcast media, new media technologies, and civil disobedience. In their study, DeLuca and Peeples isolate the broadcast media's narrative of this event, highlighting the ways in which the dominant discourse and that of the activists conflicted. What is underplayed—though acknowledged—in their account is the vital importance of alternative news sources and online communities like IndyMedia in the run up to, and organisation of, the Seattle protests. Alternative media are therefore often crucial to radical strategy.

How should such alternative media be understood? Christian Fuchs (2010) conceives of alternative media as a subaltern public sphere, whose critical perspective is its very foundation. For Fuchs, these media should "...challenge the dominant capitalist forms of media production, media structures, content, distribution, and reception" (Fuchs 2010, 178). Fuchs is particularly interested in examples that offer alternatives to the repressive messages of the mainstream media, examples that give voices to the voiceless and productive power to the powerless. However, alternative media alone cannot guarantee that effective resistance will materialise. For alternative media to bring out social change, they must, as Sandoval and Fuchs (2009) argue, exist within a network of individuals, organisations, cooperatives, and social movements pursuing a common cause. There is evidence to suggest that alternative media and networked movements are in fact related. Joshua Atkinson (2008), for instance, has shown that activists reporting higher levels of interaction with alternative media also report higher degrees of closeness with their social movement networks. Along the same lines, John Downing (2008) sees media technologies as having the potential to mobilise audiences, while simultaneously expressing doubts over the emancipatory potential of online activism. Activism—and not necessarily content—is for Downing the key ingredient for alternative media networks to bring about successful mobilisations.

However, as Atkinson (2008) argues in his analysis of the relationship between social movements and their related media channels, content is important in establishing interactivity in activist networks on a global level (though less so in intimately organised local contexts). In fact, as he and his colleague Laura Cooley later discovered (Atkinson and Cooley 2010), the relation between social movements and alternative media depends upon what they call "narrative capacity," which refers to the capacity for message dissemination through an activist network—in essence, an activist network's ability to tell its own story to its members. Thus, as "narrative capacity" increases, so too do levels of closeness and interaction within the activist network. The performance of resistance, Atkinson and Cooley show, depends heavily on an activist's perceived "closeness" with their network, this "closeness" being established through the circulation of common narratives.

Adbusters, Occupy, and the Billion People March

This relationship between perception and action, as mediated by alternative media, is illustrated by the case of *Adbusters*, a Vancouver-based counter-cultural magazine and website dedicated to the disruption of consumer society (Nomai 2011). *Adbusters* is widely known for its own brand of cultural resistance, "culture jamming": the appropriation of consumer imagery for resistance purposes, inspired by the dissident actions of the Situationists in the late 1960s. Essentially, the magazine critiques consumer society while simultaneously packaging individualised radical politics as a lifestyle—what Max Haiven (2007) calls "privatised resistance" and what Thomas Frank (1997) calls "commodified dissent." While *Adbusters* recognises the fragmented quality of subjectivity in the age of austerity,[1] one can question whether its attempt to stimulate resistance *on an individualised level* is an appropriate response to this condition, a question to which we shall soon return.

Occupy, according to Jodi Dean (2013), was set in motion through an anarchic mobilisation of multiple movements simultaneously. This was not privatised resistance but rather a common movement made up of disparate parts:

> Occupy made dispersed struggles register as a common struggle. To this extent, as it became a common name, it started to operate as a nascent party, one in the process of being formed and directed by people in the course of political movement. (Dean 2013, 13)

It was, in this reading and as I propose here, a movement whose force owed more to "physical" organisation on the ground than to the initial call to arms that may have sparked it. Micah White (2016), former *Adbusters* editor and the co-creator of the Occupy call, is also quick to note that the power of the *#OccupyWallStreet* meme and its subsequent rallying call "we are the 1%" lay in its openness and flexibility, reflected in its being repurposed by several movements with varying goals.

This style of non-hierarchical organisation reflects Haiven's conceptualisation of the radical imagination as not an individual attribute—something that one possesses—but as a collective process, something developed through shared practice. The radical imagination, for Haiven and Khasnabish (2014), derives from autonomous experimentation in social movements and activist communities. This is borne by the case of Occupy and especially in the imaginative forms of community organisation seen in free libraries, artistic collectives, and community kitchens. Thus, the story of Occupy is not the story of alternative media. It is not the story of

Adbusters. Rather, it is the story of collective imagining and of autonomous organisation. It is the story of community and of activist experimentation. Though *Adbusters* provided a catalyst, an idea to mobilise around, the work of the imagination was borne collectively in the streets and public squares.

In 2015, *Adbusters* attempted to reprise its leading role in the theatre of protest. Late that spring, it put out a new call for a "Billion People March," to take place on December 19.[2] "Maybe marching in the streets isn't for you," one of the messages reads. "You like prowling alone, or with a few close friends… But you can be <u>one</u> in a billion too" (*Adbusters* 2016). This call, to be *one* in a billion, attempted to recreate the phenomenon of Occupy—of individuals forming part of a larger movement, a "part of the swarm" as *Adbusters* once put it. Billed as a decentralised mobilisation on a global scale, the calls for the "Billion People March" proposed a "global big-bang moment" (Adbusters 2015). What interests me here is how or if this individualistic, lifestyle-ist brand of resistance actually contributed to the collective forming of the radical imagination. Does such a politics of the self and of the (anti-)consumer actually promote solidarity, or does it appeal to an atomised impulsivity, a yearning to rage against the machine as a "lone wolf," a brand of commodified dissent one might expect from the isolated and unconnected denizens of our age of austerity?

To begin to answer these questions let us consider what actually happened on 19 December 2015, the proposed date of the Billion People March. According to *Adbusters* (2016), "On #D19 forty grassroots groups around the world took to the streets in dozens of cities on five continents to demand deep down, paradigm-shifting change to our global system." This sounds impressive. However, searches of LexisNexis, Google News, and various individual news outlets produced no hits whatsoever for the following terms in the days and weeks after those purported protests: *Adbusters*, Billion People March, #d19, and *#BillionPeopleMarch*. Moreover, the same searches on Twitter and Facebook revealed just a handful of small local actions. An individual here, a small group there, but little evidence that December 19 was much other than business as usual. According to the rather limited social media chatter on the movement, demonstrations took place in Fort Wayne, Indiana; Savannah, Georgia; and Denver, Colorado. Photos reveal between 8 and 15 participants at each event. As far as can be discerned, the turnout was, to put it mildly, rather short of a billion people. It is of course possible and even likely that demonstrations also occurred elsewhere. But that said, there is almost no evidence that they had any impact.

In the Billion People March, we therefore find an attempt to recreate a past success,[3] namely Occupy, a movement estimated to have incorporated protests in as many as 1000 cities and a hundred countries across the world, united by a struggle for social equality and "real democracy." Why did so few heed this later call? Perhaps it was the perceived lack of novelty. Perhaps it did not resonate with the movements of the moment—the messaging did not, for instance, seem to address the ongoing struggle for racial justice in the USA and elsewhere as exemplified by Black Lives Matter. Perhaps the cause was too nebulous, coming as it did so many years after the financial crisis of 2008 and Occupy.

This seeming failure is, of course, no fault of those few activists who did take to the streets on December 19. After all, without the 300 or so demonstrators who initially occupied Zuccotti Park in 2011, it is likely that we would have never even heard of Occupy (White 2016).

Indeed, Micah White recently reflected on a similar *Adbusters* initiative, the Carnivalesque Rebellion, which was to take place in 2010 and with broadly similar aims (2016). "The Carnivalesque Rebellion," remembers White, "was a flop, and the protest fizzled [...] We failed because we were too early" (White 2016, 13). This was an idea whose time had not yet come. For White, the lesson he learned from the failure was that he and Kalle Lasn, *Adbusters* co-founder, were "ahead of the curve" of contemporary protest. But could the same be said of the Billion People March in 2015, which followed Occupy and was based upon similar demands for inequality reduction and democracy? Is it too great a stretch to suppose that in fact it was the organisers who were behind the curve? Is it really so great a surprise that an attempted repeat of Occupy did not result in another mass insurrection? After all, is not the struggle for a reimagined social order dependent upon a *creative* spark?

Concluding Remarks

In an era characterised by seemingly continual crises, there are noticeable tensions in the institutions of social reproduction which grant opportunities for critique and resistance. In the preceding pages, I have explored the interrelation of alternative media and social movements by focusing on the ways in which activist praxis prefigures the creation of alternatives to the status quo. The radical imagination, the creation of new ways of seeing and of being, finds its inception in communication and in practice. As such, we should acknowledge that there is no *formula* for catalysing resistance. What worked once in igniting the spark of the radical imagination might not work in a different time, a different place, or different context.

What the case of *Adbusters* teaches us is that the autonomous community organising of Occupy and other manifestations that it inspired do have the capacity to change the perception of what is possible. Of course, this will not happen in every instance. The Billion People March is a stark reminder of this reality. New media technologies and alternative media messages do not alone generate resistance movements, still less successful ones. While they are a critical ingredient in the awakening of the radical imagination, they depend on social movements for their success.

I should stress that although *Adbusters'* most recent call did not result in a global movement, that is no indictment of alternative media. As conditions worsen or stagnate for most of the world's population, the unquestionable will continue to be questioned. Discontent will continue to drive many to read radical theory and consume alternative media (Fuchs 2014a), and large numbers of the economically marginalised may begin to find more credible the many ideologies and movements that challenge the basis and purported virtues of capitalism (Wright 2010, 287). Alternative media will continue to play a crucial role as a megaphone for the on-the-ground organising that proliferates during periods of increased political tension. But rather than assuming that these can create new movements all on their own, we should instead try to identify ways to support them as sites for consciousness raising, community building, strategic planning, and sparks of the radical imagination. For it takes only one idea, brought into being at the right moment and carried by a social movement of sufficient dynamism, to alter our perceptions of what is possible.

Recognising this, we need a reinvigorated push to unify alternative media and activist communities. Of course, this requires a coordinated effort from both communities. What this investigation suggests is a lesson for the former: that alternative media must be reflexive and respond to the demands and programmes of the movements of the moment. Simply putting out a meme will not be enough. What alternative media should strive for is interactivity with social movements, locally and globally. Through direct involvement with movements and activists, alternative media can serve as both the spreader of narratives, and the platform through which strategies can be developed.

The time to build this coalition is now. The last year has shown a surge in far-right organising.[4] From Brexit to Trump, this upsurge in regressive political activity signals a dramatic shift in the global political landscape. For many, hope is likely to be in short supply, though it remains alive in a few vibrant movements that have formed in resistance to this turn to the hard-right. The treatment of these struggles in alternative media will be a crucial ingredient in influencing the ways in which they are perceived. In coalition, activists and media can create a united front from which to challenge regressive policies and systems while, simultaneously, envisioning alternatives to replace them.

Notes

1. See the *Adbusters* publication *Meme wars: The creative destruction of Neoclassical Economics* for an accessible yet nuanced interpretation of the neoliberal condition (Lasn 2012).
2. As a devoted follower of *Adbusters* on both Twitter and Facebook, I welcomed this idea hoping that this time the movement might transcend some of the challenges of Occupy and catch on to an even greater degree.
3. Success in this context refers to the Occupy movement's ability to mobilise an impressive and diverse number of activists under a single banner.
4. It's worth noting that this surge corresponds with new levels of regressive media production and consumption.

Works Cited

Adbusters. 2015. *Get ready for the billion people march*. http://www.adbusters.org/article/get-ready-for-the-billion-people-march/. Accessed 24 Apr 2017.

———. 2016. *Billion people march*. http://www.billionpeoplemarch.org. Accessed 24 Apr 2017.

Atkinson, Joshua D. 2008. Towards a model of interactivity in alternative media: A multilevel analysis of audiences and producers in a new social movement network. *Mass Communication and Society* 11 (3): 227–247.

Atkinson, Joshua D., and Laura Cooley. 2010. Narrative capacity, resistance performance, and the "shape" of new social movement networks. *Communications Studies* 61 (3): 321–338.

Benjamin, Walter. 1968. Theses on the philosophy of history. In *Illuminations*, ed. Hannah Arendt, 217–252. New York: Schocken.

Castells, Manuel. 2012. *Networks of outrage and hope: Social movements in the internet age*. Cambridge: Polity Press.

Dean, Jodi. 2013. Occupy Wall Street: After the anarchist moment. *Socialist Register* 49: 52–62.

DeLuca, Kevin Michael, and Jennifer Peeples. 2002. From public sphere to public screen: Democracy, activism, and the "violence" of Seattle. *Critical Studies in Media Communication* 19 (2): 125–151.

Downing, John. 2008. Social movement theories and alternative media: An evaluation and critique. *Communication, Culture & Critique* 1 (1): 40–50.

Fleming, Andrew 2011. Adbusters sparks Wall Street protest: Vancouver-based activists behind street actions in the US. *Vancouver Courier*, September 27.

Frank, Thomas. 1997. Opening salvo: The new gilded age. In *Commodify your dissent: Salvos from the Baffler*, ed. Thomas Frank and Matt Weiland, 23–28. New York: WW Norton & Company.

Fuchs, Christian. 2010. Alternative media as critical media. *European Journal of Social Theory* 13 (2): 173–192.

———. 2014a. *Digital labour and Karl Marx*. London: Routledge.

———. 2014b. *Occupymedia!: The Occupy movement and social media in crisis capitalism*. Winchester: Zero Books.

Habermas, Jürgen. 1973. *Legitimation crisis*. Boston: Beacon Press.

Haiven, Max. 2007. Privatized resistance: AdBusters and the culture of neoliberalism. *The Review of Education, Pedagogy and Cultural Studies* 29: 85–110.

———. 2014. *Crises of imagination, crises of power: Capitalism, creativity and the commons*. Halifax/Winnipeg, London/New York: Fernwood Publishing and Zed Books.

Haiven, Max, and Alex Khasnabish. 2014. *The radical imagination: Social movement research in the age of austerity*. London: Zed Books.
Lasn, Kalle. 2012. *Meme wars: The creative destruction of neoclassical economics*. New York: Seven Stories Press.
Nomai, Afsheen. 2011. Adbusters Media Foundation (Canada). In *Encyclopedia of social movement media*, ed. John Derek Hall Downing, 3–4. Los Angeles: Sage.
Sandoval, Marisol, and Christian Fuchs. 2009. Towards a critical theory of alternative media. *Telematics and Informatics* 27: 141–150.
Srnicek, Nick, and Alex Williams. 2015. *Inventing the future: Postcapitalism and a world without work*. London: Verso.
White, Micah M. 2016. *The end of protest: A new playbook for revolution*. Toronto: Knopf Canada.
Wright, Erik Olin. 2010. *Envisioning real utopias*. London: Verso.
Žižek, Slavoj. 2012. *The year of dreaming dangerously*. London: Verso.

[illegible]

The Battle of Barton Moss

Steven Speed

In November 2013, a group of environmental activists set up a camp at Barton Moss, Salford, in the northwest of England. Their aim was to protest exploratory drilling at a potential hydraulic fracturing (fracking) well by a leading British oil and gas exploration company, IGas. At the core of their varied protest activity were daily 'slow-walks'[1]: organised group walks down a public footpath in front of the trucks and lorries attempting to enter the drilling site through Barton Moss Road to deliver materials and equipment for drilling operations. Between 30 and 100 people participated, twice a day, four days a week, and they lasted until April 2014—when IGas called off their drilling. During this five-month period, the activists of Barton Moss had succeeded in overcoming the resistance of the local council, Greater Manchester Police (hereafter GMP), IGas, and Peel Holdings, one of the largest landowners in the North of England. Their efforts may also be traced to a marked galvanising of local activist groups in Greater Manchester and even a general increase in the politicisation of the wider community.

S. Speed (✉)
Staffordshire University, Stoke-on-Trent, UK

T. Geelan et al. (eds.), *From Financial Crisis to Social Change*,
https://doi.org/10.1007/978-3-319-70600-9_8

This chapter tells the story of the Battle of Barton Moss and shows how a local protest movement in England was able to halt the drilling of a fracking well using innovative methods of protest, and despite mounting government and corporate pressure. It draws on the many weeks I spent as an observer of the camp and the protest walks, in which I took photographs and conducted interviews with activists (whom I have anonymised).

I begin by discussing briefly the relationship between the protest at Barton Moss and the earlier Occupy movement, which connects the details of our case to a broader pattern of political protest in England. In so doing, I outline some of the distinguishing qualities of the Barton Moss protest, focusing on its aims and scope, its spatial characteristics, and many kinds of tactics. I then switch attention to the opposing side, without whom there could be no battle. My spotlight falls on the 'foot-soldiers', that is, the GMP, and what their methods in policing the demonstrations tell us about the nature of the state, specifically its attitude and strategy vis-à-vis protesters, and the motivations underpinning them. In the third part of this chapter, I advance a five-part explanation of the campaign's remarkable success, before giving, in part four, an indication of its ripple effects. Finally, in the fifth and final part, I consider the wider meaning and import of the Battle of Barton Moss, and suggest what might be learned from it.

Its Relationship to Occupy

To some extent, the protest camp at Barton Moss can be seen to have evolved out of the Occupy movement of 2011. In the first place, several of its members had participated in various Occupy camps across the UK, and applied the lessons of their experience to the situation at Barton Moss. As one protester from Greater Manchester who resided in the Barton Moss Camp explained:

> The knock-on effects of what happened at Occupy still resonate today. If you go to any eviction hearing for activists, they will automatically refer to the City of London's eviction of Occupy. That camp was there to show that

> people weren't happy and were ready to start rising up saying 'we are not going to move unless you change'… Occupy may not have worked the way that people wanted it to work because it was the first time many of us had done anything like that, but to be able to learn you have got to make mistakes… We have learnt from those mistakes… It also brought a lot of people together that wouldn't have been together without it. It is through these things that we have learnt what to look out for and what we are not going to do in the future, and how we can keep getting the message across. (Telephone interview, 20 January 2015)

While the protests at Barton Moss revealed that the embers of Occupy still glowed some two years after its fires had been extinguished, there are nevertheless some important differences between Barton Moss and Occupy. First, the protests at Barton Moss were time- and issue-specific; they opposed exploratory drilling expected to take place over a limited period, with initial estimates of 12 weeks. By contrast, Occupy had in its sights a much more diffuse, even nebulous, target: social injustice, as manifested in runaway social inequality, unprecedented concentrations of corporate power, and a lack of meaningful democracy. These grievances admit of no easily defined enemy—like IGas—still less a clear timetable for action.

Second, in response to the protests, the landowners, Peel Holdings, made numerous attempts to have the camp evicted. Supported in their efforts by the British government and corporations, they worked to stifle dissent through one recourse in particular: the criminal legal system. Yet this proved ineffective; in contrast to the Occupy camps, the environmental activists of Barton Moss were able to avoid eviction, maintaining the camp until the drilling was abandoned. At that point, on surveying the deserted drilling site and after having dismantled their camp such that only tent-peg holes evidenced their five-month stay, the protesters could at last share in a feeling of victory that lifted them all and instilled an almost palpable sense of optimism for the future.

The third, and perhaps most significant difference, was the protest's *spatial* character. At Barton Moss, the activists occupied a space with not only the tents that made up their camp, as is the norm in almost all such protests, but *with their bodies*. By simply exercising their legal right to walk along a public footpath, the protesters occupied the space in front of the supply vehicles entering the drilling site, obstructing and delaying their arrival. But this was no blockade; no human wall or chain was formed.

To be sure, slow-walking was supplemented by numerous other methods of direct action, fundamental to the repertoire of the modern protester—though occasionally receiving in Barton Moss some innovative twists. These included blocking the entrance to the drilling site—with wind turbines. Also deployed were the time-honoured 'lock-on' techniques, whereby protesters glue, lock, or chain themselves to immobile objects. For our protesters these included steel pipes, fences, a red bus, IGas trucks, and—where a little creativity was called for—a coffin. But in the end, it was the most mundane of techniques—walking along a public footpath, an everyday activity that anyone could participate in—that appeared to have best disrupted IGas' exploratory drilling. The genius of this tactic, in hindsight, was its immunity to GMP's preferred means of suppression: arrest and prosecution. But occupying a physical and legal space beyond criminalisation, the protesters of Barton Moss, unlike those of Occupy, were free of the state's prior (successful) attempts to control dissent through the manipulations of law enforcement.

Political Policing

What happened at Barton Moss did not only make fracking visible to a wider public; it also exposed the mechanisms of state repression, rendering them not only visible but, from the perspective of the activists, *experiential* and *tangible*. For they bore the physical brunt of GMP action and overreaction: from threats to the brutalities and distress of arrest. Thus, the typically abstract casting of ideas about the relationship between the state and commerce, which are for most people devoid of ready frames of reference, and hence meaningless, were given at Barton Moss a more concrete instantiation—in police oppression. When protesters came later to view their suffering at the hands of the police as arising out of the GMP's service of corporate interests above those of 'the people' (the evidence for which we shall soon examine), they consequently came to interpret each act in their suppression—and its associated physical and mental consequences: pain, bruising, fear, humiliation—as manifestations—if not the very substance—of that alliance between government and big business. This realisation was for some transformative, allowing them to suddenly apprehend via their experience the full significance of 'corporatocracy' or 'crony capitalism', and to see with greater clarity why they are worth opposing.

It is not without justification that the policing at Barton Moss has been compared for its disproportionate use of force to that of the miners' strike.[2] There were many absurd, unjust, and brutal arrests at Barton Moss. To provide merely an illustrative list of examples that the reader can themselves check against online amateur video footage, these included the arrest of a Legal Observer—a trained representative of a human rights organisation, who attends public protests to monitor and report police conduct—for drink driving while he was filming the arrest of another protester on 14 January 2014[3]; the brutal arrest of Legal Observer Kris O'Donnel, while he tried to speak to an officer about a traffic offence[4]; and the case of Vanda Gillet,[5] who was injured during her brutal arrest but refused medical attention for over an hour.

However, while the miners, being deprived of their income during the strike, were susceptible to being starved out in a war of attrition with the state, at Barton Moss it was IGas which were being 'starved out'. Their increased operating costs brought by protesters' disruption of their near-daily convoys, and mounting negative publicity, which was exacerbated by the severity of the policing, would, in the end, prove too great to bear.

And while protest actions elsewhere, as in Canary Wharf, suffered under their successful criminalisation by the authorities, at Barton Moss the GMP struggled to find for the slow-walkers a suitable criminal charge. Each time an arrest on a new charge ended up in court, the actions of the protesters were judged to be lawful.

The first charges levelled against the slow-walkers were for Obstruction of the Highway. These cases collapsed following a hearing on 12 February 2014 at Manchester and Salford Magistrates' Court, when District Judge Qureshi ruled that the land in question was not a public highway. Later charges of obstructing a police officer were dismissed on the grounds that the arrests and the force used by police to 'push' protesters down the road were unlawful.

The third most common charge was aggravated trespass. At the time of writing, many of the cases for this charge are still ongoing. However, the first of them, which was being used as a test case, concluded with the acquittal of both defendants. In his judgement, District Judge Sanders said the protesters were:

> Entitled to demonstrate, were entitled to walk along Barton Moss Road, had been generally compliant with the police, and their actions were specifically directed towards the object of their protest and not the wider public. (Sanders 2016, 13)

The judge also went on to express how the nature of the policing had led directly to the arrests:

> Without any warning (or indeed clear rationale) the police changed their tactics and sought to significantly increase the pace of the protesters. Neither of the defendants wished to progress at this faster pace and resisted attempts to make them walk faster. In both cases, but separated by time, they had the misfortune to find themselves in front of PC Genge who interpreted this resistance as deliberate pushing back. (Sanders 2016, 13)

The majority of arrests of slow-walkers has been deemed unlawful. Solicitor Simon Pook, of Robert Lizar's, who represented pro bono many of the arrested protesters, called for a public enquiry into the policing of the demonstration:

> Since November 2013, Richard Brigden and I advised the Court on the nature of Barton Moss Road. GMP continued to act without lawful authority for a number of months… We cannot permit, in an established democracy, police forces arresting and detaining citizens with the knowledge that their actions are themselves unlawful. Such a position only undermines confidence in the police and justice system. (Telephone interview, Simon Pook, 24 September 2014)

The sense among protesters that GMP had been serving the interests of IGas was first stirred following the release of a memorandum of understanding between GMP, Salford City Council, and IGas (Greater

Manchester Police 2014). The memorandum disclosed that GMP's purpose was to 'facilitate peaceful protest' and that 'Police Officers must only use the minimum amount of lawful force' (Greater Manchester Police 2014, 13, 23)—an aim clearly at odds with the experiences of protesters, their corroboration by amateur video footage of police abuse, and the strikingly high number of dropped charges. Much more revealing was what the memorandum set out next: that IGas would 'lead on all media communication, both proactive and reactive' (Greater Manchester Police 2014, 10). For Simon Pook, this explains why GMP's published press releases, which were circulated in the public domain, exhibited a decidedly pro-IGas, anti-protester bias: 'GMP has to balance the right of the protesters and the rights of the community and workers,' said Pook, while 'in practice GMP appears to have given IGas direct access to their gold and silver command, and IGas had the lead role in regards to press' (Telephone interview, Simon Pook, 24 September 2014).

The nature of the policing at Barton Moss may be seen as a continuation of the policing of the 2013 anti-fracking protests at Cuadrilla Resources' exploratory drilling well in the village of Balcombe, West Sussex. A review by Hertfordshire Constabulary and Essex Police found that the operation at Balcombe had several deficiencies—which might be all too familiar to Barton Moss' slow-walkers. The report discloses that at Balcombe, too, numerous police charges would later be dropped due to 'the absence of initial clear charging guidelines and standards' (Adams 2014, 9). The report also states, tellingly, that following a briefing by Sussex Constabulary to Cuadrilla, the company's response 'became a significant political/economic issue related to subsequent involvement at a *more senior political level*' (Adams 2014, 4). The report then goes on to describe the relationship between Cuadrilla and Sussex police as needing to be 'more transparent and less open to subsequent influence' (Adams 2014, 4).

The claims of 'political policing' at Barton Moss gained traction due to its remarkably large police consignment, and, more than this, the heavy-handedness of their approach, which attracted allegations of police brutality (Telephone interview, Simon Pook, 24 September 2014). They were also fuelled by the conspicuous ways in which the police assisted IGas in its business, with escorts to and from Barton Moss Road, and traffic disruptions to enable IGas convoys to arrive earlier—perhaps to evade protesters. And then there were the outcomes of police arrests, already highly suspect in the eyes of many. As the charges upon which these arrests were made would come, one after the other, to be dropped, thrown out of court, or ruled against, the protesters' belief that policing had been political became increasingly difficult to deny. After all, they had statistics on their side. The average conviction rate across public order offences in the UK stands at 96%. What was the conviction rate for arrests made during the Barton Moss protests, the majority of which were made in relation to public order offences? Just 29% (33 out of 93 prosecuted protesters; see Gilmore et al. 2016, 39–40).

What is the significance of that statistic? A report by the Centre for the Study of Crime, Criminalisation and Social Exclusion, by Liverpool John Moores University, and the Centre for URBan Research (CURB), University of York (and to which I contributed the photographs), examines the gap between GMP's published objective of police operations at Barton Moss and the actual results:

> Given the low conviction rates, arrest under Operation Geraldton did not appear to have been carried out with a view to securing convictions. Rather, mass arrest and blanket bail served to create a de facto protest exclusion zone around the fracking site – an action that would otherwise have no basis in law as well as being a clear violation of the protesters' right to freedom of assembly under Article 11 of the European Convention on Human Rights. (Gilmore et al. 2016, 41)

The report goes on to dispute the lawfulness of the arrests and questions the aims and tactics of police operations, lending credence to the opinion of many protesters that the state was using the GMP to silence dissent and facilitate business. As the report further suggested:

> The dubious legality under which arrests were carried out, evidenced by the readiness of the courts to challenge their legal basis, raises important questions about the extent to which the policing operation was driven by interests other than public order and crime prevention. It is clear from the above analysis that mass arrest was a central component of Operation Geraldton. The tactic served to physically clear protesters from the site, to

> deter others from attending the camp and to reinforce the construction of protesters as violent criminals and thereby legitimize the intensity of the policing operation. (Gilmore et al. 2016, 41)

Of course, what would have been clear to all involved in these moments of 'intense' policing was that one did not need a degree in politics to understand what was happening. Anyone taking part or witnessing these events could see and hear what was going on; and what is more, some could feel it, too. Each time an arrest on a new charge was judged to be unlawful, protesters' long-held sense of indignance at the absurdity, injustice, and brutality of their treatment received an additional exclamation point.

Over these five months, the attempts of the Greater Manchester Police to criminalise the actions of the Barton Moss protesters became increasingly desperate—but no more successful. This failure might be thought a source of morale for protesters, even while its obverse reinforced a depressing truth: that the criminal justice system was being used as a tool in their oppression, and which was especially galling, to serve the interests of IGas. The protesters were not demoralised. In fact, the unity of the activists continued to grow. Moreover, the dissemination via social media of amateur videos depicting police malpractice galvanised support from other interest groups, most notably the Greater Manchester Association of Trades Union Councils (GMATUC), an association of trade unions with 18,000 members. In a public letter from that group to Tony Lloyd, the Greater Manchester Police and Crime Commissioner, the GMP was excoriated for its 'horrendous' policing at Barton Moss, with opposition raised to 'legitimate protest' being 'criminalised in an attempt to silence dissent' (Haworth 2014, 1). The letter also stated that '[t]here are citizens in our county who because of this episode now find it impossible to trust any man or woman wearing the GMP badge' (Haworth 2014, 1).

In attempts to investigate further the allegation of political policing, the research team behind the *'Keep moving!' Report on the policing of the Barton Moss community protection camp* have issued several Freedom of Information Act (FOIA) requests for such data. The GMP and the Crown Prosecution Service (CPS) have continued to refuse the team's requests for this information, involving them in an ongoing case with the

Information Commissioner (IC) who has instructed the CPS to provide the information. At the end of April, the CPS agreed, on threat of court action, to respond to FOIA requests. However, to date the Greater Manchester Police and the Crown Prosecution Service have refused all requests for the final figures on arrests at Barton Moss.

Explaining the Protests' Success

What started as a routine environmental protest about fracking had, by the time the protesters had left the site, become something much more. Among other things, it had metamorphosed into a quasi-heroic tale of the 'ordinary citizen's' struggle against corrupt and oppressive government-corporate power.

This transformation happened gradually. At the start of the campaign, local opinion seemed to support the proposed fracking. In a poll conducted in December 2013 by BBC North West Tonight, only 34% said they were opposed to fracking 'in the north west', while 44% supported it and 22% were undecided (BBC 2013). By contrast, in the wake of the protests, a local newspaper, the *Manchester Evening News*, conducted a poll in March 2014 in which 73% of respondents said they were opposed to fracking (Thompson 2014)—39% more opposition than was reported in the earlier survey.

It is important to recognise that these surveys were conducted by different organisations. The BBC commissioned the market research company TNS to carry out its poll, while the *Manchester Evening News* appears to have conducted theirs in-house through their website. Because the surveys used different methodologies, their data cannot be assumed to be comparable and special caution should be exercised in making all but the most general of inferences across the data sets. One such general inference, which I think one may be justified in drawing with confidence, is that the surveys' results reflect a genuine and marked shift in public opinion. This has, in turn, put significant pressure on local politicians to oppose any future applications for fracking.

The presence of such consequential effects raises the question of how we are to account for the remarkable achievements of what was conceived as a fairly unremarkable anti-fracking protest? In what follows, I outline what I take to be the five factors most instrumental to the Battle of Barton Moss ending—against expectation—in victory for its environmental protesters and corporate-governmental defeat. I also try to explain the protest's cause of an enduring shift in the public's opinion of fracking in the northwest of England, and possibly further afield, from general approval or indifference, to widespread opposition.

First and foremost was the innovative 'slow-walk' method of protest, which involved walking in front of the IGas convoys along Barton Moss Road before their entrance into the drilling site. Knowing that this would reduce productivity at the drilling site gave protesters a sense of having accomplished something tangible. Incorporating participants into active, coordinated protests also helped contribute to a sense of camaraderie, not only among protesters, which is always critical to protest success, but also between protesters and local residents. The value of this form of comradeship is exemplified by the remarks of one experienced protester, who participated in the Occupy London protest at the Stock Exchange and lived on the camp site at Barton Moss:

> The people of Salford turned out in support of our attempts to prevent IGas from fracking at Barton moss. They came every morning and walked in front of lorries with us, they were arrested with us, they were brutalised by police with us. When we were arrested, they came to police stations in solidarity with us. They have attended our court cases to support us. Many locals offered showers, meals and beds for the night if we needed them. They brought us goods and blankets and all sorts of things the camp needed. The love and solidarity from local residents was amazing. In fact, I and many others formed strong bonds with many during the campaign at Barton moss, for me to such a degree that I couldn't leave them and remained in Manchester after our camp was disbanded [...] The love, support and solidarity shown to us by the local community, many of who were attending their very first protest was incredible. I have no doubt that if or when the frackers return, this community will be more than ready to resist. (Telephone interview, 26 June 2014)

Second, and more remarkably, after local activists had commenced the anti-fracking protests at Barton Moss, people from across the country soon arrived to swell the number of camp residents, citing similar concerns about environmental degradation. Hence, the 20 or 30 protesters who occupied the camp on any given night always comprised a mix of locals and those from further afield. This relationship, between the camp's occupants and the wider community, appears to have been crucial in maintaining the daily rhythm of the protests, as well as the growth of a broader anti-fracking campaign. As a resident of the nearby Cadishead explained:

> The relationship between the 'protectors' [the name given to protesters who stayed at the camp] who came to live on the camp and the local residents was electric. Without the 'protectors', locals wouldn't have had the knowledge and skills in how to survive, how to protest, legal knowledge, how to work together for the greater cause. Overall [it was] a phenomenal, dynamic experience that changed the lives of the local residents forever. It was like the cavalry coming. It was confirmation that we were doing the right thing in trying to save our Moss and showed we weren't alone in trying to stop the destruction of the environment. It made everything change and our determination to continue the fight is resolute. (Interview, 20 March 2014)

The third factor was the unlawful, unjust, sometimes brutal nature of the policing, reflected partly in the frequency of arrests. This generated among activists a great sense of injustice, which strengthened their resolve and compelled others to get involved, even where, as was the case for many participants, they had never protested before. Unsurprisingly, many reported becoming politicised by the experience, a process described by a protester from Irlam, a suburb in Salford:

> I'm a local resident, a peaceful person. I've never demonstrated before in my life. I'm not a politically aware person, just easy going, believe the Government, believe people, but do you know what? I am staggered with what I've seen… It breaks my heart. The previous day I attended the protest to see what was going on. I came down, watched it go past, stood on the side and just cried, watching the police just pushing people down this footpath. Today I came and joined the group. (Interview, 19 February 2014)

Another protester, a Manchester resident and regular slow-walker, similarly emphasised the self-defeating nature of the repressive policing which strengthened the resolve of the local community. He also revealed that it was the behaviour of the GMP that motivated him to engage in a more direct form of action: gluing his arm and that of a friend to the inside of a metal tube, before lying down on the road, forcing delays upon a convoy of trucks as they tried to enter the drilling site.

> It was very, very congested which created loads of confrontation. At the end when I did my direct action and why I did my direct action, apart from being about the dangers of fracking, was because it felt like we were in a police state [… I had tried many times to speak to the inspector about their behaviour and the way they would take it upon themselves to get us up the road in record time when the day before it had taken 45 minutes to an hour. As a direct result of that, and when they lost control and ran at people like myself and others, I thought I am going to make a stand because they shouldn't be able to push people around like that. (Interview, 19 April 2014)

Our fourth factor is the camp itself. As an observer, it was clear that having a physical space in which protesters could convene, plan, socialise, and learn from one another was a major boon. It gave the campaign a kind of 'headquarters', or 'base of operations' to use the more apt military metaphor, which acted as a focal point for protest organisation and socialisation, without which the campaign may have lacked binding co-ordination. For example, through meetings with legal advisors at the camp, many protesters discovered what their rights were during the 'slow-walks'. Further, those who were unable to stay or participate on a daily basis could drop in to the camp at their convenience, receive instruction, and thereafter immediately take up a protest function. Finally, having a physical space provided a channel through which the local community was able to express its solidarity with the protesters via donations of food, water, clothing, medicine, skills (such as construction), and expertise (such as in media and law).

One protester, who travelled from Liverpool to reside in the camp and who had never attended a protest before, suggested that the camp also served an important visual/symbolic function:

> The most important thing that the camp gives to the local community is that it is a visual of the issue. Once something appears, the media comes down because it is new news and they want to know what is going on.

> Then you get it on your local TV news. Plus, if you look, all the community places are shut so people haven't got a place to gather any more [...] I am looking for ways to change public perception of issues and the only way to do that is making the issues visible. You have to make it visible for people to start moving. (Telephone interview, 19 January 2015)

It should also be noted that in looking beyond the bounded space of the camp site, one finds the emergence and growth of a broader anti-fracking network that has, in turn, galvanised a still wider activist community in Greater Manchester, as Martin Porter from Frack Free Greater Manchester[6] explained:

> The success of the anti-fracking movement has sucked in experienced campaigners from Greenpeace, Reclaim the Power, Friends of the Earth and so on but also, and this is what makes it unique as an environmental protest in my experience, the trade unions and other left wing political groups. I still don't think the big NGOs realise how important the links we have made in Manchester are. Non-hierarchical 'direct action' people, Green NGOs and trade unions working together is very rare, and I think a huge innovation by Greater Manchester, all thanks to Barton Moss. (Telephone interview, 19 May 2014)

The fifth factor was the strategic sophistication of the protest, which included the use of various cutting-edge online platforms, and which one protester, a Manchester resident who regularly attended the protest walks, suggested that IGas and GMP were not adequately prepared to deal with:

> The location and the route was a flaw but in actual fact they had never come up against the sort of sophistication of these protectors... which really laid them bare and made them look very, very amateurish, especially when compared to the policing that I know goes on in communities. (Interview, 19 April 2014)

While it has been well documented that social media is beneficial for organising protests, Barton Moss being no exception, lesser-known platforms like Bambuser,[7] which enabled users to film protests and record police behaviour, proved decisive. The principal benefit of Bambuser is that footage is not stored on the recording device but online, so that footage remains secure and accessible in instances where devices are confiscated by the police. The many hours of footage recorded in this way were used to great effect by solicitors representing the protesters. Although the GMP tried to counter this by confronting people during their livestreams, and trying to switch off confiscated devices while questioning protesters, this also produced the counter-productive effect of stimulating additional anti-police, pro-activist sentiment and action.

Bambuser and related social media platforms, like Twitter and Facebook, as well as independent publications (online and paper-based), such as the Salford Star, including in both online and paper-based formats, provided protesters with a means of contesting the narrative of the mainstream media, which characterised those living at the camp as 'professional protesters': self-serving and mercenary troublemakers who profit from stirring up social discord. Consider also the public pronouncement of GMP Chief Superintendent Mark Roberts that 'the majority of people who are arriving on the site are not there to protest against fracking but are there to disrupt and intimidate the local community and to antagonise police' (*Manchester Evening News* 2014). Other sources told a different story, with members of the local community praising protesters' conviction politics (in stark contrast, one is tempted to observe, with the many 'career politicians' against whom the public turned during the protests). The challenge is in spreading the alternative perspectives, which is where these innovative platforms of networked communication come in. These were used by protesters to disseminate to a big audience via the Internet damning evidence of the aggressive policing of peaceful protesters—thereby countering the establishment narrative. These 'weapons of information warfare' would appear to be of truly game-changing significance in their endowment of activists with a power unimaginable to earlier generations of protesters: the ability for the *individual* to respond readily and at minimum cost to disinformation intended to undermine the legitimacy of a campaign, and to do so in ways that reach a large audience.

Battles Beyond Barton Moss

Over the past few years, I have witnessed a number of protests that owe their vitality—if not their very existence—to the networks that grew out of the protests at Barton Moss. A campaign to reduce homelessness is one example, in which activists from Barton Moss have participated. This recently livestreamed a homeless camp in Nottingham, and run homeless camps on the streets and in occupied buildings in Manchester. They have also been involved in camps that have been set up to tackle the effects of climate change in North Wales, Cheshire, Central Lancashire, East Yorkshire, South Yorkshire, and Fylde. What the anti-fracking campaign at Barton Moss has done for the North, then, is create a prototypical movement that through its emulation, replication, and adaptation may be deployed in new locales and repurposed in other campaigns.

One protester, a camper at Barton Moss now residing in Greater Manchester, has paid close attention to these developments, explaining it as follows:

> What the anti-fracking campaign at Barton Moss has done is brought everyone under one roof and to realise that we are all fighting for the same thing. No matter what campaign you are fighting for we are all fighting for a redistribution of resources. We all just want things to be dealt out more evenly. We have got homeless people that we have helped to get housing who are now fighting on other campaigns. There are people who we couldn't get housed who have gone to anti-fracking sites and flourished. No matter what campaign we are working on it is always giving people the drive to go on and do something else. (Telephone interview, 20 January 2015)

Another camp protester, who made the trip from Liverpool, described how Barton Moss had changed his life:

> It was the first time I'd ever been on a protest. I'd never even been to a local demonstration, so Barton Moss did change my life. From what I learnt there it has taken me on to other things with campaigns all around the

> country. And from never having been on a protest before, I have set up protest camps at Upton in Cheshire and in East Yorkshire. I have spoken at public meetings in front of packed halls which six or seven months earlier was a million miles away in my life. (Telephone interview, 19 January 2015)

Galvanising the Local Activist Community

In the 15 years that I have documented social movements, I have seen no other campaign achieve as much as did Barton Moss. The impact it has had on the wider community has been simply astounding. Its incorporation of many people from all walks of life, due largely to its innovative slow-walks, also set the protests of Barton Moss apart. Everyone who 'slow-walked' a truck, or lorry (or sometimes cement mixer), into the IGas site felt—*knew*—that they had achieved something. Many came back for more. Whether a walk expressed resistance to the repressive practices of the Greater Manchester Police or represented one more cost to be borne by the fracking industry—each symbolised a minor victory. When the GMP forced protesters to walk at unreasonable or unsafe speeds, the campaign's response—not to shrink in intimidation, but to grow in courage, commitment, and numbers—was and is inspiring.

Those moments in front of the trucks at Barton Moss seemed collectively to form a space in which people with diverse backgrounds and biographies were united by their concerns over what fracking might do to our environment. And yet in this space, peaceful protesters found themselves under siege, treated by the state as a danger to society, a problem to be solved through fair means or—as happened all too often—foul. Yet amid the rough treatment at the hands of the police—public servants tasked to uphold the law, not break it—we find a space that provided a unique vantage point from which the actions of the state could be clearly apprehended, its close relationship with industry, on whose behest it abused its powers, laid bare for all with open eyes to see. This was also a space whose conditions, in retrospect, must have been particularly hospitable to the emergence and evolution of what can reasonably be described as a special kind of virus, which once loosed upon the world could be expected by virtue of its dynamism and vigour only to spread, inexorably, from one person to the next, with the power to bring down organisms far greater in size and strength—and with seemingly no cure in sight.

What happened at Barton Moss is a reminder of just how powerful participatory forms of protest can be, especially at a time when people feel disillusioned by the political process and disengaged from the usual forms of political participation. It has shown how a band of ordinary committed citizens, despite government and corporate resistance, can use peaceful tactics accessible to all, to defeat corporate interests and challenge repressive policing. At the same time, we must caution ourselves against the seductive but erroneous view that success at Barton Moss was inevitable and that the spread of protest movements, as if by viral contagion, is literally inexorable—however things might seem in self-congratulatory hindsight. As proof of this, consider what might have transpired if Barton Moss Road was not a public footpath upon which protesters could lawfully walk (or slow-walk).

Putting aside for the moment the intractable contingency of political protests and the uncertainty of their consequences, and looking to the future of social movements, in northern England and beyond, what might Barton Moss teach us? All too briefly: that social movements rely for their efficacy upon their ability to exploit the holes liable to exist in any complex system of power. Such exploitation should therefore be a primary focus of any protest's strategic development. A second strategic aim should be to develop protests that expose the (often unpalatable) intentions of the state and reveal (as is typically the case) the speed with which its agencies and agents are willing to dispense with legality and morality in favour of the free exercise of power. And remember: the more ingenious the campaign, the more enlightening will be the protest.

Notes

1. The term 'slow-walk' appears to derive not from the speed of the walk, which is not necessarily slower than normal walking, but because slow-walkers walk in front of vehicles, obstructing their passage, and *slowing*

them down. At Barton Moss, activists would speak of 'slow-walking' vehicles, which usually meant walking in front of the IGas convoys and vehicles that arrived perpetually at the site.

2. In an article for *Salford Star* on 6 February 2014, Simon Pook of Robert Lizar Solicitors compared the policing of the protests at Barton Moss to the policing of the Miners' Strike: '[t]he last time I saw this sort of behaviour was in the Miners' Strike of the 1980s where we saw identical police tactics being used, pushing at miners, brutalising peaceful protest [...] I am very, very concerned' (Salford Star 2014).
3. [Retrieved 24 March 2014] https://www.youtube.com/watch?v=3gxI4ToNKGQ.
4. [Retrieved 24 March 2014] https://www.youtube.com/watch?v=9HWy4BegZqw.
5. [Retrieved 24 March 2014] https://www.youtube.com/watch?v=AwU2zapAfJ8.
6. Frack Free Greater Manchester is a group from Greater Manchester that opposes any attempts to explore or undertake any high volume slickwater hydraulic fracturing for extracting coal bed methane, shale gas, or underground coal gasification. See http://frackfreegtrmanchester.org.uk.
7. Bambuser is a free to use live video streaming platform that enables users to upload live video recorded through mobile devices such as phones and tablets. An example of one video that was viewed more than 5000 times can be found here: http://bambuser.com/v/4450505.

Works Cited

Adams, Andy. 2014. *Peer group review of operation Mansell anti fracking protest Sussex Police*. Hertfordshire: Hertfordshire Constabulary/Essex Police.

BBC. 2013. BBC survey suggests support for fracking in North West. *BBC News*, December 3. http://www.bbc.co.uk/news/uk-england-25157239. Accessed 24 Apr 2017.

Gilmore, Joanna, Will Jackson, and Helen Monk. 2016. *'Keep moving!': Report on the policing of the Barton Moss community protection camp, November 2013–April 2014*. York: Centre for the Study of Crime, Criminalisation and Social Exclusion.

Greater Manchester Police. 2014. *Memorandum of understanding between Greater Manchester Police, Greater Manchester Fire and Rescue Service, North*

West Ambulance Service, Salford City Council, Association of Greater Manchester Authorities, Highways Agency, Igas, Peel Holdings/Estates and Manchester Barton Aerodrome. Greater Manchester: Greater Manchester Police.

Haworth, Susan. 2014. *Re: policing of protest, human rights and justice*. Greater Manchester Association of Trades Councils, July 18. https://netpol.org/wp-content/uploads/2014/08/GMATUC-to-GMPCC-July-2014.pdf. Accessed 24 Apr 2017.

Manchester Evening News. 2014. Most fracking protesters are there to 'intimidate the local community' and 'antagonise' the force, police claim. *Manchester Evening News*, January 23. http://www.manchestereveningnews.co.uk/news/greater-manchester-news/salford-fracking-protesters-intimidate-local-6554055. Accessed 24 Apr 2017.

Sanders, Nicholas. 2016. *Report of Regina V Boris Roscin, John Wasilewski, and David Cohen*. Manchester: The Manchester Magistrates' Court. https://netpol.org/wp-content/uploads/2016/01/Judgment-Roscin-etc-130116-Frackers.pdf. Accessed 24 Apr 2017.

Thompson, Dan. 2014. Three quarters of Mancunians oppose fracking, an M.E.N survey finds. *Manchester Evening News*, March 6. http://www.manchestereveningnews.co.uk/news/greater-manchester-news/three-quarters-mancunians-oppose-fracking-6778067. Accessed 24 Apr 2017.

Section III

Recasting Politics

The Limits of Populism: Mills, Marcuse and 1960s Radicalism and Occupy

Mike O'Donnell

Introduction: Scope and Terminology

This chapter explores three main themes. Firstly, extrapolating from the work of Craig Calhoun, it offers a description of radicalism, focusing particularly on populism. This section pertains especially to early nineteenth-century England, but Calhoun considers that the features of radicalism he observes—with due regard for differences of issues and context—tend to recur in certain later social movements (Calhoun 2012, 6–11; 88–92). Secondly, this chapter highlights aspects in the work of Charles Wright Mills and Herbert Marcuse compatible with populism and discusses their relationships to 1960s American radicalism, which is also found to have populist aspects. Thirdly, it examines the 'Occupy' movement using Calhoun's observations on populism and the work of Mills and Marcuse as points of reference. Populism refers to particular, identifiable characteristics, but is not a settled ideology, and

With Observations from Bryn Jones.

M. O'Donnell (✉)
University of Westminster, London, UK

T. Geelan et al. (eds.), *From Financial Crisis to Social Change*,
https://doi.org/10.1007/978-3-319-70600-9_9

both 1960s radicalism and Occupy—like early nineteenth-century English radicalism—encompassed other, more clearly defined ideological strands. While social movements arise outside of, and typically in tension with, formal political systems, I conclude by emphasising the importance of transforming the populist impulse into support for progressive rather than repressive change.

The purpose of this book is to make a contribution to imagining social change: the same motive that inspired Mills and Marcuse. In that spirit, this chapter critically describes the interweaving of radical and progressive theory and action in two peak periods, mainly in the United States. It points to certain pitfalls of social movement activism as well as its recurrent strengths. Among the former are the disadvantages of settling for gesture and protest at the expense of sustained and organised struggle. Among the latter is the unyielding search to maintain and extend democratic freedoms and social justice. While history is rarely repeated in precise detail, patterns do recur and it makes sense to learn from them.

The title of Calhoun's book *The Roots of Radicalism: Tradition, the Public Sphere, and Early Nineteenth-Century Social Movements* (2012) indicates a concern with the reactive and defensive elements of radicalism during that period. He states that 'early modern thinkers described analyses as radical when they went to foundations, first principles, or what was essential' (Calhoun 2012, 12). With reference to the popular level of struggle, he goes on to state:

> [A]mong many ordinary people, traditions informed radical protests, community provided a base for sustained radical struggles, and appeals to morality and history were basic tools for reaching beyond present circumstances to claim a chance at better lives. (Calhoun 2012, 19)

Calhoun emphasises that radicalism 'is not best understood as a stable ideological position' and rejects the more recent left-right model of political differentiation as an inappropriate framework for analysing it (Calhoun 2012, 6). He adopts the term populist to describe the character of much radical protest of the period, stressing that such broad ideological and expressive currents predate modern socialism. Craft-workers, artisans and peasants are among the social groups within which populism might flourish. A desire to regain autonomy undermined as result of industrial and agrarian capitalism was typical of these and other groups affected by early capitalism. He emphasises that:

> the working people excluded from the 'respectable' public were every bit as committed to the idea of autonomy and perhaps more so. Over and again they reiterated the value of independence and castigated elite writers and parliamentarians for depending on patronage. (Calhoun 2012, 128–129)

He observes that 'ideas of autonomy were considerably more prominent than notions of exploitation among traditional English radicals' (Calhoun 2012, 92). The community of the oppressed, rather than an organised political party, is the main frame of reference of populists as they react to diminished autonomy and reduced circumstances. As well as local communities, groups based on, for instance, 'religious currents, leading philosophies, and the working class movement' sustained radical dissent and 'were distinctive in the extremes to which they took antihierarchical ideology' (Calhoun 2012, 269).

Despite his emphasis on the reactionary and traditional aspects of populism, Calhoun maintains that populists may also respond positively to the challenge of change. The struggle for greater autonomy and liberty had a positive political potential, for instance, in the support for franchise extension and the rights reforms advocated by Thomas Paine.

Calhoun challenges the common distinction between old (OSM) and new social movements (NSM), in which the former are considered mainly concerned with material issues and the latter with identity ones. He regards both these features as characteristic of social movements in general. Accordingly, he denies privileged historical status to the labour movement and reinstates the significance of non-socialist radical movements that preceded it. Although Calhoun recognises the diversity of social movements, the removal of the OSM/NSM divide also facilitates recognition of long-term continuities, including those of a populist character. He considers that the NSM formulation is 'historically shallow' and partly responsible for populism being 'commonly treated as an anomaly – not a central and recurrent response to large scale capitalist and centralizing state power' (Calhoun 2012, 285).

The Cambridge Dictionary of Sociology refers to populism as 'an ambiguous term' (CDS 2006, 448). Both the CDS and Calhoun opt to describe and illustrate populism rather than attempt to provide a precise definition. However, Calhoun's retrospective application of the term is justified by the impressive way he employs it to clarify particular continuities in radicalism. In the United States, populism is often thought to have arisen in the late nineteenth century, as small farmers' opposition in the South and mid-West to northern industrialists and bankers. Nowadays, the term is frequently used to describe broad currents of anti-elitist or 'anti-establishment' sentiment with roots in civil society, typically with some impact on the formal political system. The term is often employed disparagingly by established politicians and commentators and, somewhat confusingly, by populists of the right and left.

The typically reactive and ideologically diffuse characteristics of populism cause problems both for theorists and for populists themselves. Populist surges might shift in various directions—reactionary or progressive, anarchist or authoritarian—rendering their trajectory unpredictable for those who seek to guide it, and making it difficult for commentators to unpick a coherent content from it. Here Calhoun's (2012, 278–279) concept of 'consolidation' is useful. The term refers to ways in which radical (including populist) sentiments and ideas might be given more concrete and sustained form. This could usefully include clarifying the common ground between what is (perhaps too rigidly) perceived as either left- or right-wing populism, thus potentially widening the electoral base of radical political parties. One possible direction of consolidation for contemporary populists of a left-radical flavour is to make common cause with democratic socialists and liberal human rights activists, thus reducing the potential for the populist impulse to simply peter out. Here Calhoun introduces a further useful concept, 'social movement field'. This describes a range of groups and smaller movements that may not be formally linked or share precisely the same values, sentiments and ideas but, at least, occur as a recognisable 'wave' of radical activity (Calhoun 2012, 253–254). The extent to which movements with some populist features may be part of such a wider field and may define the latter's character is variable, but I argue that they play a significant part in both cases discussed below.

Mills, Populism and the 1960s Radical Movement

This section discusses populist and what I term 'radical liberal' aspects of the work of Mills and their impact on 1960s radicalism. His work captured the beginnings of radical questioning and unrest, and his analysis of the main structural divide of American society in elite/mass terms led him away from Marxism towards a more populist inclined perspective. However, he did not describe his work as populist. Locating his own values within humanist thought, he helped shape the idealistic sentiments of young activists, albeit that this anchoring was lost in the later 1960s.

An initial point of terminology needs to be made. I use the terms 'New Left' to indicate the political current, 'Counter-culture' to indicate the cultural current of 1960s radicalism in the United States, and the term 'Movement' to include both. The two currents inter-mingled and complemented each other, often to the point of fusion (see Jones and O'Donnell 2010, Chap. 6; O'Donnell 2008, 242). Calhoun states that far-reaching and long-term change—he uses the term 'revolution'—requires a profound cultural as well as an institutional shift and citing Charles Taylor refers to 'strong horizons' of moral judgement (2012, 285). Mills understood these aspects of deep social change and his own aspirations for the future were partly rooted in traditional values. The Movement itself mixed genuine cultural innovation with a revisiting of traditional and naturalistic styles of living and values but the mainstream did little more than flirt with these boundary-challenging developments. Under pressure serious radical ideas and activities became submerged, but were reasserted again more publicly in the 1990s.

Although he died in March 1962 some years before the Movement reached its peak, Mills arguably remained the major ideological influence on it until it began to fragment into ultimately contradictory strands. Many of Mills' themes and arguments, and even some phrases he used, reappear in the speeches and writings of Movement activists. Unsurprisingly, Mills achieved a more sophisticated critique of American society than the generally young Movement activists, but the latter were better placed to test and develop ideas through practice, whereas Mills remained primarily an academic voice, albeit a powerful one.

Neither Mills' work nor the Movement was 'populist' in any simplistic sense, but the term is useful in understanding significant aspects of both. Mills' writings helped to clarify rising but ill-defined radical sentiment by integrating a range of moral, cultural, psycho-social and political themes: the association between individually felt problems and social structure; the relationship of values to political ideology and action; a growing cultural dimension to the emerging radicalism; the forms and distribution of power in the United States and the country's position in the world.

In *The Sociological Imagination* (1959a), Mills articulated the often-repeated association between personal problems and public issues, a link later powerfully echoed in the feminist dictum, 'the personal is the political'. The potential relationship between personal troubles and public issues that Mills notes chimes with Calhoun's observation that populists' initial 'gut reactions' could prompt collective public responses. From the 1960s, the personal-social-political dimension became a major aspect of emerging identity politics. Mills' sharp psychological awareness and sensitivity to emotional experience are also apparent in his emphasis on the role of culture and values in formulating radical ideology and practice as the following comment made in his *Letter to the New Left* illustrates (the 'magazines' he refers to are two journals that eventually merged to form the *New Left Review*):

> As for the articulation of ideals, there I think your magazines have done their best work so far. That is your meaning – is it not – of the emphasis on cultural affairs? (Mills 1960a, reprinted in Horowitz 1967, 252)

Mills went on to state that the left should be 'guided morally by the humanistic and secular values of Western civilisation – above all by the ideals of reason, freedom and love' (Mills 1960a, in Horowitz 1967, 253).

Mills' coupling of humanistic and secular values reflected and reinforced an established theme in radical thought—one that has current resonance when these values are under challenge from Islamic State's theocratic ideology. Viscerally anti-authoritarian, Mills dismissed the

Soviet regime and the American power elite as undemocratic, albeit in different ways (Mills 1959b). Otherwise, he maintained a dialogical relationship with both socialism and liberalism. He directed some of his fiercest rhetoric towards an influential cluster of American liberals whom he considered no longer represented progressive ideals but were promoting a technocratic and elitist liberalism, which he regarded as a fundamentally 'conservative' accommodation to the status quo (1956, Chap. 14). In particular, he berated Daniel Bell, whose 'end of ideology' thesis he referred to as 'a slogan of complacency' and 'a refusal to work out an explicit political philosophy' (Mills 1960a, in Horowitz 1967, 249–51). Mills' *The Power Elite* (1956) is an attempt to fill this vacuum.

Mills' examination of 'the power elite' (1956) is often discussed in juxtaposition to Marxist class analysis especially in relation to his debate with Marxist Ralph Miliband (Miliband 1969). However, its main proposition that the fundamental division in American society is between the elite and the mass is closer to a populist perspective. Although Mills dismissed the notion of the working class as the main agent of change and seemed unable to prevent himself from ridiculing the conformity of the emerging white-collar class, his sympathies nevertheless lay with these less powerful groups, and he reserved his most scathing criticism for the power elite. The combination of Mills moral tone and anti-elitism has an echo of William Jennings Bryan, the most populist of major American politicians. Bryan's anti-elitism was succinctly expressed in the old Jacksonian motto that he often quoted: 'Equal rights to all and special privileges to none' (in Hofstadter 1967, 188).

Mills focused more on inequality of power, particularly the lack of personal and group autonomy, than on material inequality. This resonates with historic and contemporary populism that has also prioritised individual and communal freedoms and grassroots democracy. Mills did not regard the United States as a fully or adequately democratic society. His critique of the power elite hardly needs revisiting, but his thoughts on what might constitute a more democratic society are less familiar (1956, 318–24). He was a consistent advocate of 'publics', by which he meant the informed engagement of individuals and groups in civil and political life. This is a similar scenario to that favoured by contemporary supporters of civil society as the cradle of change. In Mills' case, his advocacy of publics has a distinct whiff of nostalgia for small-town and rural America, and he expressed doubts about whether such public political participation is compatible with large-scale society. These sentiments have a populist flavour but he most often uses the word 'liberal' to describe the kind of democratic society he advocates, repeatedly contrasting 'a genuinely liberal public' with mass society.

> The idea of a mass society suggests an elite of power. The idea of the public in contrast suggests the liberal tradition of a society without any power elite, or at any rate of shifting elites of no sovereign consequence. (Mills 1956, 323)

Mills' understanding of 'genuine' liberalism cannot be equated with populism but resonates with the latter's characteristic emphasis on popular participation and complementary anti-elitism and with the tendency for populist ideological strands to overlap and intertwine with more developed ideologies. Equally, Mills' secular humanism reflects the ideals of the enlightenment and jars with the ideologically sceptical liberalism of Daniel Bell (1988[1960]) and Seymour Martin Lipset (1972).

Unable to envisage a convincing agency of change in American society, Mills did not even sketch an outline agenda for social transformation. Casting around for signs of radical stirring, he was supportive of the rising tide of dissent among intellectuals and students (Mills 1960a, in Horowitz 1967, 256–9), and, in the last years of his life, he also looked to emerging nations as potential agents of radical progress (1960b).

Mills' comments on bureaucracy find him at his most populist:

> Great and rational forms of organisations – in brief, bureaucracies – have indeed increased, but the substantive reason of individuals at large has not. Caught in the limited milieux of their everyday lives, ordinary men often cannot reason about great structures – rational and irrational – of which their milieux are subordinate parts. Accordingly they often carry out series of apparently rational action without any idea of the ends they serve, and there is an increasing suspicion that those at the top as well – like Tolstoy's generals – only pretend they know. (Mills 1959c, in Horowitz 1967, 237–238)

With typical bravado, Mills jibed at those he regarded as technocratic liberals as 'crackpot realists' and the conformist mass as 'cheerful robots' reprising Kafka and Weber's depiction of modernity as impersonal and dehumanising.

Mills' work, then, provided a broad sense of direction to the new radicals, but not a developed strategy or vision of destination. Unsurprisingly, many got lost on the way to utopia. It is necessary to put the Movement in context before setting out aspects of Mills' influence on it. Typical of a social movement field, it was a collection of more or less loosely connected and mutually supportive groups and organisations. In the early stages of the Movement, the main issues were segregation and the denial of black people's rights in the South, and the Cold War with its associated risk of nuclear annihilation. Both illustrate Calhoun's argument that incipient populism typically involves reaction to perceived injustice or threat rather than the emergence of a fully fledged ideology. While the social base of the Movement was, of course, different from early nineteenth-century English radicalism, as what follows illustrates, the dynamics of modern social movement development offer parallels.

An early positional document reflective of the Movement's emerging perspectives was *The Port Huron Statement* (PHS), written in 1962 by a group from the Students for a Democratic Society (SDS). It opens by referring to a generation looking 'uncomfortably to the world' it inherited (Jacobs and Landau 1967, 154). In addition to the issues of racism and the nuclear threat, unease was expressed about the state of American democracy in an appeal for 'truly democratic alternatives to the present, and a commitment to social experimentation with them' (Jacobs and Landau 1967, 157).

The section titled 'Values' in the PHS closely reflects Mills' concern with the moral motivations underlying politics. After commenting that 'not even the liberal and socialist preachments of the past seem adequate to the forms of the present', it repeats verbatim Mills' belief that people have unfulfilled capacities 'for reason, freedom and love' (Jacobs and Landau 1967, 158). A later section, titled 'Politics without Publics', claims in recognisably Millsian terms that the 'American political system is not the democratic model of which its glorifiers speak' (Jacobs and Landau 1967, 164). The document then substantially recounts Mills' analysis that congressional politics function predominantly at a middle level of power, while the power elite controls the heights (Jacobs and Landau 1967, 164–7). However, the PHS mainly focuses on the lower levels of power. Participatory democracy was the young radicals' attempt to address the putative democratic deficit that had so perturbed Mills but to which he was unable to offer a solution.

Among the Movement organisations that adopted participatory democratic forms were the Student Non-violent Coordinating Committee (SNCC) and the Economic Research and Action Project (ERAP) set up by SDS. There is synchronicity between Mills' ideas and many of the practices of the emerging activists. Although the two organisations overlapped in personal and shared similar grassroots values and strategy, they reflected the different parts of the social movement field in which they were mainly located. SNCC was founded in 1960 to promote the democratic goal of ensuring one person one vote in the still largely segregationist South. Initially its practice reflected the pacifism and intimate political manner fostered by Martin Luther King rather than Mills' combative style. Its participatory and discursive decision-making approach and organisation became widely influential across the early Movement. Its ethos is well reflected in the following reflections of SNCC activist Bob Moses:

> What we have begun to learn and are trying to explore about people is how they can come together in groups, small groups and large groups, and talk to each other and make decisions about basic things, about their lives, I think that has application everywhere in the country. (Jacobs and Landau 1967, 129)

Moses goes on to comment on the inadequacy of democracy in the United States:

> Whatever we [i.e., the American people] currently mean by democracy, we don't mean that people should come together, discuss their main problems that they all know about and be able to do something about themselves. (Jacobs and Landau 1967, 129)

Instead, Moses advocates open public discussions to enable participants to establish their own priorities rather than be presented with prearranged ones. More directly influenced by Mills, the ERAP project tried to implement and test the principles proposed in *The Port Huron Statement* advocating for a democracy of individual participation in which people shared in the decisions determining the direction and quality of their lives, principles that resonate with the populist tradition. The SDS set up 12 projects in areas of socio-economic disadvantage, with the intention of supporting people to empower themselves. Only a couple of projects lasted more than a few years, which is not surprising given their exploratory nature. Some activists concluded that fundamental improvement in the condition of the poor required structural change.

In different ways, Mills and Martin Luther King provided the kind of charismatic focus that can give direction and impact to social movements. Mills' influence is also highly apparent on the Free Speech Movement (FSM) of 1964 at Berkeley University.

The FSM is a classic case of a movement defending perceived fundamental rights and freedoms against vested interests and bureaucratic control. The initial conflict between students and administration concerned the right of students to political advocacy on a particular area of university-owned property. The debate soon brought into play the relationship between higher education to industry and the nature of bureaucracy. On the former matter, the President of the University, Clark Kerr, was a noted public advocate of close cooperation between the educational and business sectors (Kerr 2001[1963]), whereas FSM spokespeople linked their advocacy of free speech to the principle of academic freedom, notably from capital and the State.

Partly because of activist Mario Savio's celebrated speech attacking the 'end of ideology' thesis which he dubbed 'the end of history' thesis, an issue closely associated with the FSM is the alienating effects of bureaucracy. Savio's immediate target was Kerr and the Berkeley administration but he extended his argument to include bureaucracy as an organisational form, pleading with his co-protestors to put their bodies 'on the levers, upon all the apparatus … and make it stop' (quoted in Teodori 1970, 156). Rhetorics aside, Savio was addressing what he saw as the increasing reliance of modern society on administrative and technological procedures rather than on democratic communication and direct engagement. His attack on 'the end of history' thesis echoes powerfully Mills' dismissal of Bell's 'end of ideology' thesis (1988[1960]) and the kind of liberalism he represented. Tempting fate, Frances Fukuyama later wrote what can be read as an extended version of Bell's thesis in his influential book, *The End of History and the Last Man* (Fukuyama 1992).

By the mid-1960s, the Vietnam War had persuaded prominent new left thinkers into developing a more defined ideological position, particularly in relation to foreign policy. In a major speech, *Trapped in a System*, Carl Oglesby, the President of SDS, named 'corporate liberalism' which he considered to be 'illiberal liberalism' as a worldwide system of exploitation and inhumanity (in Teodori 1970, 186). Instead, he appealed to humanistic liberalism as Mills had done in the closing pages of *The Power Elite*. Oglesby put the matter bluntly:

> Corporatism or humanism: which? He then evokes the American revolutionary tradition appealing to simple human decency and democracy and the vision that wise and brave men saw in the time of our own revolution. (Oglesby 1970, 187)

A European new leftist might well have presented a socialist position in relation to corporate liberalism. In contrast, like Mills, Oglesby reiterated the progressive tradition of American liberalism. Although Oglesby's position was broadly similar to that taken by Eugene McCarthy and Robert Kennedy in 1968, relatively few of the increasingly disenchanted activists immediately 'consolidated' around it as the Movement began to fork into a variety of directions.

Marcuse, Populism and the 1960s Radical Movement

A refugee from Fascist Germany, Marcuse was a critical theorist of the Freudian-Marxist Frankfurt School. Similar to Mills he adopted a quasi-populist elite/mass perspective on the structure of American society, regarding the majority of the population as subject to material exploitation and manipulated cultural delusion. Much less of an institutional analyst than Mills, he insisted that a change of 'consciousness' was a precondition to social revolution (1964, 47). Although his seminal work, *Eros and Civilization*, appeared in 1955, it was the publication of *One-Dimensional Man* in 1964 with its vision of cultural liberation that made him an iconic figure to the emerging Counterculture.

Like Mills, Marcuse trawled American social strata for signs of rebellion. *One-Dimensional Man* refers to 'the outcasts and outsiders, the exploited and persecuted of other races and other colours, the unemployed and the unemployable' as 'revolutionary' in 'their opposition to one dimensional society even if their consciousness is not' (Marcuse 1964, 200). He is realistic enough to know that these socially disparate and poorly organised people had little hope of effecting systemic change without the involvement of more powerful groups. He comments in his concluding chapter that '[t]he critical theory of society possesses no concepts that could bridge the gap between the present and the future' (Marcuse 1964, 201). In his *An Essay on Liberation*, first published in 1968, his mood is lifted by the activities of young radicals although he still offers no outline of how change might occur (Marcuse 1968).

Marcuse's pessimism, even more than Mills', was based on the idea that '[r]eason has conquered the world in the image of repression' (1955, 60). Both saw repressive rationality as embodied in large-scale corporate and governmental bureaucracies that treated human beings as functional means. Marcuse went further than Mills, arguing that American liberal capitalism had produced a totalitarian, 'one dimensional society' reflective of a rationality based on *thanatos*, on aggressive competitiveness and repression rather than on *eros*—love, compassion and cooperation. The originality and power of Marcuse's work lies in his proposition that the central tension in human nature is not, as is often thought, between instinct and reason but within instinct itself, between *eros* and *thanatos*. Reason might be harnessed in the cause of either but Marcuse advocated a society reflecting a rationality based on the pleasure principle, that is, as far as practical on the life instincts rather than *thanatos*.

How far Marcuse's work directly influenced the Counterculture is uncertain, but the lifestyle radicalism of the second half of the 1960s synchronised with his theories, at least until many of its practices morphed into the mainstream becoming imitative, mere radical chic and less an indicator of a radical orientation. The Counterculture did not exactly follow his carefully theorised notions of cultural and social liberation. When 'the lid blew off the *id*' as well as creativity, anger and excess also poured out, sometimes confusingly interwoven with idealism. By the late 1960s, liberals of what Mills had designated as the 'end of ideology' school were lining up to condemn the direction the Movement was taking, some seeing it as quasi Fascist (see Bettleheim 1969; Lipset 1972).

In adopting a radical elite/mass theoretical approach and in designating 'the masses' as the focus of their moral and political concern, Mills and Marcuse anticipated perspectives widely expressed in the social movements following the crash of 2007–2008. Further, they were influential in arguing that fundamental social change should be rooted in the values and practice of activists themselves. The diffuse social movement field of which the Counterculture was an often anarchic part reflected these insights, intuitively as much as intellectually. What Calhoun refers to as 'aesthetic production and reception' was important in signifying alternative lifestyles and an aspirational direction of social change (2012, 274–275). However, without parallel political and institutional change of the kind advocated by Mills, alternative culture is at risk of being absorbed, trivialised or remaining peripheral.

Populism and *Occupy*

The elite/masses theme of Mills and Marcuse, influential on the American New Left, recurred in the Occupy movement. Post the 2008–2009 crash, both radical activists and theorists appeared to use the term elite (or elites) more than ruling class although the terms are not necessarily incompatible. However, terms such as 'the 99 per cent' or 'the rest' were generally preferred to the somewhat patronising 'the masses' that is also associated with conservative political theory. However, the key point from a radical perspective is that the majority of people are seen as exploited, not merely one social stratum. As far as elite theory is concerned, the interlocking of the economic/financial, political and military elites offers an account of power and exploitation less prone to economic reductionism than cruder forms of ruling class theory. These analytical trends prompted some radicals of the left to adopt the term populist in describing their political orientation.

The term 'anarcho-populist' was successfully floated to describe Occupy and other movements that appeared across the Americas, Europe and elsewhere following the financial crash of 2007–2008 (Gerbaudo 2013). While Occupy reflected other ideological strands including Marxism, as did the 1960s Movement, the term 'anarcho-populism' comes closest to describing its direct action tactics, targeting of mass support and communitarian tendencies.

The Occupy movement fits Calhoun's broad description of populism and shares similarities with the 1960s radical movement in the United States. Its reactive element was anger, especially of young people, at the behaviour of the financial elite and at the relentless shrinking of their career and life prospects. The slogan '99% and the 1%' signalled, well before Piketty (2014), the emergence of a global elite increasingly remote materially and culturally from the majority of the world's population.

Todd Gitlin, a former New Left activist and President of SDS, provides a closely observed account of the Occupy protests in the United States. Gitlin avoids overstating the similarities between Occupy and the radical movement of the 1960s. However, the parallels are considerable, and in Gitlin's terms the two movements are part of the same radical tradition that he refers to as '[a] kind of anarchism of direct participation' (2012, 80) but which could as accurately be described as 'anarcho-populist'.

In tones reminiscent of Bob Moses (quoted above), he describes this tradition further:

> There is lineage even longer. Decision making by consensus is of Quaker inspiration, as if to say: Speak and listen, listen and speak, until the spirit of the whole emerges. (Gitlin 2012, 80)

Occupy's tactic of occupying public space, in some cases by camping, evokes those adopted in the 1960s, resembling a cross between a sit-in and a commune. Direct democratic forms of participation were adopted by Occupy and other radical groups including, in Britain, 38 Degrees. The potential for networking increased where the same activists participated in various protests and actions (Diani 2000). The Web greatly facilitated horizontal communication, enabling a global flow of information and ideas and the co-ordination of activities.

As Gitlin describes it, Occupy Wall Street attempted, not always successfully, to model what a different society might look like through integrating ideology and practice. He quotes one activist:

> Occupation is more than just a tactic [...] Many participants are prefiguring the kind of society they want to live in. (Gitlin 2012, 73)

The same sentiments were often expressed by activists in the 1960s. By the end of that decade, the idea that a fundamental socio-cultural change in American society was at hand had gone 'viral'. Books such as Theodore Roszak's *The Making of the Counter Culture* (1968) speculated that the influence of the young radicals might transform dominant culture. A survey by the mainstream journal *Fortune* categorised three million out of eight million respondents aged 18–24 as 'forerunners' who took a good quality of life as a given and were motivated by moral idealism and a desire for career fulfilment (Seligman 1969). In reality, even as these works were published, the Movement was in rapid decline. Change on the scale and in the radical form envisaged did not occur. The demise of the Movement and the current low visibility of Occupy raise the issue of whether in order to make long-term impact, social movements should address more directly the task of gaining institutional power. This is not to downplay their historic role as a stimulant to society's conscience and moral imagination. Less well-known than Occupy's symbolic 'performance' in Zuccotti Park is that, in a distant echo of the community projects of SDS, it generated a number of grassroots actions, including a major disaster-relief effort following Superstorm Sandy.

Conclusion

Populism is a significant and formative current in the stream of radical politics. Often it is considered to 'muddy the waters' of radicalism, introducing confusing and disturbing elements of ideological incoherence, mass disorder and authoritarian leadership. Albeit referring to populism of the left, even a *Daily Telegraph* editorial frets about 'worrying populism' (2016). However, as Calhoun argues and this chapter illustrates, populism can voice genuinely democratic sentiments, particularly when drawn into the larger flow of progressive politics. The desire for freedom, negatively from self-seeking elites and positively to establish a meaningful degree of autonomy across personal and public life, deserves to be taken seriously.

The tough challenge to radical thinkers and activists is to focus the democratic potential of populism and to formulate concrete policies that can deliver on sometimes valid but often vague aspirations: thus consolidating populism within the progressive fold. In both the United States and parts of Europe the post-war decline in traditional 'right/left' divisions is reflected in more fluid patterns of political identification and voting behaviour. This creates an opportunity for progressive radicals (as it does for reactionary ones) to win over new constituencies, including from among populist movements. Further, the regular failure in Britain of about a third of the electorate to vote, particularly among the young, offers a so far untapped opportunity to reshape and revitalise the political landscape. Already the social movement sector is giving a lead in the direction of enhanced institutional democracy. Equality is also being re-envisaged in terms that might have wide appeal, for instance, in the form of a participatory citizens' income. Such possibilities offer a glimmer of a realistic utopia. Alain Touraine in *After the Crisis* (2014) attempts to sketch a fuller picture of transformation. He reflects that there remains no single class interest that defines radical politics and that the conflict is now between the global elite and the 'interests of the population' (Touraine 2014, 156). He envisages a crucial role for social movements to pursue not merely sectional interests but universal human rights. This is a long-term vision that transcends populism but also has the capacity to channel the populist impulse in a direction of moral and practical reconstruction.

Works Cited

Bell, Daniel. 1988[1960]. *The end of ideology: On the exhaustion of political ideas in the fifties*. Cambridge: Harvard University Press.

Bettleheim, Bruno. 1969. Obsolete youth: Towards a psychograph of adolescent rebellion. *Encounter* 32 (September): 29–42.

Calhoun, Craig. 2012. *The roots of radicalism: Tradition, the public sphere and early nineteenth century social movements*. Chicago: University of Chicago Press.

Cambridge Dictionary of Sociology (CDS). 2006. *Cambridge dictionary of sociology*. Ed. Bryan Turner. Cambridge/New York: Cambridge University Press.

Daily Telegraph. 2016. Worrying populism. *Daily Telegraph*, February 28, 17.

Diani, Mario. 2000. Simmel to Rokkan and beyond: Towards a network theory of new social movements. *European Journal of Social Theory* 3 (4): 387–406.

Fukuyama, Francis. 1992. *The end of history and the last man*. London: Penguin Books.

Gerbaudo, Paolo. 2013. When anarchism goes pop. *Open Democracy*. https://www.opendemocracy.net/paolo-gerbaudo/when-anarchism-goes-pop. Accessed 23 June 2014.

Gitlin, Todd. 2012. *Occupy nation: The roots, the spirit, and the promise of Occupy Wall Street*. New York: itbooks.

Hofstadter, Richard. 1967. *The American political tradition and the men who made it*. London: Jonathan Cape.

Horowitz, Irving. 1967. *Power, politics and people: The collected essays of Charles Wright Mills*. Oxford: Oxford University Press.

Jacobs, Paul, and Saul Landau. 1967. *The new radicals*. Harmondsworth: Penguin.

Jones, Bryn, and Michael O'Donnell. 2010. *Radicalism and social movement activism: Retreat and resurgence*. London: Anthem.

Kerr, Clark. 2001[1963]. *The uses of the university*. Massachusetts: Harvard University Press.

Lipset, Seymour Martin. 1972. Ideology and no end: The controversy till now. *Encounter* 39 (6): 17–22.

Marcuse, Herbert. 1955. *Eros and civilisation*. London: Sphere Books.

———. 1964. *One dimensional man*. London: Routledge and Kegan Paul.

———. 1968. *An essay on liberation*. Boston: Beacon Books.

Miliband, Ralph. 1969. *The state in capitalist society*. London: Weidenfeld and Nicolson.

Mills, Charles Wright. 1956. *The power elite*. New York: Oxford University Press.

———. 1959a. *The sociological imagination*. New York: Oxford University Press.

———. 1959b. *The causes of world war three*. London: Martin Secker and Warburg.

———. 1959c. Culture and politics: The fourth epoch. In *Power, politics and people: The collected essays of Charles Wright Mills*, ed. Irving Horowitz, 236–246. Oxford: Oxford University Press.

———. 1960a. Letter to the New Left. In *Power, politics and people: The collected essays of Charles Wright Mills*, ed. Irving Horowitz, 247–259. Oxford: Oxford University Press.

———. 1960b. *Listen Yankee: The revolution in Cuba*. New York: Ballantine Books.

O'Donnell, Michael. 2008. Nineteen sixties radicalism and its critics: Utopian radicals, liberal realists and postmodern sceptics. *Psychoanalysis, Culture and Society* 13 (3): 240–260.

Oglesby, Carl. 1970. Trapped in a system. In *The New Left: A documentary history*, ed. Massimo Teodori, 182–188. London: Jonathan Cape.

Piketty, Thomas. 2014. *Capitalism in the twenty-first century*. Massachusetts: Harvard University Press.

Roszac, Theodore. 1968. *The making of the counter-culture: Reflections on the technocratic society and its youthful opposition*. New York: Doubleday.

Seligman, Daniel. 1969. A special kind of rebellion. In *Youth in turmoil: Adapted from a special issue of Fortune*, ed. Louis Banks. New York: Time Incorporated. https://www.amazon.com/Youth-Turmoil-Adapted-Special-Fortune/dp/B000ND0N60.

Teodori, Massimo. 1970. *The New Left: A documentary history*. London: Jonathan Cape.

Touraine, Alain. 2014. *After the crisis*. Cambridge: Polity.

The Myth of Bourgeois Democracy

Andreas Møller Mulvad and Rune Møller Stahl

Introduction

This chapter challenges the claim that parliamentary democratic institutions are either inherently 'bourgeois' or 'liberal'. Unfortunately, this claim retains considerable traction among Marxists and in cognate emancipatory political theories. In what follows we argue that the notion of a necessary structural connection between capitalism and parliamentary democracy, while problematic even when applied to the post-war epoch, is becoming increasingly counterproductive today. First, because it provides a barrier to understanding the current unravelling of the post-Second World War compact of relative harmony between capitalism and national parliamentary democracies. Second, because it stands in the way of a productive theoretical engagement with post-2011 popular movements to reinvigorate and expand representative democratic institutions

A. M. Mulvad (✉)
Copenhagen Business School, Copenhagen, Denmark

R. M. Stahl
University of Copenhagen, Copenhagen, Denmark

T. Geelan et al. (eds.), *From Financial Crisis to Social Change*,
https://doi.org/10.1007/978-3-319-70600-9_10

against oligarchic elites. Thus, we argue that anti-capitalists today should reaffirm the radical republican tradition that Marx saw himself as a part of, as a philosophical basis for a democratic project to overturn capitalism in an age of increasing threat to parliamentary institutions.

In his 2010 book *Envisioning Real Utopias*, Erik Olin Wright distinguishes three ideal-typical strategies for achieving systemic transformation beyond capitalism: ruptural ('revolutionary socialist/communist'), interstitial metamorphosis ('anarchist') and symbiotic metamorphosis ('social democratic') (Wright 2010, 304). While Wright's typology provides a clear analytical framework for discussions about strategy, what falls through the gaps left open by the typology is the historical experience of parts of the socialist workers' movement in rejecting the rupture/symbiosis dichotomy (also known as 'revolution vs. reform'). We posit that while the dichotomy between the Leninist path of class war and the Bernsteinian path of evolutionary change[1] has dominated debates in the last century, there is an older tradition in the workers' movement that transcends this fruitless binary, and which can be useful for anti-capitalist movements today. As we will demonstrate below, this original Marxian strategy sought to use the state to gradually achieve ruptural change of property relations. It was neither extra-legally 'ruptural' nor naïvely evolutionist, and, contrary to the impression that Olin Wright's model leaves us with, it certainly did not build on 'class compromise' in any meaningful sense. It is perhaps best described as a pro-constitutionalist strategy of using democratic republics as vehicles for the gradual abolition of capitalism.

Thus, as we challenge below the perhaps most prolific contemporary exponent of the Neo-Leninist 'rupturism', Slavoj Žižek, we simultaneously hope to add a modicum of historical nuance to Olin Wright's theoretical model.

Perhaps the most prominent intellectual proponent of the claim of the bourgeois character of parliamentary democracy in contemporary academic and political discussions is the Slovenian philosopher Slavoj Žižek. Hence, we devote considerable space to a discussion of the content and implications of his political analyses. While Žižek is himself a lifelong critic of the former communist countries, he nevertheless argues that contemporary anti-capitalists should reformulate the issue of taking over

State power through a reengagement with the extra-legal vision of the Leninist tradition (Žižek 2002, 3). For example, in the afterword to *Living in the End Times*, he writes:

> Radical changes in [social relations of production] need to be made outside the sphere of legal "rights." In "democratic" procedures [...], no matter how radical our anti-capitalism, solutions are sought solely through those democratic mechanisms which themselves form part of the apparatuses of the "bourgeois" state that guarantees the undisturbed reproduction of capital. (Žižek 2011, 450)

Žižek here construes the state as a monolithic and purely capitalist entity. While this reading is clad in superficially Marxist terms, by drawing on the Communist Manifesto slogan of the State as the executive committee of the bourgeoisie, it is hardly representative of the more nuanced view of the State in the Marxist tradition. Of course, the state can and often does serve as an instrument for capitalist class control. But the state is also, as Nicos Poulantzas (2001) and Bob Jessop (1990) have argued with inspiration from Antonio Gramsci, itself a site of class struggle. On this more refined strategic-relational view, the pro-capitalist functionality of state apparatuses is a research hypothesis, not an a priori truth. Moreover, the parliamentary institutions we know today are the product of past but still ongoing struggles between different social classes and political-ideological movements that know very well that their class-specific effects depend on institutional set-ups. Furthermore, as we shall argue, although Žižek evokes Marx to support his position, his stance does not represent the views that Marx himself held on parliamentary democracy.[2] On the contrary, Marx consistently stressed that supporting constitutional reforms towards political democracy is a vital part of socialist politics.

In terms of strategy, the simplistic notion of the State as a pro-capitalist entity leads Žižek to the inevitable conclusion that the very notions of constitutionality and legality stand in the way of any real socialist transformation. Instead he demands a return to the insurrectionary stance of Lenin, where the break with constitutionality becomes the guarantor of a 'politics of truth' (Žižek 2002, 167).

Rejecting all existing forms of legal and constitutional frames as rigged beyond repair in favour of the bourgeoisie, Žižek regards the extra-legal revolutionary coup as an indispensable part of revolutionary politics.[3] For Žižek the depth of the interpellation of the population and the working class under capitalist ideology makes a revolutionary break absolutely necessary as a means of breaking ideological dominance. Thus, the rupture with the institutional and legal order in itself becomes a way of creating a new form of politics, through the instigation of a State of exception. This idea seems more indebted to Carl Schmitt's decisionism (see Schmitt 2007)—an affinity which Žižek himself openly endorses (Žižek 1999)—than to that of Karl Marx.

Žižek's position is problematic in three respects. First, it neglects the radical mobilising potentials that lie in struggles to achieve democratic rights. Second, it reinforces the ideological conception of a natural connection between capitalism and democracy—an ideological connection he often criticises in his works but inadvertently reinforces through his flirtation with Schmitt's anti-parliamentary theories. Third, it neglects the necessity for anti-capitalists to engage with the constitutional question. Serious consideration for exactly what institutional character a project of radical democracy shall take can, if we follow Žižek, apparently be postponed until after the transformative act of revolution. However, by rejecting the relevance of legal rights and democratic procedures, Žižek not only runs the risk of discarding the main lessons from the horrible mistakes of the Leninist revolutions of the twentieth century. He also inadvertently equates legal and democratic procedures with bourgeois rule, and argues that such procedures must be circumvented if the goal is the profound transformation of social relations of production.

In what follows, we provide a historically grounded argument for why anti-capitalists should defend parliamentary democracy and fight to expand its socio-economic constitutional reach, rather than reject it entirely. In doing so, we highlight an alternative set of theoretical resources within the Marxist tradition—particularly those of the historically conscious Marxist historian Eric Hobsbawm and the Republican-socialist Spanish intellectual historian Antoni Domènech (see Hobsbawm 1973; Domènech 2004)—in order to provide a more constructive platform for thinking about parliamentary democracy in the twenty-first century.

In the section entitled 'Before the First World War: Liberalism Against Democracy', we dispute the notion that parliamentary democracy—defined as the constitutionalisation of state executive power under a legislative body with regular elections and universal suffrage—was originally a liberal or bourgeois invention. We look at historical examples of how democratic enfranchisement was achieved as the product of protracted struggles of workers', women's and civil rights movements. The section entitled 'Marx on Parliamentary Democracy' engages directly with the works of Karl Marx. Through a rereading of his 'Third Address' on the Paris Commune (Marx 1871), we demonstrate that Žižek's rejection of parliamentary democracy is at odds with the pro-parliamentary democratic-republican allegiances that Marx himself expressed. The section entitled '1917 Onwards: Emergence of the Myth of "Bourgeois Democracy"' investigates how the assessment of parliamentary democracy within the socialist workers' movement was polarised in the period after the First World War, due to the tragic split between Bolshevik 'rupturalists' and evolutionist social democrats. We show how the Marxist left, under the influence of Lenin, became progressively alienated from parliamentary democracy in the aftermath of the October revolution, while liberals developed a new and profoundly ahistorical interpretation of parliamentary democracy as their own brainchild—an interpretation which achieved hegemony after 1945 as it was accepted by both liberals, social democrats and communists in the Cold War period. The final section draws on this historical reappraisal to investigate the predicament for anti-capitalists in today's neoliberal conjuncture, where tensions between capitalism and democracy are becoming politically urgent once again. The emerging divorce between capitalism and democracy provides anti-capitalists with a golden opportunity to deconstruct the myth that parliamentary democracy is inherently bourgeois, and instead invest their energies in the construction of a counter-hegemonic popular project to restore and expand the democratic capacity of States against unregulated global markets.

Before the First World War: Liberalism Against Democracy

Before the twentieth century, the term democracy did not primarily refer to a specific set of political institutions or decision-making procedures. Rather, democracy was identified as a type of social class rule, namely, the rule by and power of the popular class—the poor—against the noble and propertied classes.[4] In Aristotle's famous typology of State forms, 'democracy' as it existed in the city state of Athens only indirectly referred to the institutional procedure of majority-based decision-making—insofar as the class of poor freemen made up the vast majority of the population. In the first instance, democracy was defined by social class, rather than in institutional terms, as government in the interest of the poor, and, as such, it constituted a deviation from the kind of mixed constitution with aristocratic elements that Aristotle preferred (Aristotle 1995, III, v.4 [1279B]). This equation of democracy as a majority rule with the political power of the 'Party of the Poor', and hence with egalitarian policies, is evident throughout history. It reappears both with opponents of popular rule, such as aristocratic republican Cicero (Wood 2008, 143), and with the early modern proponents of democratic constitutions, such as popular republicans in the North Italian city states (McCormick 2011) or the Levellers and Diggers of the English Civil War (Robertson 2007).

The radical phase of the French Revolution, led by Robespierre and the Jacobins, marked the (re)introduction of the idea of democracy as the rule of common people into the heart of the political scene in Europe. Crucially, the ideology of liberalism first emerged precisely as a reaction to the radical-democratic republicanism of the French Revolution. The term 'liberalism' was coined in 1812, designating an ideologically centrist position on the constitutional question, in the spectrum between radical republican democrats and conservatives who defended absolutist monarchy. Liberals favoured keeping monarchs but curtailing their arbitrary power through constitutions (Domènech 2004). The new ideology of liberalism emerged out of a century-old tradition of liberal thought, represented by thinkers such as Locke and Montesquieu who voiced a critique of monarchy without demanding a fully democratic-republican constitution (Skinner 1998; Wood 2012). The latter became an influential force with his notion of 'moderate government', based on a division of power by the combination of monarchy and constitutional elements (Montesquieu 1794, book 5§14). This liberalism became the ideology of the rising bourgeoisie of Western Europe. Self-declared liberals played a leading role in the moderate government after France's 1830 Revolution, and in Great Britain the Whig Party finally changed its name to the Liberal Party in 1859 (Hobsbawm 1973).

The primary goal of the liberals was to secure private property from the potential encroachment of the absolutist State and to open the feudal economic structures to commercial development. Rule of law and the control of State power were the ultimate goals of the liberals of the nineteenth century, and popular participation was only an instrument to achieve this aim.[5] Sometimes this quest for a constrained State and personal liberty demanded alignment with the popular classes against conservatives, such as in the revolutions of the 1830s and 1848. However, whenever the threat from the reactionary forces of absolutism became less serious, there was no desire of the liberals to introduce general political participation. For instance, in Germany after the revolutionary fervour of 1848, liberals joined in an alliance with the Junkers, and were quite content with the restricted parliamentarism of the Bismarck years, when the law restricted not only suffrage, but also, through the so-called Sozialistengesetze (anti-socialist laws), the organisation of popular resistance to these restrictions via a partial ban on the rising SPD (Blackbourn and Eley 1984, 255).

Even John Stuart Mill, arguably the strongest nineteenth-century proponent of an inclusive liberalism, feared the prospect of majority rule (Losurdo 2011, 254). In *Considerations on Representative Government* (1861), he states: 'But even in this democracy, absolute power, if they chose to exercise it, would rest with the numerical majority; and these would be composed exclusively of a single class' (Mill 1861). The class Mill had in mind is of course the poor and unpropertied: The 'demos', which in England in the nineteenth century had taken the form of the industrial proletariat. In order to get a model of democracy which would be compatible with his liberal inclinations, Mill had to transform the notion of democracy from the rule of the majority to the divided rule between the majority and the propertied minority.[6]

Thus, the preferred constitution for nineteenth-century liberals was not one that entailed a system of full parliamentary sovereignty and universal suffrage but rather a mixed constitution with elements of monarchy, democracy and aristocracy. Remembering this genesis of liberalism is important, because it demonstrates that the terms 'liberal democracy' and 'bourgeois democracy' are, historically speaking, oxymorons.

If the founders of political liberalism did not envision the broadening of enfranchisement much beyond their own class of the wealthy and the educated, and conservatives opposed the idea of constitutionalism altogether, how then did we nevertheless see a continued expansion of the suffrage to wider and wider groups from 1848 onwards? The reason was the pressure from a variety of popular social movements, manifesting themselves with increasing ferocity through campaigns, riots and even revolutions, fighting for a say in public policy through gaining the right to vote. Popular force was already present in the Sans-Culotte wing of the French Revolution, but it was with the rise of the organised working class that the pressure became consistent and permanent. The first manifestation of this was the Chartist movement in Britain, through which millions of craftsmen and industrial workers joined in the support of a programme for general suffrage which had as its central demands 'a vote for every man twenty one years of age and [...] [n]o Property Qualification for members of Parliament' (London Working Men's Association 1838). The Chartist movement led a decade-long campaign with demonstrations, strikes and petitions, and was fiercely opposed by liberals and conservatives in parliament. As a result, a substantial widening of political enfranchisement was not realised until Disraeli's reform in 1867, and anything resembling full male suffrage only in 1918 (Hobsbawm 1973, 152).

Crucially, the struggle for universal suffrage and parliamentary power was not abandoned with the rise of Marxism and the workers' movement in the later decades of the nineteenth century. On the contrary, the demand for representation and universal suffrage remained a key part of the programmes of national workers' parties until the First World War. In the last decades of the nineteenth century, the Suffragettes also entered the scene, demanding the vote for women (Hobsbawm 2005).

Marx on Parliamentary Democracy

In order to understand the significance of the constitutional question in the nineteenth century, it is useful to take a closer look at how it is treated in the political writings of Karl Marx. We propose to treat these not as supra-historical oeuvres of political theory, but as works of their time, interventions written in a specific historical context. Some Marxists, including Žižek, interpret Marx's stance towards constitutional democracy as one of dismissal. However, their interpretation actually fits poorly with a closer reading of his works.

Our aim here is not to suggest that a pro-parliamentary reading of Marx is the only acceptable one. We do, however, think that our analysis can at least lay to rest the erroneous claim that Marx saw parliamentary democratic institutions as intrinsically pro-capitalist. Moreover, we do consider—as forcefully argued by Hobsbawm (1973) and Domènech (2004)—the interpretation of Marx as a lifelong democratic republican worthy of renewed consideration. Put simply, this reading posits that Marx consistently propagated the view that constitutional republics with elected parliaments—even if dominated by bourgeois classes in the short term—were clearly preferable to monarchies and empires seen from the perspective of the working class. A republican and parliamentary democratic solution to the constitutional question of the social distribution of political power within modern states was quite simply a sine qua non—a necessary but not sufficient condition—for a communist solution to the social question of class divisions under capitalism.[7] As Hobsbawm points out 'Marx and Engels had always seen the democratic republic, though plainly "bourgeois", as the ante-chamber of socialism, since it permitted, and even encouraged, the political mobilisation of the proletariat as a class' (Hobsbawm 2005, 110). Indeed, the mature Marx remained true to the youthful conviction that led him to make the introduction of a German republic with a parliament and universal suffrage the first demand of his 1848 proposal for the Program of the German Communist Party (Marx and Engels 1848).

One key text that is certainly consonant with the democratic-republican interpretation of Marx is his lengthy comment on the Paris Commune, the 'Third Address' to the International Workingmen's Association, published in May 1871 (Marx 1871). The 'Third Address' has been interpreted as Marx's ultimate denouncement of the 'bourgeois state'—including all its representative democratic institutions—favouring instead the construction of an entirely new political system created in the image of the proletariat (see Lenin 1917). In particular, the formulation that 'the working class cannot simply lay hold of the ready-made state machinery, and wield it for its own purposes', has been taken to mean that Marx saw the need for a working-class strategy pivoted on a complete rupture with all aspects and institutions of 'the bourgeois state' (Lenin 1917, 419f.) However, careful scrutiny of Marx's 'Third Address' reveals that he does not in fact demand that the workers' movement give up the republican form of national constitutional government as such, nor the practice of elections or the principle of representation:

> The Commune was formed of the municipal councilors, chosen by *universal suffrage* in the various wards of the town, responsible and revocable at short terms. The majority of its members were naturally working men, or acknowledged representatives of the working class. The Commune was to be a working, not a parliamentary body, executive and legislative at the same time. (*ibid.*, 331, our emphasis)

We note here how universal suffrage was implemented in the Commune and that this allowed for a majority of 'poor freemen' in the representative organs—which were, however, not exclusively made up of workers. Second, although it may appear as if Marx denounces parliamentary democracy in the last sentence, he actually argues that true parliamentary democracy requires that the parliamentary body is not checked by a State apparatus acting on its own behalf, with the ability to selectively execute the decisions made by parliamentary majorities. What Marx celebrates is that, unlike the bourgeois-controlled republic which came before Louis Bonaparte's coup in December 1851, the Commune (1871) was structured in such a way as to bring executive power under the firm control of the elected legislature. The prior system had divided those functions into two, so that on one hand there was a parliament (to which only rich men could vote) and on the other there was an independent State executive, including a heavily politicised police force, independent of popular control (Marx 1986 [1871], 331–332).

Indeed, the Paris Commune that Marx celebrates as an exemplary case of a new kind of unexploitative, popular-controlled political order retains a written constitution, a national parliamentary assembly and even institutions to maintain a monopoly of violence and national territorial integrity (a police force under democratic control and a popular army, the National Guard). Specifically, the republican idea of a popular (cross-class) National Assembly, through which popular will is expressed, is clearly not rejected by Marx as an inherently bourgeois invention. What has been changed, however, is rather the class-relevant mode of functioning of key State institutions, indeed of the State apparatus in its entirety.

Nor did Marx envision the dismantling of the nation-state. To the contrary, he frames the Paris Commune as setting the example for the rest of France, even down to 'the smallest country hamlet'. The Paris Commune does provide an innovative model for a federal system of bottom-up democratic government. Importantly, however, this system of local Communes would still function with the larger confines of a parliamentarised nation-state:

> The rural communities of every district were to administer their common affairs by an assembly of delegates in the central town, and these district assemblies were again to send deputies to the National Delegation in Paris [...] The unity of the nation was not to be broken, but, on the contrary, to be organised by Communal Constitution. (*ibid.*, 332)

Given this, seeing Marx as an opponent of parliamentary, representative democracy at the level of actually existing States becomes untenable. His affirmation of the Paris Commune's method of re-organising national unity on a bottom-up democratic basis shows that it was not parliamentary democracy per se he derided, but a particular way of implementing it in countries with bourgeois dominance. Even his oft-cited rejection of 'deciding once in three or six years which member of the ruling class was to misrepresent the people in Parliament (*ibid.*, 333)' turns out, on closer inspection, to be a call for the deepening of representative democracy and not a rejection of it:

> While the merely repressive organs of the old governmental power were to be amputated, its legitimate functions were to be wrested from an authority usurping pre-eminence over society itself, and restored to the responsible agents of society. Instead of deciding once in three or six years which member of the ruling class was to misrepresent the people in Parliament, universal suffrage was to serve the people, constituted in Communes (*ibid.*, 333).

Marx thus explicitly favoured a system of universal suffrage for electing local representatives for a national parliament—only with much wider powers to recall and replace representatives than was given in the bourgeois-dominated republics or indeed in 'liberal democratic' systems today. Marx did not consider parliamentary democracy a bourgeois illusion best thrown on the scrapheap of history but wanted to use—and deepen—it as a key tool for social transformation. Indeed, supporters of the representative system in the twentieth century, with suffrage for all regardless of gender or social position, would find much more support for their views in the writings of Marx than in those of his liberal contemporaries.

1917 Onwards: Emergence of the Myth of 'Bourgeois Democracy'

A conundrum emerges: If Marx was indeed in favour of parliamentary democracy at the level of the nation-state, then how come many of his modern-day followers consider it an essentially bourgeois phenomenon? To explain this, we need to return to Lenin. After 1917, the socialist labour movement experienced a tragic split produced by the October revolution and the lacking mirror revolutions in Western Europe. Consequently, Lenin's Bolsheviks abandoned belief in the constitutional assembly as the institutional means to achieve socialism.

In his most systematic discussion of the State and democracy, 'Revolution and the State' (1917), written shortly before the Russian Revolution, Lenin did not yet attack the idea of representative, parliamentary democracy as such. On the contrary, he unequivocally declared, 'We cannot imagine democracy, even proletarian democracy, without representative institutions' (Lenin 1917). However, in the post-revolutionary turmoil, he quickly shifted his position. An example of this hardened stance towards parliamentary democracy can be found in Lenin's (1919) inaugural address to the First Congress of the Communist International in March 1919. After announcing the 'absurdity of promising freedom of assembly to exploiters' (thesis 7), Lenin—a year after the Bolshevik suspension of the Constituent Assembly and in the midst of the Civil War—has come to conceptualise the relationship between the models of the Paris Commune and the Soviet State not as parallel options but as a historical progression—'the first epoch making step' vs. 'the second [step]' (thesis 19). Thus, Lenin goes on to suggest that 'genuine democracy' is achievable 'only through Soviet, or proletarian, democracy' (thesis 20, our emphasis). Indeed, while the 'Soviet System' now embodies Lenin's ideal of proletarian dictatorship, the institution of a 'National Assembly'—which, as shown in section 'Marx on Parliamentary Democracy', was part of Marx's grassroots vision of a model of democracy built on the principles of the Paris Commune—is now branded simply as 'bourgeois dictatorship' (thesis 21).

Eric Hobsbawm, himself a lifelong communist, makes the case that Lenin's interventions constitute a root cause for large parts of the socialist labour movement forgetting its parliamentary democratic past:

> 'A democratic republic', argued Lenin in 1917, 'is the best possible shell for capitalism, and therefore, once capitalism has gained control of this very best shell...it establishes its power so securely, so firmly, that no change, either of persons, of institutions, or of parties in the bourgeois-democratic republic can shake it'. As always, Lenin was concerned not so much with political analysis in general, as with finding effective arguments for a specific political situation, in this instance against the provisional government of revolutionary Russia and for Soviet power. In any case, we are not concerned with the validity of this claim, which is highly debatable, not least,

> because it fails to distinguish between the economic and social circumstances which have safeguarded states from social upheaval, and the institutions which have helped them to do so. We are concerned with its plausibility. Before 1880, such a claim would have seemed equally implausible to either supporters or opponents of capitalism insofar as they were committed to political activity. Even on the political ultra-left, so negative a judgment on 'the democratic republic' would have been almost inconceivable. (Hobsbawm 2005, 110)

In this passage, Hobsbawm notes how Lenin's position constitutes a break with the thought of Marx. Moreover, he cuts through a key analytical problem with the Žižekian position on democracy, which remains faithful to Lenin's idea that the very institutional form of the democratic republic makes any social revolution impossible. The failure to distinguish institutional forms from material factors—such as the economically grounded power relationships between specific social classes at given stages of capitalist development—leads Lenin to blame the practice of general elections for what could also be the result of the industrial working class being too structurally weak to succeed in overturning capitalism at a particular historical stage.[8] The Leninist position amounts to a peculiar kind of 'institutional fetishism' and ignorance of economic and social circumstances for a theorist who supposedly values historical materialism highly. Still, we can identify in Lenin the original philosophical articulation of the 'Marxist' rejection of parliamentary democracy.

However, we also need to understand how Lenin's rejection of 'bourgeois democracy'—which morphed into a more general rejection of parliamentary democracy as such—could gain hegemonic status on the radical left. This development appears surprising, because the idea seemed to be running against the practical experience of popular movements for democracy across Europe for several decades. It also went against fierce theoretical opposition from within the Marxist movement, especially from Karl Kautsky who attacked Lenin's new dismissive stance towards democracy and representation in his pamphlet *The Dictatorship of the Proletariat* (Kautsky 1964).

On this issue, Antoni Domènech has posited that the propaganda of the young Soviet state 'launched in self-defence against the harassment of the powers of the Entente' was 'so successful that it literally ended up becoming a majority viewpoint even among social democrats' (Domènech 2009, 99f., our translation).[9] In any case, it is evident that during the interwar years, the radical-democratic position of socialist republicanism—which sought to use and stretch existing constitutional frameworks for socialist purposes—went on the defensive. This, however, was not just a question of it being pressured discursively by the propaganda of the Third International but also had to do with the rise of the fascist movement, which made the promise of annihilating working-class attempts of building socialism through radical-democratic republicanism (e.g. in Germany, Austria and Spain). It is an irony of history that the entrenchment of Bolshevik discourse describing parliamentary democracy as essentially 'bourgeois' happened during the decades of the 1920s and 1930s, a time when a significant fraction of the capitalist class turned to a tacit or explicit support of fascism as the ultimate solution to the threat to private property and social stability posed by parliamentary democracy.[10]

We are not arguing, however, that the assumption of an intrinsic connection between capitalism and 'liberal' democracy should simply be turned on its head and that the true political nature of capitalism is that of some sort of despotic, disciplinary regime in the style of fascism. Our argument is rather that finance and large corporations tend to lend support to whatever system they perceive to be the best safeguard for stable capital accumulation. In the context of general social upheaval and the unprecedented level of workers' radicalism after the First World War, a significant fraction of the capitalist class rejected parliamentary democracy (Domènech 2004). While in continental Europe, many capitalists sided with the fascist movement to quell the popular threat to property, a different strategy prevailed in the UK and the USA. There the sections of business that leaned towards fascism never gained a strong standing. Instead, the propertied classes developed an understanding with the new fact of popular involvement and general suffrage (Hobsbawm 1994). Indeed, as continental Europe's newly parliamentarised republics, many with radical republican constitutions, started to fall apart, the moderate republic of the US and the 'parliamentarised' monarchy of the UK remained strong.

Meanwhile, the idea that there was something inherently liberal about the parliamentary representation and democratic participation, as opposed to the totalitarian systems of Communism and Nazism, began to resonate both among social democrats and among Anglo-American liberals. The idea was born that there existed a natural connection between capitalism, liberalism and democracy—all bound together by the concept of liberty. This attitude was perhaps most clearly expressed in Friedrich von Hayek's *The Road to Serfdom* (1944), in which liberal capitalism was put forward as the only system capable of securing a stable foundation of democracy and individual liberty. This was in contrast both to the collectivised planning he saw in the new regimes of Europe and to the emerging Keynesian welfare states of the West. Without 'a competitive system based on free disposal of private property', Hayek argued, 'democracy would inevitably destroy itself' (Hayek 1944, 52). The implication was that, for democracy to survive, it had to be restricted, with strong constitutional restraints on all forms of majority rule, to secure the principles of individual property rights and limited government (Hayek 1993[1960], 103ff).

It was not Hayek's neoliberalism that came to dominate the post-war decades, however. It was rather the Anglo-American model of embedded liberalism, which emerged out of the depression and the New Deal (Ruggie 1982). This embedded liberalism involved a compromise between labour and capital, where the survival of private ownership in the economy was combined with a strong widening of welfare services and rising wages. This compromise not only included economic aspects as often acknowledged but also a specific constitutional arrangement based on parliamentarism and universal suffrage (see Streeck 2011). Before the Second World War, the capitalist class in the developed world was divided over the issue of democracy. But after the war this changed in favour of general support for universal suffrage under democratic constitutions, which on the one hand protected private property and on the other guaranteed certain social rights and a general right to political participation.[11] The novel character of this institutional compromise was quickly forgotten, along with the recent support for non-democratic regimes by large parts of the capitalist class. Instead, the newfound, contingent connection between capitalism and democracy (in the US-dominated West at least) soon came to be seen as the natural order of things.

This development was, in no small part, a product of the thinking of the left. In the heavily polarised climate of the Cold War, social democratic parties emphasised that they were democratic socialists as a way of distinguishing themselves from the communists (Padgett and Paterson 1991, 8). At the same time, communists, as a way of defending Soviet dominance over Eastern Europe, deepened their opposition to the so-called bourgeois and shallow democracy of the Western States, and contrasted it with the genuine popular democracies that they alleged to have set up (Hobsbawm 1994, 372). Through this double movement, the social democrats moved into the camp that celebrated the marriage of capitalism and parliamentary democracy in the guise of the social market economy, whereas the communists rejected both. Thus, both the social democratic and the communist wings of 'the left', each in their way, inadvertently assisted the liberals in strengthening the pedigree of the newborn bastard of 'democratic capitalism'.

Democracy in the Age of Neoliberalism

In recent decades the post-war compromise—which contingently tied capitalism and a particular variant of parliamentary democracy together—has been steadily unravelling. The epoch of neoliberalism is marked by growing tensions between an increasingly unfettered capitalism and the institutions of parliamentary representation. The USA has been the front-runner in this development. From the 1970s onwards, the country experienced an unprecedented mobilisation of business interests with the aim of restoring the squeezed profits of corporate America, through a direct involvement in federal and State politics (Duménil and Lévy 2004; Harvey 2005). This paved the way for the political landscape of the last decades, during which economic inequality has spiked and the power of business has trumped all other interest groups in both of the two major political parties (Hacker and Pierson 2010). Meanwhile, Europe has not been far behind. The introduction of the Common Market and the Euro has drastically decreased the scope of parliamentary and democratic politics, with issues of monetary policy being left to the unelected ECB while the scope of fiscal policy is severely restricted (Lapavitsas 2012).

In recent years, however, the tension between capitalism and parliamentary democracy has moved from indirect to direct confrontation, as has been demonstrated most forcefully with the harsh reaction of the EU elite to popular attempts at reversing austerity through the election of anti-austerity blocs in Greece and Portugal. The emerging divorce is further strengthened by the emergence of the 'Chinese Model', by which China's Communist Party has so far managed to combine a successful capitalist accumulation strategy with sustained authoritarian control of the State (Harvey 2005).

We agree with Žižek's diagnosis that the 'virus' of authoritarian capitalism is indeed spreading globally (Žižek 2009a, 132). This is precisely why we disagree with this attempt to build an anti-capitalist movement based on rejecting the relevance of parliamentary democracy to emancipatory struggle. Imperfect as parliamentary institutions and democratic constitutions might be, they nonetheless serve as means for popular organisations to put checks on the arbitrary power of State and corporations and protect against resurgent forms of authoritarian elite rule.

The urgency of the issue is heightened by the fact that the demand for truly functional representative democracy has been a central factor of motivation in the post-Crisis global wave of protests. One common denominator of the popular movements emerging since 2011 has been a concern with fixing broken political systems by reinstating popular democratic control against the global financial oligarchy and their local allies. This was the case in the various pro-democracy movements of the Arab Spring that called for democratic elections and the rule of law, as well as the *Indignados* in Spain, and subsequently the party of Podemos, whose stated aim is to build a truly democratic political system in the spirit of the Second Republic of the interwar years. In Greece, the rise and fall of Syriza was the story of a forceful popular rejection of the social consequences of a neoliberal plan for debt reduction on the explicitly political-legal grounds of the moral invalidity of any supranational economic policy that overrides the democratic autonomy of a people. Most recently, both Jeremy Corbyn and Bernie Sanders embody strongly pro-democratic reactions to neoliberalism.

The problem anti-capitalists ought to deal with is not how to start popular mobilisations against the status quo—because this is already happening. It is, rather, to propose radical strategies and aims to the protestors and to outline a feasible plan for global transformations beyond capitalism. Here, we find that the contemporary theoretical poverty regarding the constitutional question and the role of parliaments and representative structures in a socialist transformation constitutes a severe hindrance. By flatly denying that issues of political representation and parliamentary democratic institutions are at all relevant for progressive change, influential theorists like Žižek render their position unintelligible to the millions who have taken to the streets in recent years precisely to protest the lack of truly representative political systems.

Žižek portrays his turn to the act of subjective transgression of the law—as the guarantor of proper political change—as Marxian. But in reality he owes more to the political decisionism of Carl Schmitt and Lenin than to the work and practice of Marx and the early labour movement.

Two central problems remain with this attitude, one theoretical and the other strategic. First, it strengthens the myth of the bourgeois character of any form of parliamentary democracy, and thus makes it harder to mount constitutional challenges to the status quo. As we have argued, this myth is not justified by the historical record and should be challenged through a historical awareness of the essential role of workers' parties and popular movements in creating a system of parliamentary sovereignty and universal suffrage. Furthermore, without a proper understanding of the State and of parliamentary democracy, this myth cannot be effectively challenged. Taking on the myth of bourgeois democracy, hence, not only requires a deconstruction of bourgeois ideology but also of certain ideas which have become prevalent within contemporary anti-capitalist theory.

In his book *Did Somebody Say Totalitarianism?*, Žižek (2001) laments that the liberal ideology of our time manages to exclude any proposals for radical political change by evoking the fear of a descent into totalitarianism if the liberal consensus or the sanctity of private property is in any way challenged by radical political movements. We agree with this analysis. However, Žižek seems unaware that he himself is contributing to strengthening this very ideological mechanism by insisting that any break with capitalism must be characterised by extra-legal measures. In this way, he reinforces the message of Hayek and his followers that the severely limited democracy endorsed by liberalism is the only attainable form of democracy, because any attempt to fundamentally change the social or economic basis of capitalism threatens the possibility of a constitutional order. Through insistence on this anti-legalism, Žižek cedes the ground of democratic constitutionalism to the liberal tradition, which has always been sceptical towards the prospects of unfettered democracy and majority rule.

The second strategic problem is that if one desires a 'ruptural' break with the capitalist mode of production in order to pave the way for 'real democracy', it is both counterintuitive and dangerous to begin by destroying all existing institutional fragments of a democratic society, however incomplete they may be. In other words, even though the intent of a Leninist 'ruptural' strategy might be to find a new political order of 'real democracy', taking a road which involves neglecting constitutional procedures and restraints in favour of faith in the transformative power of the party seems doomed to lead to the same sort of antidemocratic regimes that emerged from the communist revolutions of the twentieth century.

Instead, contemporary anti-capitalists should return to the radical-democratic and constitutional roots of Marx and the early labour movements. In a period when the connection between democracy and capitalism is unravelling, the task of the left is to defend existing representative institutions against persistent attacks and to call for their reinforcement and further development rather than their disbandment. Truly popular control is always constitutional and bound by laws, and the revolutionary transformation we desire is exactly the extension of this control to the entire social and economic system.

If the left is to play a significant role in the social struggles of the coming decades, it needs to formulate a coherent counter-hegemonic project that encompasses both the demands for greater social justice and the belief in the fundamental role of democratic representation. Here we need theory to mirror the political practices developing in the battle against the emergence of post-democratic neoliberalism. And here it seems counterproductive to follow Žižek in denying the significance of the institutions of parliamentary democracy at the exact historical moment when growing fractions of the capitalist class appear willing to abandon their (contingent) embrace of 'liberal democracy'.

Furthermore, it would be a tactical error to throw away the banner of democracy in the middle of a conjuncture of crisis, in which the most potent expressions of popular mass discontent pivot on the need for democratic constitutions, which serve the broad majority rather than the plutocratic elites. There are, of course, many ways for the left to rise to this challenge. Yet, as we have argued, dismantling the myth of the bourgeois essence of parliamentary democracy is an essential task. This also leads back to a necessary rediscovery of the radical potential of unfettered democracy that forms part of the Marxist and radical republican tradition.

Notes

1. Summarised by Olin Wright (2010, 304) as: 'attack the state' and 'confront the bourgeoisie' vs. 'use the state' and 'collaborate with the bourgeoisie'.
2. The in-depth analysis of Marx's works in this chapter does not imply that we view him as an infallible voice of trans-historical philosophical authority on issues of theory and strategy. Rather, this approach is chosen because of a discontent with the fact that fragments of his thought are distorted and used to support strategic conclusions which would have been quite foreign to Marx himself. Furthermore, we actually think that Marx (and Engels)—if read with proper contextual understanding—actually provides useful points of orientation (but not, of course, a definitive guide) for the organisational and intellectual challenges of our generation.
3. Žižek's concepts of egalitarian terror (2007, xi) and divine violence (2009b) both point to the transformative character of the revolutionary act itself.

4. For two important contributions which argue this point, see Domènech (2004, 25) and Wood (2008, 39).
5. Benjamin Constant describes this 'modern liberty' of liberalism as essentially the right to 'peaceful enjoyment and private independence', as opposed to 'the liberty of the ancient', which consisted in political participation (Constant 1988[1816]).
6. The main method was the introduction of qualification on the vote. Most often this took the form of property qualification, but even Mill's inclusive model gives extra votes to the educated and informed (which included owners of property) and restricts it from servants and recipients of public relief (Mill 2010 [1861], Chap. 8, Sects. 1–2).
7. In making this argument, we are indebted to the insights of Hal Draper (cf. Johnson 2011).
8. Or even—dare one say it—the socialist workers' movement lacking the ability (because of its dogmatically hostile attitude towards the 'petit bourgeoisie' and to peasants) to make itself the head of an anti-oligarchic movement with a popular backing solid enough to decisively tip the balance of social power against capitalist interests.
9. Domènech (ibid.) furthermore contends that: "neither for [Edward] Bernstein, nor for Rosa Luxembourg, and nor for the Lenin of '*What is to be done?* (1902)' [...] did 'bourgeois democracy' refer to a form of state or government introduced by the bourgeoisie and characteristic of an entire epoch of capitalist political dominance and triumph—as it later would to the main part of vulgar and de-memorised twentieth century Marxism. Even less did it refer to a political 'superstructure' which necessarily emerges out of the development of capitalist economic life. To encounter Marxists willing to give away 'democracy'—and the workers movement's long and painful struggle of to obtain it—so cheaply to the 'bourgeoisie' and to an inveterately anti-democratic liberalism, one would have to await the ending of the Great War and to the desperate Bolshevik propaganda."
10. For an investigation of the role of (parts of) the German grand bourgeoisie in funding Hitler, see, for example, Domènech (2004, 340–350).
11. Claus Offe (1983, 25) has described how this compromise as 'mass participation through a competitive party system makes democracy safe for capitalism and Keynesianism and the welfare state makes capitalism safe for democracy'.

Works Cited

Aristotle. 1995. *The complete works of Aristotle: The revised Oxford translation*. Princeton: Princeton University Press.

Blackbourn, David, and Geoff Eley. 1984. *The peculiarities of German history: Bourgeois society and politics in nineteenth-century Germany*. Oxford: Oxford University Press.

Constant, Benjamin. 1988[1816]. The liberty of the ancients compared with that of the moderns. In *The political writings of Benjamin Constant*, 309–328. http://www.uark.edu/depts/comminfo/cambridge/ancients.html. Accessed 10 Oct 2013.

Domènech, Antoni. 2004. *El eclipse de la fraternidad: Una revisión republicana de la tradición socialista*. Barcelona: Crítica.

———. 2009. Democrácia burguesa: nota sobre la génesis del oxímoron y la necedad del regalo. *Viento Sur* 100 (January): 95–100.

Duménil, Gérard, and Dominique Lévy. 2004. *Capital resurgent: Roots of the neoliberal revolution*. Cambridge, MA: Harvard University Press.

Hacker, Jacob S., and Paul Pierson. 2010. Winner-take-all politics: Public policy, political organization, and the precipitous rise of top incomes in the United States. *Politics and Society* 38 (2): 152–204.

Harvey, David. 2005. *A brief history of Neoliberalism*. Oxford: Oxford University Press.

Hayek, Friedrich A. 1944. *The road to serfdom*. London: Routledge.

———. 1993[1960]. *The constitution of liberty*. London: Routledge.

Hobsbawm, Eric. 1973. *The age of revolutions*. London: Abacus.

———. 1994. *The age of extremes: The short 20th century, 1914–1991*. London: Abacus.

———. 2005. *Age of Empire, 1875–1914*. London: Abacus.

Jessop, Bob. 1990. *State theory: Putting the capitalist state in its place*. Philadelphia: Pennsylvania State University Press.

Johnson, Alan. 2011. The power of nonsense. *Jacobin Magazine*, July. http://jacobinmag.com/2011/07/the-power-of-nonsense/. Accessed 14 Dec 2013.

Kautsky, Karl. 1964 [1918]. *The dictatorship of the proletariat*. Ann Arbor: University of Michigan Press.

Lapavitsas, Costas. 2012. *Crisis in the eurozone*. London: Verso.

Lenin, Vladimir I. 1917. The state and revolution. In *Collected works, Vol. 25*, 381–492. http://www.marxists.org/archive/lenin/works/1917/staterev/. Accessed 15 Dec 2013.

———. 1919. First congress of the Communist International. In *Collected works, Vol. 28*, 455–477. http://www.marxists.org/archive/lenin/works/1919/mar/comintern.htm. Accessed 15 Dec 2013.

London Working Men's Association. 1838. *The people's charter*. http://www.bl.uk/learning/histcitizen/21cc/struggle/chartists1/historicalsources/source4/peoplescharter.html. Accessed 15 Dec 2013.

Losurdo, Domenico. 2011. *Liberalism: A counter-history*. London: Verso.

Marx, Karl. 1986 [1871]. The civil war in France: Address of the General Council of the International Working Men's Association. In *Karl Marx and Friedrich Engels' collected works, Vol. 22*, ed. Tatyana Grishina, 307–359. London: Lawrence & Wishart.

Marx, Karl, and Friedrich Engels. 1848. *Demands of the Communist Party in Germany*. http://www.marxists.org/archive/marx/works/1848/03/24.htm. Accessed 15 Dec 2013.

McCormick, John P. 2011. *Machiavellian democracy*. Cambridge: Cambridge University Press.

Mill, John Stuart. 2010[1861]. *Considerations on representative government*. https://doi.org/10.1017/CBO9780511783128. Accessed 15 Dec 2013.

Montesquieu, Charles-Louis de Secondat, Baron de. 1794. *The spirit of laws*. Translated from French, Montesquieu Eighteenth Century Collection Online Database. http://find.galegroup.com/ecco/infomark.do?&source=gale&prodId=ECCO&userGroupName=dkb&tabID=T001&docId=CW3324479092&type=multipage&contentSet=ECCOArticles&version=1.0&docLevel=FASCIMILE. Accessed 10 Dec 2013.

Offe, Claus. 1983. Competitive party democracy and the Keynesian welfare state: Factors of stability and disorganization. *Policy Sciences* 15 (3): 225–246.

Padgett, Stephen, and William E. Paterson. 1991. *A history of social democracy in postwar Europe*. London: Longman.

Poulantzas, Nicos. 2001. *State, power, socialism, Vol. 29*. London: Verso.

Robertson, Geoffrey. 2007. *The Putney debates: The Levellers*. London: Verso.

Ruggie, John Gerald. 1982. International regimes, transactions, and change: Embedded liberalism in the postwar economic order. *International Organization* 36 (2): 379–415.

Schmitt, Carl. 2007. *The concept of the political, expanded edition*. Chicago: University of Chicago Press.

Skinner, Quentin. 1998. *Liberty before liberalism*. Cambridge: Cambridge University Press.

Streeck, Wolfgang. 2011. The crisis of democratic capitalism. *New Left Review* 71: 5–29.

Wood, Ellen Meiksins. 2008. *Citizens to lords: A social history of Western political thought from antiquity to the late middle ages*. London: Verso.
———. 2012. *Liberty and property: A social history of Western political thought from the Renaissance to Enlightenment*. London: Verso.
Wright, Erik Olin. 2010. *Envisioning real utopias*. London: Verso.
Žižek, Slavoj. 1999. Carl Schmitt in the age of post-politics. In *The challenge of Carl Schmitt*, ed. Chantal Mouffe. London: Verso.
———. 2001. *Did somebody say totalitarianism*. London: Verso.
———. 2002. *Revolution at the gates—Žižek on Lenin*. London: Verso.
———. 2007. *Slavoj Žižek presents Robespierre: Virtue and terror*. London: Verso.
———. 2009a. *Violence*. London: Profile Books.
———. 2009b. *First as tragedy, then as farce*. London: Verso.
———. 2011. *Living in the end times*. London: Verso.

Seeing Like a PIG: The Crisis in Greece as a Tale of Hope and Disillusionment

Rosa Vasilaki

In the past six years, Greece has been at the epicentre of debates about the future of Europe, the viability of the Eurozone and the divisions between North and South. In many ways, it has become a metaphor for the European crisis itself. In these turbulent times, 'crisis' has become simultaneously a descriptive and explanatory framework, a synecdoche which embodies fears, hopes, rapid transformations, precarisation, the rise of extremisms, insecurity, civil disorder, repression, resistance, solidarity, xenophobia and scapegoating. In short, the term signals to one of the most significant—yet difficult to fully evaluate—historical moments in Europe's living memory. This chapter is an attempt to document but also reflect upon this peculiar historical juncture, this ongoing story, using Greece as a case study and putting forward the perspective of those who have been central figures—albeit with limited agency and ability to confront the full force of the changes inflicted upon them—in the six years that shook the Greek world. If, from the dominant ideological point of view, Greece is the prime example of crisis and dysfunction, it is also,

R. Vasilaki (✉)
Panteion University of Social and Political Sciences, Athens, Greece

T. Geelan et al. (eds.), *From Financial Crisis to Social Change*,
https://doi.org/10.1007/978-3-319-70600-9_11

from a different perspective which I present here, a major example of resistance and of the hope that another way out of the crisis is possible.

The title of this chapter aims to question the assumptions embedded in the acronym PIGS, used in economic and diplomatic circles to refer to the economies of Portugal, Ireland (initially Italy), Greece and Spain. The present historical occurrence represents a significant challenge for all political movements which propose a different, more socially centred approach to the dominant economic rationality of our days. As I hope will become obvious, my contribution to this volume is not only about Greece. *Seeing like a PIG* is a vehicle for deconstructing the hegemonic economistic view of society and assessing possibilities as well as pointing to limitations, especially given the trajectory taken by radical political movements in Greece once in possession of State power. It is above all an opening to the progressive political movements of today, and an invitation to assess the promise embodied in practices of resistance to the dehumanisation of economy and the precarisation of life itself. But it is also a call to reflect on the limitations of those social movements of resistance which made it into State power, and the perils related to their trajectory.

In my view, radical thinking is the ability to question dominant narratives which naturalise inequality—and hence injustice—and which disempower dissent by systematically assigning the possibility of alternatives to the realm of the 'unrealistic'. It is the ability to think beyond the dominant ideology and hence to speak back to the hegemonic economic and social paradigms of our times. Critical thinking is essential in times of crisis, when a prevailing, dangerous ideology has subsumed society and those values that make us distinctively human under the tyranny of the market. But it is also the ability to face our own disenchantment with regard to the rise to power of radical left political formations, not in order to give up and accept the re-affirmation of the 'There Is No Alternative' logic, but with the aim of evaluating where real possibilities of change lie in the current juncture.

For this purpose, this chapter is constructed around two narratives, two turning points in the history of the Greek crisis, aiming to open a space to think about hope and disillusionment, potentials and stalemates via focusing on specific instances in the unfolding chronicle of the global crisis of capitalism. The first story is a tale of hope: it narrates a moment of rebellion, which was represented largely by the *Indignados* movement in the 2011 summer of discontent and which culminated in the electoral victory in Greece of a radical left coalition—Syriza—in January 2015. It is a story revolving around the perspective of the PIGS and the ability of such viewpoint to deconstruct the dominant economistic narrative of the 'market' as a 'neutral' and 'fair' force and to shed light on the ways ordinary people reclaim the empty conceptual space of values, such as democracy and social rights, through their resistance. The second story is one of disillusionment: it is the story of the radical left's capitulation to the demands of an austerity agenda. It offers a critical account of the complications in the passage of a radical social movement into political, and more precisely State, power.

A Tale of Hope

Greece has appeared in international press headlines in recent years more than ever in the history of mass media. In the civilised 'North', 'Europe' or 'the West—terms which to a large extent have ceased to represent the once-called Great Powers and have increasingly become synonymous with a dominant, albeit abstract point of view, that of the 'economy'—Greece, the 'archetypical' PIG, has become a metaphor for everything threatening the 'global economy': instability, irresponsibility, social unrest. Aside from the ongoing obsession with Islamic fundamentalism, the 'Greek crisis' has become the name of the most fundamental fear of all: the crisis of the global capitalist economic system itself.

As a result, the omnipresent accounts of economic, political and diplomatic experts have been underpinned by a general feeling of urgency to the imminent global catastrophe to which we must react 'now'. Analysts from all over the world, together with the unpopular creditors, constantly bombard their publics with admonitions that time is running out, that now is the time to act, that the whole world is on the verge of collapsing if the Greeks (and by extension the other three little PIGS) do not rush to comply with the increasingly predatory demands for the privatisation of public goods, the commercialisation of the State, the curtailment of social rights—in short, with the precarisation of life itself—as requested by the authorities of the IMF, the Central European Bank and the World Bank.

This sense of urgency to act against the looming disaster—if we follow Žižek (2009), a deeply anti-theoretical and in that sense *anti-critical move*, which, as we shall see below, is instrumental in discouraging any critical reflection about the situation—goes together with the deployment of an impressive arsenal of stereotypical, quasi-racist representations of the PIGS in the Western media. Hierarchical binaries, long associated with the political, economic and ideological supremacy of the West, have been given new leases of life: the developed North versus the backward South, the orderly West versus the unruly Orient, and the disciplined, peaceful protests in civilised Europe versus the violent and chaotic riots in the Mediterranean. Indeed, the evocation of the image of the clean 'real Europe' versus the dirty European periphery in the invention of the acronym PIGS says a great deal about the deeply ingrained binary stereotyping constructions at the heart of the EU.

It goes without saying that framing the discussion about the 'Greek crisis' in this way allows the legitimation of the discourse of 'fair punishment'. Probably the most employed stereotype by politicians and the media, the one that seems to speak directly to the minds and hearts of those European citizens who express indignation and anger against the Greek protesters, is the 'hard-working' Northern European versus the 'lazy' Southerner. This binary is itself underpinned by one of the most potent myths of capitalist ethics, meritocracy, which asserts that in our (neo)liberal societies everyone gets what they deserve. What if the Greeks work on average 2119 hours per year whilst the Germans 1390?[1] As the media know only too well, facts are too feeble against the power of stereotypes: after all, does not everybody know that Greeks are 'lazy', Italians 'corrupted', Germans 'efficient' and the English 'fair'?

One would be even tempted to think of the PIGS, and more precisely the Greeks who have been at the spotlight of world attention lately, as a contemporary version of the *homo sacer*. As Agamben analyses in his famous study in Roman law, the *homo sacer* was a man who, having committed a certain kind of crime, was banned from society and all his rights were revoked. As a consequence, he became *homo sacer*, and could be killed by anyone, whilst his life, which was henceforth considered sacred, could be sacrificed in a ritual ceremony. Agamben defined the *homo sacer's* life as 'human life [...] included in the juridical order [ordinamento] solely in the form of its exclusion (that is, of its capacity to be killed)'.[2] Much like a contemporary *homo sacer*, Greece's crime to default on her debts has led to her ostracism from a 'society', that is, European community, and—as constantly repeated by the media—the market, with her rights as an autonomous, sovereign country retracted. The cold, unapologetic indifference demonstrated by technocrats concerning the dreadful consequences of the 'austerity package' to the lives of real people, namely an *accelerated* pauperisation as a form of punishment, reflects to a certain extent the logic and practice of the *homo sacer*.

However, framing the discussion in terms of racism or Orientalism and the discursive practices of inclusion and exclusion they sustain, important as it may be in the current climate of scapegoating, has little to say about the nature of the current predicament. Northern European racism here feels too narrow a focus, not the least because Greece, as well as the other countries which are the object of the Western negative stereotyping, does not fall short of inventing scapegoats and culprits for their national plights—invariably immigrants, refugees and asylum seekers. The unbearable pain of the pogroms perpetrated by extreme right groups against immigrants in Greece (Christopoulos 2014; Kirtsoglou 2013; Psarras 2012), coupled with the unbearable shame of those public intellectuals—incidentally, the enthusiasts of the neoliberal reforms—who legitimise these acts by deploring the 'fall of Athens' to the hands of 'undefined tribes, which regardless of their origin, race or religion, have a common trait: crime',[3] suggests the significance of the Greek predicament cannot be totally encapsulated by the framework of imperial racism inflicted by the West on the Rest. The exacerbation of inequalities and the rapid pauperisation caused by the application of the logic of neoliberalism seems to be bound to lead to the kind of public reasoning that seeks scapegoats. For this reason, the task of any critical engagement towards current power relations is to point out that the positions of the dominant and the dominated are not fixed nor reducible to any binary of good and evil, to any essentialised good or bad people or nations.

What could be more helpful to understand the predicament and promise of the 'Greek crisis' would be to take critical distance from the dominant perspective. This perspective—that is, the 'economy'—has become so hegemonic, so naturalised, that the mere act of thinking outside its framework—for instance, in terms of collective good—is automatically rejected as heretic, lunatic, dangerous or naïve. It is within this viewpoint of the 'economy' that international economic and political experts scold the Greeks as bad students failing their neoliberal re-education,[4] praise the brutality of the sweeping 'reforms' and the 'boldness' of the Greek governments that implemented the creditors' demands, deplore the 'backwardness' of the Welfare State, blackmail the resisting Greek people with reprisals of total disaster and present the tremendously unfair, anti-social 'bailout packages' as the only viable solution. Greece is currently implementing its third.

Stepping out of the 'objective' framework of the 'economy' would allow us to assume a different position and enable us to see what is at stake in the 'Greek crisis'. It would also allow us to reflect upon the meaning and intentions of the Greek protests, rather than easily attribute them to an essentialised fiery Greek character, or the presumed lack of rule of law in the Orient,[5] therefore reducing them to a senseless burst of violence. But let us for a moment resist the frantic calls of urgency to save the 'economy' and adopt, tentatively, the perspective of the PIGS. Perhaps then we can ask a couple of critical questions, such as: what is it really that the Greeks and the other three little PIGS are so vociferously accused of? What is the meaning of Greek resistance, what does this necessarily amorphous, heterogeneous and recently radicalised crowd so vigorously defend?[6]

Demystifying the abstractness of the 'economy' with the specificity of history would allow us to see that what we are witnessing is the engineering of the accelerated death of the twentieth century and its promise of a better, more equal, society. The dismantling of the Welfare State, the devaluation of public (and in Greece, free) education, the commodification of health, the systematic shrinking of the public sector and the demonisation of the poor as failing because of personal choices and shortcomings are all typical symptoms of the neoliberalisation of political (State) power, already experienced in other parts of the world since the

1970s. What is unusual in the Greek case is the brutal rapidity, one could even say the rage, with which neoliberal reforms are implemented. The reform of the alleged Welfare State, usually qualified as 'bold' and 'innovative' by technocrats and supporters of neoliberal politics, is a good example of what gets conveniently masked when the complexity of the social gets reduced to the economistic, instrumental one-dimensionality: the fact that the State is not merely an instance of bureaucratic efficiency. Embedded in the Welfare State, not only symbolically but literally, are the social rights that made the twentieth century the most egalitarian, the most progressive, the most democratic in the history of the 'West' (at the expense of the Rest, as the postcolonial critics rightfully never cease to remind us). What is at stake in Greece is a core aspect of the political tradition of the Enlightenment that made it worthy to be called universal and inspired the national and social revolutions of modernity: that is the commitment to social egalitarianism rather than social privilege, to the redistribution of wealth rather than its accumulation at the top. The much-maligned Welfare State is the practical application of these ideals.

What the Greek protesters are defending—and what they are accused of—is not a return to the past, the residue of a traditional attachment to the 'redundant' Welfare State that is deemed too slow and old-fashioned for the fast financial capitalism whose most cruel manifestation has been the current economic crisis. Quite the contrary: the meaning of the protests should be read as a political move oriented to the future, a future which must keep the promise of egalitarianism, not only as a legalistic concept nor limited to universal franchise and parliamentarism. Giving substantive content to concepts such as egalitarianism means resisting against the selling out of the national—and non-negotiable—*common* wealth, such as water, electricity and transport. It means defending labour rights and the right to education and healthcare. It means resisting the commodification of basic human values, such as care for the elderly, the poor, the ill, the unemployed. Ultimately, it means resisting the dehumanisation of society itself. What we witness in Greece is a remarkable resistance to the manipulation of those ideals on which the political edifice of modernity stands and a struggle for their meaningful application.

'REAL DEMOCRACY NOW'—the slogan that emerged in Puerta del Sol to conquer the squares of European cities—is not a claim looking at the past, as many neoliberal supporters claim. It is not mere discontent for the loss of 'privileges' of the Welfare, quasi-socialist in certain aspects, Greek state, for the simple reason that accessible and adequate education, healthcare, transport, the protection of the weak, the disadvantaged and the marginalised are not 'privileges' but undeniable social rights from any perspective which puts society rather than profit at its centre. The Welfare State and its provisions materialised, to a certain extent, the struggles for social equality. These provisions are the result of ongoing struggle against a formal understanding of equality which boils down to voting rights. Social rights are the answer to privilege in our unequal societies, not a privilege granted by the powerful and wealthy to the 'lazy' and 'unworthy' poor. The Greek resistance is a battle for their protection, even for the widening of their inclusivity, at least for the most progressive ones amongst the protesters. 'REAL DEMOCRACY NOW' is a claim embodying a political desire for a future which needs to be imagined radically different from the precarisation of life, from the accelerated economic, cultural, social and intellectual deprivation imposed on the Greeks.

From this perspective, Greek protesters can be seen as defenders of the universalist ideals of the Enlightenment: the ones who reimagine their future in human rather than economic terms, who dream of a meaningful rather than bureaucratic democracy—whose content has shrunk into the formal affirmation of predetermined decisions and fake choices, such as the ones related to the prevailing logic of austerity. Despite the rhetoric of 'innovation' and 'change', it is the neoliberal devotees who are committed to the past, to a perverted amalgam of pre-political social privilege and post-political economic instrumentality. Therefore, the real possibility of change lies in the concreteness of resistance to pauperisation, in the subjectivity of the Greek rioters and not in the 'objective' abstractness of the 'economy' and its political representatives. In that sense one could even see the Greek resistance as an exemplary instance of what is called *catachresis* in postcolonial theory. As Spivak (1990) explains, *catachresis* as a strategy of displacing and seizing the value of concepts such as democracy or equality, whose 'correct', authoritative content was decided elsewhere, in the social formations of Western Europe and its contemporary bureaucratic configuration, the EU. In this perspective, what gets seized and displaced is also the conceptual topography of Europe. Today, the site of progress and political future is where the battle for the meaning of universal concepts—such as democracy and equality—and resistance to the submission of the economy to the market is taking place: in the periphery of Europe, in the PIGS' lands, rather than the West.

In this logic, *Seeing like a PIG* may not sound as foolish, irresponsible and misguided as it is often represented, and the resistance of the Greek protesters may seem as something more than a residue from the past, or a quasi-Luddite reaction to the wonders of neoliberal capitalism. *Seeing like a PIG* may also mean that it is time to stop regarding the basic social rights gained through political struggles of past generations as privileges to be sacrificed so that plutocrats limit their losses whilst the rest of us, all of us, are called to pay a bill that is not ours to pay.

A Tale of Disillusionment

As far as Greece is concerned, this mobilisation, this political energy and hope, which was manifested via the social movement of *aganaktismenoi* (the equivalent of the *Indignados* movement), culminated with the victory of Syriza—a coalition of the radical left which in past decades typically scored between 3% and 5%—in January 2015.[7] A party of left-wing intellectuals, Marxist in terms of economic analysis, progressive in terms of social rights and causes, emerged as the most potent, innovative political power challenging the hegemony of austerity politics in Greece. Syriza embraced those who were hit by the crisis, mainly the lower and middle classes. Widespread identification with Syriza was not only due to their anti-austerity agenda and promise of change but was also a response to what was perceived as a corrupt political system which functioned along the lines of clientelism (Featherstone 2008; Cinar 2016). Syriza's victory was a reaction against the two dominant parties, the centre-right New Democracy and the centre-left PASOK, which dominated the Greek political scene since the collapse of the Colonels' dictatorship in 1974. Widespread support for Syriza was as much a response to austerity as a reaction to the political system which had led the country to the crisis.

During the first months of its mandate, Syriza enjoyed popular support whilst being pressured to prove itself from day one. This did not mean Greeks became Marxist overnight, but revealed the immense level of discontent with the austerity policies followed by the previous governments along with a certain willingness to see what a left governance may look like. Naturally, economic matters were at the centre of attention of analysts before and after the elections. However, there are political as well as symbolic developments stemming from the nature of the coalition government, which have often been overlooked. This was the case of Syriza's choice to form a coalition with right-of-centre ANEL (Independent Greeks), which received much criticism from the opposition and the mainstream press alike. ANEL seemed like an unnatural ally, given the dividing lines of internationalism versus patriotism defining the political landscape throughout the twentieth century, as well as sharp differences on cultural issues that typically determine the imaginaries of the Left and the Right. In joining forces with ANEL, Syriza was accused of making an opportunistic and possibly dangerous choice. However, placing Syriza's decision within the political and historical context which made it possible, and perhaps inevitable, may allow for a different reading of the situation.

Syriza and Alexis Tsipras—Syriza's president and prime minister—himself have often been compared, respectively, to PASOK and Andreas Papandreou (the Socialist Party which had dominated the political scene in the past 40 years and its leader). Although this is a problematic comparison, there is certainly an analogy to be drawn in terms of their responses to popular demands. If for 1981 '*allagi*' (change)[8]—meaning democratisation after the authoritarian rule of the Colonels along with the overdue liberalisation of Greek society—was the central issue at stake, justice was the popular demand in the 2015 election. Syriza not only captured the public's mood but capitalised on it by choosing as a partner a political party which was 'clean' in terms of involvement with the austerity policies of the previous government and with the political elites who led the country to economic disaster. Justice in this historical moment was defined by a widespread conviction regarding the unfair nature of austerity economics, which hit the already disadvantaged much harder than the privileged. But justice in this context is more than economic relief and the restoration of life standards *tout court*. Demands for justice also need to be understood as anger against the political and economic elites who led the country to the crisis, and against the failure to persecute corruption scandals involving government officials, local and international businesses and the justice system itself.

Syriza succeeded in capturing the popular mood, and in that sense, the choice of ANEL—given the refusal of the Communist Party to participate in a coalition—made sense. ANEL, itself a product of the crisis, is a nationalist party (and, as far as cultural matters are concerned, a far-right one) which has held a clear anti-austerity line since 2012. Indeed, the cultural makeup and agenda of ANEL could not be more far removed from those of Syriza, which has a consistently progressive programme in cultural and social issues such as immigration and integration policies, gay and minority rights, or the separation between State and Church. However, given the extraordinary circumstances, the economy, anti-austerity and the popular mood for justice determined the agenda, Syriza's pool of choice was extremely small. Strategically, Syriza's choice of ANEL was proven right at the time: support for the government was overwhelming. This is partly because this move demonstrated to sympathisers, but most importantly to opponents, that the government seemed to be something more than a 'government of the Left for the Left'. Symbolically, the choice of ANEL was catalytic in engaging right-wing voters, who felt that they had a stake in the government, and in creating a vast national consensus.

Lastly, these developments indicated a significant transformation of the political landscape in Greece. The dividing lines between the Left and the Right seem to be being renegotiated and re-drawn. What happened in Greece was the reinvention of politics on purely and unapologetically economic terms: after almost three decades in which the culturalisation of politics prevailed in the West, the economy seems to be setting the tone of the debate. In that sense, we seem to have moved from the post-Cold War definitions of the Left and Right to the lines of life politics (Giddens 1991). Such redefinition of politics, however, has cost Syriza—along with other anti-austerity parties—the accusation of populism. However, reducing the analysis of such re-orientation of politics to populism hinders a proper recognition of the devastating effects of economic necessity and hastily reduces the desire for national dignity to nationalism, the rejection of the austerity agenda to xenophobia and the support for Welfare policies to backwardness.

In that sense, Syriza seemed, at least until July 2015, to represent not just simply a change of government but a change of *regime*. Certainly, its advent to power marked the end of an era, which started with Metapolitefsi[9] in 1974 and the hope of 'allagi' (change) in 1981 and ended in economic disaster. Syriza's victory—as well as its post-election support—suggests that the persuasive power of the austerity narrative was weaning rapidly. This remarkable popular support, however, as well as trust in Syriza's ability to challenge the austerity agenda, began to fade in July 2015. The Syriza government's negotiation with creditors led to a stalemate and was followed by a referendum, where despite the immense popular support for the rejection of the austerity package (61.31% NO and 38.69% YES to the proposed agreement) did not materialise into a much desired political and economic break. On the contrary, it led to the signing of yet another memorandum within austerity lines, few days after the referendum was held. In the September 2015 elections following the referendum, Syriza made an effort to deal with the contradictions between the terms of the memorandum and its anti-neoliberal ideological orientation by putting forward the idea of implementing an austerity package with a 'human face'. However, as austerity tends to impact hardest on those who are most in need by weakening the safety net provided by the Welfare State, this idea was proved impossible to implement in terms of concrete policies. Syriza's capitulation against the creditors led to further retreat in a number of crucial fronts—such as the privatisation of public assets, the deregulation of labour relations, pensions, wages, policies to counter unemployment—and has been experienced by the majority of the public as a 'betrayal'.

However, 'betrayal' belongs to the moral rather than the analytical realm, and, as such, it can do little to promote critical reflection, even if such feelings are understandable. A certain analytical distance is necessary to understand rather that condemn. Beyond the obvious consequences of Syriza's capitulation to the demands of creditors, I would like to highlight the particularly problematic political and ideological aspects of Syriza's transformation in power into a political party of the system.

Syriza's failed attempt does not only represent the return with a vengeance of the TINA ('there is no alternative') dogma, but also deprives ideological legitimacy, popular support and hope to the very idea of radical change. It also promotes a climate of political confusion, if not paranoia. Facing a widespread wave of discontent, strikes and protests, Syriza found the only recourse to be the narrative of 'unwilling yet necessary' to follow what austerity demands. Legitimacy is built on the government's emphasis of its disagreement with the same policies it brings into parliament for validation. This contradictory political stance is further heightened by the party's open support for the protesting social and professional groups which are hit by the austerity measures. Demonstrations and social strikes are embraced by the government and represented as the government's arsenal against the demands of creditors. Anti-systemic discourse is adopted by the members of the government and party officials as if they were representing the opposition rather than State power.

In this climate, words, promises and actions seem to lose their meaning. When austerity and further pauperisation of the population are re-labelled 'salvation from disaster' and when protests and strikes against the government are re-labelled 'manifestations of support', one has to ask how close we risk resembling peculiar forms of 1984-style public discourse. Nonetheless—and despite Syriza's failure to materialise a meaningful break with the neoliberal structures and institutions—the momentum before the party's ascension into State power, as well as the people's mobilisation around the idea of rejecting the austerity politics (as expressed by the NO vote of the July 2015 referendum), gave a glimpse of what an alternative may look like. One where people resist the over-determination of their lives by the dicta of profit, 'efficiency' and prosperity for the few, and recast the meaning of democracy as politics which protects the commons and serves society first.

Conclusion

Since history does not end, despite Fukuyama's (1992) melancholic proposition,[10] where can we identify spaces and forces which can generate hope and possibilities of transformation? Where can we identify trajectories of unintended social change in the current predicament? Has the radical left's capitulation in Greece signalled the dead end of alternative horizons for the time being?

The final chapter of the Greek story—and as such of anti-austerity, society-centred politics—has not been written yet. Syriza's retreat, after the initial puzzlement and disorientation, which kept people off the streets for a few months, radicalised the Greek public once again. Professional and social groups took to the streets in one of the most well-attended general strikes on 4 February 2016. In this ongoing crisis, it seems that social battles are given and won in the streets, because the organised political system and its parties are, for the time being, totally dominated by economic forces which lie beyond the nation-state, at least as far as Europe is concerned.

Syriza's experiment demonstrated that alternative politics needs to be reimagined in a different, un-systemic rather than anti-systemic manner. Mere antagonism to the 'system' seems too susceptible to being engulfed by it once power is seized. Anti-systemic politics have been proven effective in overthrowing structures of power throughout the twentieth century. Gender equality and anti-racist movements, as well as the anticolonial struggle—to mention but a few notable cases—have challenged structures of power which sustain relations of domination. To a certain extent, anti-systemic politics could be said to be similar to the history of revolts against inequality, exclusion and subordination. However, much like these movements, radical politics of the crisis era have failed to transform the unequal relations of power and work towards alternative horizons for profound social change. Indeed, anti-systemic movements have a one-dimensional conception of the system and see one type of power as the basis of all other forms, without, however, challenging power itself (Fotopoulos 2001).

This could be the reason behind these movements' failure to reimagine power after it is seized. The Syriza experience in Greece suggests that radical politics of the crisis era seem willing to replicate the existing power model, by simply replacing the people in positions of power, being unable to deliver an alternative project. Anti-systemic thinking may succeed in challenging existing power relations, but it tends to reflect the very system they oppose once the existing relations of domination are toppled.

For this reason, Kouvelakis (2016) may be right when he argues that it is a mistake for the radical left to follow a line which is merely complementary to social democracy. For a meaningful and viable alternative, the horizon needs to be extended beyond 'corrective' measures to the existing power structures. In this perspective, un-systemic thinking—in other words, thinking that challenges power itself, once power is seized, and deconstructs its articulations—seems as a necessary path for any possibility of imagining alternative horizons.

Notes

1. [Retrieved 12 March 2016] http://www.tovima.gr/politics/article/?aid=407156.
2. Agamben 1998, 12.
3. [Retrieved 12 March 2016] http://www.tanea.gr/empisteytika/?aid=4630465.
4. As Harvey (2005) has been persistently arguing, neoliberalism is above all a political project of disciplining of the self to the logic of 'the market'.
5. The idea that Greece's peculiarity vis-à-vis 'civilised Europe' is due to a deficiency of modernising spirit, and as such incomplete modernisation is a recurrent theme in the field of Greek studies (e.g. Diamantouros 1994; Mavrogordatos 1997). For a critique of modernisation theories employed by scholars of modern Greek history and politics, see Andriakiana (2016). For an analysis of the deployment of this explanatory scheme for the 2008 Athens riots, see Vasilaki (2017).
6. A clarification about resistance is necessary here: I do not mean to idealise resistance or to see resistance as necessarily conducive to progressive politics. Besides, the Greek resistance to austerity has produced its own dark side—namely, the rise of the far-Right, xenophobia and racism—and it is not entirely disconnected with the popularisation of conspiracy theories, even in its progressive versions. For an astute analysis of the ambivalence of the Greek resistance to the crisis, see Thedossopoulos (2014a, 2014b). Foucault's writings are indicative in bringing to the fore the ambivalent nature of power and, consequently, resistance. For an interesting discussion on the political and ethical underpinning of

resistance and the distinction between liberation and freedom and the kind of politics they sustain, see Armstrong (2008), Heller (1996) and Pickett (1996).

7. For an extensive account of Syriza's trajectory from fringe party to State power and its course in the past year, see Ovenden (2015) and Kouvelakis (2016).
8. 'Change' in the particular context of 1981 was meant both as a change of regime—democratic rule was only established in Greece in 1974—and in terms of polity, institutions and culture after several years of authoritarianism and repression.
9. The post-authoritarian years is a period commonly known as 'Metapolitefsi' (literally, political transition). Many see this period ending with the 2008 riots, others with the Greek crisis (2010) and yet others with the advent of Syriza to power in January 2015. In any case, there seems to be agreement that the era of Metapolitefsi has come to an end and Greece currently undergoes another period of transition.
10. On the analysis of Fukuyama's forecast as melancholic rather than triumphant, see Ahmad (1997).

Works Cited

Agamben, Giorgio. 1998. *Homo Sacer. Sovereign power and bare life*. Stanford: Stanford University Press.

Ahmad, Aijaz. 1997. Postcolonial theory and the 'post' condition. *The Socialist Register* 33: 353–381.

Andriakiana, Eleni. 2016. Public history, 1821 revolution and greek identity. In *Defining identity and the changing scope of culture in the Digital Age*, ed. Alison Novak and Imaani Jamillah El-Burki, 56–80. Hershey: IGI Global.

Armstrong, Aurelia. 2008. Beyond resistance: A response to Žižek's critique of Foucault's subject of freedom. *Parrhesia* 5: 19–31.

Christopoulos, Dimitris. 2014. *The 'deep state' in Greece today and the far right: Police, justice, church*. Athens: Nisos—Rosa Luxemburg Stiftung.

Cinar, Kursat. 2016. A comparative analysis of clientelism in Greece, Spain, and Turkey: The rural–urban divide. *Contemporary Politics* 22 (1): 77–94.

Diamantouros, Nikiforos. 1994. *Cultural dualism and political change in postauthoritarian Greece*, Estudio/Working Paper, Center for Advanced Study in the Social Sciences. Madrid: Fundación Juan March.

Featherstone, Kevin. 2008. 'Varieties of capitalism' and the Greek case: Explaining the constraints on domestic reform. *GreeSe* Paper 11, Hellenic Observatory Papers on Greece and Southeast Europe. http://www.lse.ac.uk/europeanInstitute/research/hellenicObservatory/pdf/GreeSE/GreeSE11.pdf. Accessed 24 Apr 2017.

Fotopoulos, Takis. 2001. The end of traditional anti-systemic movements and the need for a new type of anti-systemic movement today. *Democracy and Nature* 7 (3): 415–455.

Fukuyama, Francis. 1992. *The end of history and the last man*. London: Penguin Books.

Giddens, Anthony. 1991. *Modernity and self-identity: Self and society in the late modern age*. Cambridge: Polity.

Harvey, David. 2005. *A brief history of Neoliberalism*. Oxford: Oxford University Press.

Heller, Kevin Jon. 1996. Power, subjectification and resistance in Foucault. *SubStance* 25 (1): 78–110.

Kirtsoglou, Elisabeth. 2013. The dark ages of the Golden Dawn: Anthropological analysis and responsibility in the twilight zone of the Greek crisis. *Journal of the Finnish Anthropological Society* 38 (1): 104–108.

Kouvelakis, Stathis. 2016. Syriza's rise and fall. *New Left Review* 97: 45–70.

Mavrogordatos, George T. 1997. From traditional clientelism to machine politics: The impact of PASOK populism in Greece. *South European Society and Politics* 2 (3): 1–26.

Ovenden, Kevin. 2015. *Syriza: Inside the labyrinth*. London: Pluto Press.

Pickett, Brent L. 1996. Foucault and the politics of resistance. *Polity* 28 (4): 445–466.

Psarras, Dimitris. 2012. *The black book of the Golden Dawn: Documents from the history and action of a Nazi group*. Athens: Polis.

Spivak, Gayatri. 1990. Poststructuralism, marginality, postcoloniality and value. In *Literary theory today*, ed. Peter Collier and Helga Geyer-Ryan, 198–222. New York: Cornell University Press.

Thedossopoulos, Dimitrios. 2014a. On depathologizing resistance. *History and Anthropology* 25 (4): 415–430.

———. 2014b. The ambivalence of anti-austerity indignation in Greece: Resistance, hegemony and complicity. *History and Anthropology* 25 (4): 488–506.

Vasilaki, Rosa. 2017. We are an image from the future: Reading back the Athens 2008 riots. *Acta Scientiarum* 29 (2): 153–161.

Žižek, Slavoj. 2009. *First as tragedy, then as farce*. London: Verso.

Unleashing the Emancipatory Power of the 'Spirit of Free Communal Service': G.D.H. Cole, Dialogical Coordination and Social Change

Charles Masquelier

In the preface of this volume, Göran Therborn offers a rather pessimistic diagnosis regarding the prospects for large-scale social change within the 'North-Atlantic zone'. This pessimism is, to a large extent, justified if, like Therborn, one looks at the centre and on the surface of economic and political life within the zone in question. Given the seemingly unshakable rule of neoliberal capitalism and spread of far-right political movements, the current economic and political climates do seem to offer little hope for a genuinely progressive form of social change. It is also too early to know with certainty whether the unexpected entry of Bernie Sanders and Jeremy Corbyn into mainstream politics will make a lasting impact on American and British political life, respectively. But in order to find the seeds of social change, one need not restrict the focus of analysis on developments taking place at the centre of economic and political practices and discourses within the North-Atlantic zone. Changes can indeed find their origins in the margins. In this chapter, I shall propose to look for

C. Masquelier (✉)
University of Exeter, Exeter, UK

T. Geelan et al. (eds.), *From Financial Crisis to Social Change*,
https://doi.org/10.1007/978-3-319-70600-9_12

'glimmers of hope' in the definite tendencies emerging within the confines of the solidarity and digital economy which offer possible avenues for the institutionalisation of some of the central components of G.D.H. Cole's libertarian socialist alternative.

As a leading figure of the early twentieth-century guild socialist movement, Cole was keen to circumvent the aporias of mere negation and was unwilling to find comfort in the belief in capitalism's self-destruction. In his early works, he expressed a particular concern with the perversion of innate 'creative' and 'communal' impulses by the logic of the capitalist market while highlighting the democratic deficit of pre-existing political institutions. To these he opposed a system of allocation of resources and political representation based on the 'spirit of free communal service' (Cole 1980, 44). In this chapter I aim to demonstrate that Cole's own alternative not only captures the spirit of pre-existing marginal economic practices and contemporary global social movements but can also offer an invaluable source of inspiration for their coordination in a strategy for large-scale social transformation. I shall proceed by first reviewing some of the core components of his critique of capitalism and liberal democracy. I will then discuss the features of the 'spirit of free communal service' Cole had in mind and draw the contours of his libertarian socialist alternative. In the third and final section, I shall provide some reflections on the prospects for social transformation by exploring the manifestations of the 'spirit' in question in the margins of economic life and a contemporary global social movement like Occupy Wall Street, which will lead to a discussion of possible strategies of coordination.

Cole's Critique: A Tale of Two Repressed Impulses

Cole was highly critical of the type of institutions upholding the capitalist mode of production and liberal forms of democratic representation. A central concern underpins his critique, namely, the fact that these institutions fail 'to be so organised as to afford greatest possible opportunity for individual and collective self-expression to all its members' (Cole 1980, 13). For Cole, the plight facing individuals in capitalist and liberal democratic societies is not merely characterised by 'limits to individual autonomy' but also by 'hindrances to the collective realisation of autonomy'. In what follows, both the origins and nature of these limits within the economic and political spheres will be exposed.

Let me start with his critique of capitalist economic life. Cole expressed his key concern as follows:

> The crowning indictment of capitalism is that it destroys freedom and individuality in the worker, that it reduces man to a machine, and that it treats human beings as means to production instead of subordinating production to the well-being of the producer. (Cole 1917, 24)

So, for Cole, capitalism rests on an intolerable logic, according to which workers' autonomy in the sphere of production comes to be severely restricted. Such a restriction is explained by the subsumption of the labour process under the 'invisible hand' of a supply and demand mechanism upheld by private ownership, driven by the profit motive and competitive ethos, imposing imperatives of productivity and efficiency upon the workplace. Translated into a rigid division of labour imposed by the private owners on workers in an attempt to maximise their gain, these imperatives undermine the latter's capacity to unleash, freely, what Cole described as 'the creative impulse' (Cole 1917, 302). Like William Morris, whom he admired greatly, Cole severely condemned the fact that the 'impulse to self-expression [has been] thwarted by commercialism' (Cole 1917, 119).

But, in addition to the repression of the 'creative impulse', the capitalist workplace has given rise to an equally problematic phenomenon: the repression of the 'impulse of the communal spirit' (Cole 1980, 49). Inspired by Rousseau, who 'put an immense emphasis on this sentiment [...] as a force in the shaping of human affairs' (Cole 1950, 128), Cole conceptualised solidarity as a fundamental human impulse. The root of its repression, he claimed, can be located in both the 'motives of greed and fear' (Cole 1980, 45) upheld by an institution like the capitalist market and the worker's incapacity to enjoy 'real self-government and freedom *at his work*' (Cole 1980, 49). While the former pit workers against one another, the latter undermines the autonomy necessitated for engaging in spontaneous and self-directed cooperation. The capitalist regime of accumulation, then, not only imposes significant obstacles to self-expression but also denies the worker the capacity to align his/her individual conception of the good life with that of other workers.

Contrary to Marxian analyses of capitalism, however, Cole extended the scope of his critique beyond the sphere of production. For him, the problem of repression of the 'impulse of the communal spirit' is not limited to bonds between workers themselves. The profit motive also interferes with the way producers relate to consumers, by giving rise to a 'divergence of interests between them' (Cole 1980, 39). Under a system of production and exchange whereby producers prioritise the private maximisation of gain over the direct satisfaction of the needs of consumers, a rather striking situation emerges: the interests of producers are pitted against those of the very individuals they provide the service to, as exemplified by the various strategies devised by commercial agencies in manipulating consumer demand. The logic of the capitalist market, therefore, also undermines collective self-expression between workers and consumers. What are, in principle, two complementary sets of interests come to oppose one another—something Cole viewed as a wholly irrational and unjustifiable state of affairs. A fully rational system of satisfaction of needs, he insisted, ought to recognise the formal complementarity between producers' and consumers' interests.

Although addressed separately here, Cole regarded 'communal and personal well-being' (Cole 1920, 62) as mutually constitutive. 'Communal well-being', for example, depends on producers' capacity to unleash the 'sentiment' of solidarity. Workers deprived of personal well-being cannot, however, be expected to express it, for they will end up prioritising their own interests over those of others. If they do cooperate, however, the motive will assume a self-interested form, rather than being expressed in the form of sentiment. Personal well-being is therefore an essential precondition for communal well-being. Conversely, an individual is said to be 'most free when he [sic, and throughout the chapter] cooperates best with his equals' (Cole 1917, 227–228). Acting with other individuals in the pursuit of a shared goal can significantly increase the chances of meeting this goal. Cooperation, therefore, empowers individuals and acts as a highly favourable condition for the attainment of personal well-being. It is such a relationship between the individual and collective basis of self-expression that lies at the operational core of Cole's 'spirit of free communal service', whose additional features will be discussed in the next section.

But given Cole's particular concern with the problem of 'communal organisation' (Cole 1980, 32), his critique also sought to tackle the form of communal life unfolding under the liberal democratic mode of representation. His diagnosis of liberal democracy is in fact no less severe than his diagnosis of capitalist economic life. While the latter is so organised that it pits workers against one another and workers against consumers, the liberal democratic state is said to be 'an organ of class domination' (Cole 1980, 122). He therefore complemented his critique of the 'industrial autocracy of capitalism' (Cole 1980, 51) with a critique of political institutions he deemed 'utterly unsuitable to any really democratic community' (Cole 1980, 32).

Cole identified a key cause of liberal democracy's failures with the highly divisive character of the hostile economic life unfolding under capitalism's guise. Because 'the economic sphere of social action has become the battle-ground of contending sections [those involved in such battles] are irresistibly impelled to widen their battlefront so as to lay waste the tracts of social organisation which lie outside the economic sphere' (Cole 1920, 149–50). Socio-economic inequalities, he argued, inevitably give rise to conflicts of interests affecting the political sphere. After all, how can an authentic conception of common good be embodied by the state, if the very individuals it is meant to represent are organised into conflicting factions? Under such conditions, political institutions come to be 'perverted by the power of the capitalists' (Cole 1980, 122). In the face of such divisions, the state is forced to manufacture the common good and impose a 'conception of human society' onto its citizens through the rule of 'Force and Law' (Cole 1920, 6). The liberal democratic state therefore fails to give life to the 'desire for comradeship upon which democracy is built' (Cole 1950, 106), and cannot be expected to represent the interests of its citizens in any meaningful manner. It follows that, had Cole been around at the time of the Occupy Wall Street movement, he would have most certainly been sympathetic with their own condemnation of the perversion of political institutions by the so-called 1%.

However, Cole's critique of liberal democracy did not end there. He also expressed concerns with the very tenets of the liberal democratic theory of representation. Although 'false' in practice, it is also 'false' in theory, for '[n]o man can represent another man, and no man's will can be treated as a substitute for, or representative of, the wills of others' (Cole 1920, 103). The problem with the ideas of 'omnicompetent State [and] omnicompetent Parliament' (Cole 1980, 32) is their tendency to 'include all sorts of people, without reference to the sort of people they are, the sort of beliefs they hold, or the sort of work they do' (Cole 1920, 95). Thus, because liberal democratic theory's universalist postulates fail to accommodate the pluralism of social life in decision-making processes, its operationalisation cannot be expected to translate individual conceptions of the good life into a politically effective force.

One can now see why Cole's diagnosis of liberal democratic life is as severe as his diagnosis of capitalist economic life: both give rise to decision-making processes that distort 'individual and collective self-expression' and, as a result, hinder the release of what he regarded as two fundamental human impulses. But Cole did not succumb to resignation. Instead, he advocated the 'complete disappearance of private ownership from [...] industry' (Cole and Mellor 1933, 7) and claimed that the liberal democratic state and parliament 'must be destroyed or painlessly extinguished' (Cole 1980, 32). Both economic and political life can and must therefore be radically re-organised. In what follows, I shall draw the contours of his alternative.

Cole's Alternative: Unleashing the 'Spirit of Free Communal Service'

Despite being equally critical of both the economic and political spheres, Cole believed that the 'transformation required' is 'fundamentally not political but economic' (Cole 1980, 180). In other words, any radical re-organisation of social and political life rests on the transformation of economic life into a 'free system [that] will bring to the front man's natural qualities' (Cole 1917, 256). I shall therefore start by reviewing the economic transformations Cole had in mind.

Although Cole eventually became somewhat more sympathetic towards central planning (see Cole 1937),[1] his early works offer a very different form of re-organisation of economic life than the one found under state socialist alternatives. 'State control of production' (Cole 1920, 98), he argued, cannot adequately accommodate the plurality of needs and desires of individuals as either producers or consumers (Cole 1980). But because he, along with his fellow guild socialists, 'repudiat[ed] the profit basis and all forms of profit-sharing' (Cole 1944, 284), he also rejected the market socialist alternative. Instead, Cole sought to re-introduce, in a modernised form, the 'moral principles' of the mediaeval guilds, which are, today, 'regarded almost as intruders in the industrial sphere' (Cole 1980, 45). His own alternative aims to accomplish 'the substitution of service to the community for service for private profit' (Cole 1946, 10). It therefore guided the moral principles of a 'spirit of free communal service' entailing values, motives and practices in radical opposition to those at the root of the repression of both the 'creative' and 'communal' impulses. In fact, Cole anticipates the development of an altogether different logic from the one upon which the capitalist market rests, namely, one that, in virtue of being guided by the 'impulse of free and unfettered service' (Cole 1917, 302), can pave the way for a form of 'social empowerment' (Wright 2010, 121), comprising individuals who are not only autonomous but also 'socially good' (Cole 1950, 10). He proposed to achieve such a goal through the re-organisation of economic life into democratically organised associations of producers and consumers, coordinating the satisfaction of needs through dialogue. His proposed re-organisation is divided into two distinct, albeit connected, levels of action: the re-organisation of economic life into associations, which entails exploring actions *within* associations of producers and consumers, and their dialogical coordination, which regards actions *between* these two sets of associations. I shall start by tackling the associational level.

In an essay acknowledging his debt to, and admiration of, Jean-Jacques Rousseau, Cole exposed the underlying logic of associative action. He put it as follows:

> [W]henever [individuals] form or connect themselves with any form of association for any active purpose, [they] develop in relation to the associa-

> tion an attitude which looks to the general benefit of the association rather than their own individual benefit. This is not to say that they cease to think of their own individual advantage – only that there is, in their associative actions, an element, which may be stronger or weaker, of seeking the advantage of the whole association, or of all its members, as distinct from the element which seeks only personal advantage. (Cole 1950, 114)

In any voluntary and democratically organised association, individuals treat the interest of their association as an extension of their own. Such a type of organisation is therefore thought to be an ideal organisational form for releasing the 'impulse of communal spirit'. They are highly suitable for the cultivation of the values of 'cheerfulness, comradeliness, co-operativeness, consideration, kindness' (Cole 1950, 7) characterising 'good men' (Cole 1950, 71). Also, because it is at the workplace that 'men have the habit and tradition of working together', it is also there that the 'the spirit of association' can 'best [be] able to find expression' (Cole 1980, 49). The economy is, for Cole, the natural home of the communal spirit, which voluntary and democratic associations are in the best position to bring to life.

But by introducing 'democracy in industry', Cole also expects individual producers to find the means for authentic self-expression. A democratically organised association is one in which individuals can 'agree [...] together upon certain methods of procedure, and lay [...] down, in however rudimentary a form, rules for common action' (Cole 1920, 37). It is therefore a space where the individual worker can exert the degree of control over the labour process necessary to express 'his likes and dislikes, desires and aversions, hopes and fears, his sense of right and wrong, beauty and ugliness, and so on' (Cole 1920, 184). Democracy induces the form of cooperative practices that can, as highlighted above, empower individuals in their quest for individual self-expression. But given the benefits of democratic associative action, Cole thought that consumers, too, should be in a position to 'make articulate and definite [their] needs and desires' (Cole 1980, 89) collectively. He consequently anticipated its introduction into the spheres of production and consumption, so that individuals *qua* producers and consumers can acquire the means to achieve both individual and collective self-expression.

While associative action is an essential precondition for the alignment of individual conceptions of the good life with the common good lying at the core of the free communal spirit, it is not a sufficient one. Indeed, according to Cole, the idea that the success of producers is not measured 'in terms of profit, but in terms of rendering a good service to the consuming public' (Cole 1957, 36) can only be expected to materialise if both producers and consumers coordinate their activities through negotiations. While producers are united through the 'performance in common of some form of social service', the bond uniting consumers is that of 'receiving, using or consuming such services' (Cole 1980, 34). They make up two different but complementary sides of the same process and should consequently, Cole argues, be able to 'negotiate on equal terms' (Cole 1917, 86). The vision Cole has in mind is a system of allocation of resources whereby producers and consumers negotiate the terms and conditions of exchange—for example, prices, nature/quantity of goods and services—through their representatives in producer guilds and consumer councils. No longer motivated by profit but by the 'direct and useful contribution [...] they freely make to the service of the community' (Cole 1980, 89), producers will no longer 'seek to thwart [consumers, but instead] be eager to elicit and respond to them because [they] will have the strongest of social motives for doing so, and no sufficient motive for doing otherwise' (Cole 1980, 89). As an alternative to the 'invisible hand' of the capitalist market, Cole therefore offers the visible hand of dialogical coordination between producer guilds and consumer councils.

However, in order to guarantee the direct representation of producers' and consumers' interests or, as he put it, individual 'wills' (Cole 1920), Cole identified another essential precondition: functional representation. A function embodies the purpose or general interest of an association (*ibid.*). It is by representing its function in the local, regional and national guilds and councils that the 'social value' (Cole 1920, 55) of an association is asserted. Representation based on associations' function can, in turn, assert the 'general will' of an association at the level of dialogical coordination, which is ultimately the level where issues regarding 'men liv[ing] together in communities' (Cole 1920, 67) are addressed. Functional representation serves as a more 'real' and 'direct' mode of political representation than its liberal democratic counterpart. It is, Cole insisted, the only 'guarantee of the recognition of the fact that society is based upon the individuals' (Cole 1920, 192) and the key not only to 'social' but also to 'communal and personal well-being' (Cole 1920, 62).

According to Cole, then, the dialogically coordinated activities of functionally represented associations of producers and consumers will induce 'an immense liberation of social and individual energy' (Cole 1980, 159), opening up the scope for the release of the 'spirit of free communal service'. He was therefore a profound idealist or, as he put it, a 'social idealist' (Cole 1957, 168) who believed in the goodness of individuals and the positive role some specific institutions can play in cultivating it (Cole 1955, ix). Despite the social ills engendered by capitalist economic life and liberal democratic institutions' democratic deficit, Cole remained optimistic. But was Cole not guilty of a misplaced optimism? It is to this question that I shall now turn.

From the Margins to the Centre

Given the seemingly radical nature of his proposals, one would be forgiven to think that the emergence of an economic system organised around the spirit of free communal service is a desirable but highly improbable expectation. But is the idea of an economy in which ordinary workers can exert direct control over their working conditions treat the interests of co-producers as an extension of their own and are 'eager' to provide a free service to the community such an unrealistic prospect? Cole certainly did not think so and insisted that 'these principles themselves are not the inventions of the theorist or social philosopher, but are, however imperfectly, at work everywhere around us in Society' (Cole 1980, 203). But their mere existence is, Cole further argued, insufficient for the large-scale social transformation his alternative entails. Workers, he added, should aim for a 'policy of encroachment' involving trade unions 'wresting bit by bit from the hands of the possessing classes the economic power which they now exercise' (Cole 1980, 196).

Since he anticipated a conflict between workers and the bourgeoisie, his approach to social change appears to involve the kind of a 'ruptural' transformation identified by Wright (2010, 303). However, it fails to meet Wright's own criteria on two crucial grounds. Firstly, Cole did not expect workers to organise themselves 'through political parties' (Wright 2010, 305), but claimed that the conflict would remain within its natural home, namely, the economic sphere. Secondly, since Cole advocated a gradual transformation through 'encroachment', he did not expect change to involve a 'sharp break within existing institutions and social structures' (Wright 2010, 303).

The 'interstitial' and 'symbiotic' strategies of transformation identified by Wright also fail to accommodate Cole's own stance. Since the latter involves changes emanating from a 'class compromise' (Wright 2010, 306), Cole could not be expected to advocate it. His stance on the prospects for an 'interstitial' path towards social transformation is, on the other hand, ambiguous. Here is, for example, what Cole made of the prospects of social change through the expansion of the cooperative sector, which Wright (2010, 324) himself presented as a possible 'interstitial' strategy of transformation:

> The fuller utilisation of working-class resources for Co-operative development would do something but not enough; for Co-operators are faced by the fact that it is simply not possible, at least within any measurable period, to drive the possessing classes out of industry simply by competing with them under conditions which these classes themselves prescribe. (Cole 1980, 191)

However, despite such a pessimism regarding an 'interstitial' social change led by the cooperative sector, Cole did acknowledge the fact that 'important social changes are usually inaugurated in the parts and not in the whole of Society, and often nearer to its circumference than to its centre' (Cole 1980, 206). What, then, could these 'parts', today, be? Unlike Cole, I shall treat aspects of the cooperative sector as a potential source of large-scale social change, along with developments taking place within the contemporary digital economy.

Several works attributing a potentially transformative role to the cooperative sector have emerged in recent years (see Alperovitz 2011; Satgar 2014; Shantz and MacDonald 2013; Wyatt 2011). This sector is divided into two types of cooperatives: those making up the 'social economy' and those comprised in the 'solidarity economy' (Satgar 2014). While the former are said to represent just another business model oriented towards growth and profit, the latter is both 'a theoretical discourse and practice [that] places the needs of human and nonhuman nature [...] at the centre of social activity' (Satgar 2014, 13). Some are therefore another way of putting the values of competition and private gain into practice. Others, however, make up a 'counter-hegemonic alternative driven from below', confronting neoliberal capitalism with 'values', 'visions' and 'practices' (Satgar 2014, 12) aiming to overcome the subordination of the well-being of producers to the economy, which Cole viewed as the 'crowning indictment of capitalism'. For example, in their work on 'workers' self-managed and recovered companies', Ozarow and Croucher have shown how cooperatives can 'exhibit [...] a sharp political edge' induced by a generalised disaffection towards political and economic elites following the destructive 2001–2002 Argentinian economic crisis (Ozarow and Croucher 2014, 995). They have proven capable of becoming spaces where 'workers' alienation from themselves, from other workers, their products and society is at least partially overcome' (Ozarow and Croucher 2014, 1003). They became spaces for individual and collective self-expression.

For these reasons, several contemporary analysts of the solidarity economy expect its expansion to give the cooperatives in question the collective power to shape the values and norms of societies under their reach. The recent proliferation of values and practices of the solidarity economy in such regions as North America, Latin America, Europe and Africa (Satgar 2014) could, in this sense, be understood as developments making up a process of large-scale social transformation within these regions. Alperovitz, for example, spoke of an 'evolutionary reconstruction' that can be expected to 're-democratiz[e] the American system in general' (2011, xxv). The change anticipated here is, therefore, aligned with Cole's own calls for democratisation.

New possibilities have also opened up through developments within the digital economy. Of particular interest are some recent studies revealing the increased potential for the realisation of a communal economy. Take, for example, the practice of commons-oriented production, referring to the voluntary production and free distribution of goods such as

Free and Open Source Software (FOSS) programmes and the Wikimedia foundation. The search engine Firefox, the content management software Wordpress and Wikipedia are highly successful examples, operating on the basis of a networked and 'voluntaristic cooperation that does not depend on exclusive proprietary control or command relations as among the co-operators' (Benkler 2013, 214). Both the Mozilla and Wikipedia community comprise a minority of paid employees and a majority of volunteers. These are not-for-profit organisations, which use their revenues to be able to keep providing the free service to users and improving it, while giving their paid employees the necessary means of subsistence. These revenues are drawn either from partnerships with major search engines in the case of the former, or from donations in the case of the latter. None of these organisations relies on advertising. In fact, the facts that they provide a free service to users and '[n]o one makes a profit directly from [their] activities' (Wright 2010, 195) mean that they are able to operate outside market relations. Moreover, both heavily rely on a vast network of volunteers willing to share their knowledge and skills *for* the community. Anyone can volunteer to act as an editor of Wikipedia entries or programmer for the Mozilla Firefox web browser. The services they provide are the result of highly collaborative practices between a core of paid employees and volunteers. In the case of the online encyclopaedia, for example, no editor has 'special privileges over others in the production of content', and 'decisions are generally made directly by editors in a deliberative process with other editors without mediation by any body that has editorial or managerial control' (Wright 2010, 196).

Given such features, it is possible to view these undertakings as contemporary manifestations of Cole's 'spirit of free communal service'. The interest of the 'producer' is here construed as one and the same as the interest of the community at large. Both place a strong emphasis on decentralised and collaborative online participation, with activities aiming to 'empower and engage people around the world to collect and develop educational content'[2] in the case of Wikipedia and to 'serve [...] the public good' in such a way as to make the Internet a 'public resource that [...] remain[s] open and accessible'[3] in the case of Mozilla Firefox. Services are provided by the community, for the community. Firefox, for example, is 'built by and for a community of users who seek greater control over their own Web browsing experience' (Benkler 2013, 226). As radical alternatives to conventional economic models, then, they provide a space for the liberation of service users and providers from the proprietary, alienating, exploitative, inegalitarian and oppressive logic of the capitalist marketplace. As such, 'online peer mutualism' in the form discussed here is a 'critical social practice' that has emerged in opposition and as an alternative to neoliberal capitalist relations by 'counteracting some of its social pathologies' (Barron 2013, 597). In addition to the solidarity economy, one therefore finds a range of experiments within the digital economy marked by values and practices sharing a close affinity with those making up Cole's own alternative.

But what if these two sets of developments at the margins of contemporary economic life—solidarity economy and online commons-oriented production—could combine their transformative energies? In a recently published article Bauwens and Kostakis (2014) explored possible avenues for achieving this goal. Here, they set out a plan for the development of an 'open cooperativism' marking the convergence of commons-oriented production found in the digital economy (characterised by 'abundance') and production practices found in the cooperative movement (characterised by 'scarcity'). Driving such a model is the need to eliminate the reliance of both sets of practices on conventional for-profit organisations for their self-sustenance—a goal echoing guild socialists' repudiation of the profit motive. Underlying their strategy is a 'reciprocal economy' within which goods (both material and immaterial) would be made freely available 'to all that contribute' (Bauwens and Kostakis 2014, 358). Open cooperativists, they further argue, should 'adopt multi-stakeholders forms of governance which would include workers, users-consumers, investors and the concerned communities' (Bauwens and Kostakis 2014, 358). The strategy proposed here, then, is essentially a vision for the development of practices 'oriented towards the creation of the common good' (Bauwens and Kostakis 2014, 358) and the provision of a free service. As such, it provides a possible avenue towards the model of dialogical coordination anticipated by Cole.

What such a strategy also offers is an illustration of the kind of alliances that could convert what are, today, marginal values and practices into a source of large-scale social transformation. Several scholars keen to attribute a transformative role to the solidarity economy have insisted on the coordination of efforts between different movements. Referring to the Occupy Wall Street movement, Richard Wolff claimed that 'workers' self-directed enterprises' (WSDEs) could 'speak to those active in or inspired by Occupy struggles' (Wolff 2012, 177). Such a call is not surprising, given an 'inner core of the movement' not only calling for 'different policies' aimed at increasing socio-economic equality but also advocating 'a different way of life' (Gitlin 2013, 8). Several of the occupations making up the movement contained a 'new way of political organizing [...] revolving around the words like "General Assemblies" and "horizontals" and "consensus" and "working groups"' (Flank 2011, 8). They aimed to provide 'the most open, participatory, and democratic space possible' (Taylor et al. 2011, 5). Thus, in their occupations, members of the movement effectively brought to life the 'alternative [they] wish to see in [their] day-to-day relationships' (Taylor et al. 2011, 5)—an alternative which, as indicated by the aforementioned practices, shared an affinity with practices and values found in the solidarity economy and the alternative advocated by Cole.

But, as Chomsky observed, the movement failed to 'persist and [...] be brought into the wider community [in the form of, for example] enterprises owned and managed by the work force and the community' (Chomsky 2012, 74–75). What appeared to be missing was a broad 'strategic and theoretical vision' (Gorz 1982, 412) capable of facilitating the creation of cooperative 'start-ups'. This is where, I think, Cole's own vision can make a particularly valuable contribution. Given its affinity with the values and practices found in the solidarity economy, commons-oriented production and a global social movement like Occupy, the 'spirit of free communal service' can provide the language capable of coordinating their opposition to the current neoliberal order and translating it into a politically effective force. While WSDEs can speak to Occupy protesters, the 'spirit of free communal service' speaks to a wide range of contemporary movements and 'critical social practices' including, but not restricted to, those discussed in this chapter. But what distinguishes Cole's work from those of the different scholars discussed in this section is the close attention he paid to a re-organisation of political life. His functional mode of political representation can therefore offer the strategic and theoretical vision that, once the economic conditions are ripe, could channel individual and collective self-expression into political decision-making processes.

Conclusion

The task of diagnosing the prospects for social change in the North-Atlantic zone invites us to look both within and outside mainstream economic and political life. In this chapter, I sought to reveal that developments within the margins offer reasons for remaining optimistic about such prospects. Cole certainly was. Whether the changes taking place in these margins will indeed pave the way for the large-scale institutionalisation of the spirit of free communal service in a dialogically coordinated system of allocation of resources is, to be sure, anyone's guess. A strategic vision, in the broad form offered here, could nevertheless provide a fruitful basis upon which to move the values and practices making up these marginal operations towards the centre of economic and political discourse.

It is also worth remembering that capitalism itself began its journey in the margins of feudal economic life. Thus, there is no reason to exclude the possibility that the solidarity economy, commons-oriented production and social movements could one day coordinate their efforts and gain sufficient critical mass to drive social change. Given the range and scale of pre-existing attempts to overcome the repressive character of dominant economic and political institutions, there is, in fact, every reason to believe, like Cole himself did decades ago, in the possibility for transformations that can 'make men good' (Cole 1950, 128).

Notes

1. Cole did indeed admire the fact that central planning could treat 'the entire available supply of labour and other productive instruments solely as means to the satisfaction of human wants' (Cole 1937, 252).

2. [Retrieved 13 March 2016] http://wikimediafoundation.org/.
3. [Retrieved 13 March 2016] https://www.mozilla.org/.

Works Cited

Alperovitz, Gar. 2011. *America beyond capitalism: Reclaiming our wealth, our liberty and our democracy*. Boston: Democracy Collaborative Press.

Barron, Anne. 2013. Free software production as critical social practice. *Economy and Society* 42 (4): 597–625.

Bauwens, Michel, and Vasilis Kostakis. 2014. From the communism of capital to capital for the commons: Towards an open co-operativism. *TripleC* 12 (1): 356–361.

Benkler, Yochai. 2013. Practical anarchism: Peer mutualism, market power, and the fallible state. *Politics and Society* 41 (2): 212–251.

Chomsky, Noam. 2012. *Occupy*. London: Penguin Press.

Cole, George Douglas Howard. 1917. *Self-government in industry*. London: George Bell & Sons.

———. 1920. *Social theory*. London: Methuen & Co.

———. 1937. *Practical economics*. Middlesex: Pelican Books.

———. 1944. *A century of cooperation*. London: George Allen and Unwin.

———. 1946. *Cooperation, labour and socialism*. Co-operative Partnership Propaganda Committee, Sixth Thomas Blandford Memorial Lecture, 23rd November.

———. 1950. *Essays in social theory*. London: Macmillan.

———. 1955. Introduction. In *The social contract and discourses*, ed. Jean Jacques Rousseau. London: Everyman's Library.

———. 1957. Sociology and social policy. *British Journal of Sociology* 8 (2): 158–171.

———. 1980. *Guild socialism re-stated*. London: Transaction Books.

Cole, George Douglas Howard, and William Mellor. 1933. Workers' control and self-government. In *Industry, a memorandum prepared by a group of trade unionists and socialists as a basis for consideration by the working-class movement*, 9, ed. The New Fabian Research Bureau. London: The New Fabian Research Bureau.

Flank, Lenny. 2011. *Voices from the 99 percent: An oral history of the occupy Wall Street movement*. St Petersburg: Red and Black Publishers.

Gitlin, Todd. 2013. Occupy's predicament: The moment and the prospects for the movement. *British Journal of Sociology* 64 (1): 3–25.

Gorz, Andre. 1982. Workers' control is more than just that. In *Workplace democracy and social change*, ed. Frank Lindenfeld and Joyce Rothschild-Whitt. Boston: Porter Sargent.
Ozarow, Daniel, and Richard Croucher. 2014. Workers' self-management, recovered companies and the sociology of work. *Sociology* 48 (5): 989–1006.
Satgar, Vishwas. 2014. *The solidarity economy alternative: Emerging theory and practice*. KwaZulu-Natal: University of KwaZulu-Natal Press.
Shantz, Jeff, and José Brendan MacDonald. 2013. *Beyond capitalism: Building democratic alternatives for today and the future*. New York: Bloomsbury.
Taylor, A., et al., eds. 2011. *Occupy: Scenes from occupied America*. London: Verso.
Wolff, Richard. 2012. *Democracy at work: A cure for capitalism*. Chicago: Haymarket Books.
Wright, Erik Olin. 2010. *Envisioning real utopias*. London: Verso.
Wyatt, Chris. 2011. *The defetishised society: New economic democracy as libertarian alternative to capitalism*. New York: Bloomsbury.

Afterword

Torsten Geelan, Marcos González Hernando, and Peter William Walsh

When putting pen to paper in 2017, we were mindful that events can quickly overtake any long-term project. While preparing this volume for publication, we have nevertheless found that the trend lines of social change that Therborn (Preface "The Labyrinths and the Layers of Social Change") observed in the aftermath of the financial crisis of 2008 remain visible. On the one hand, austerity measures and neoliberal politics continue to increase inequality and erode the welfare state, and authoritarianism, nationalism, racism, xenophobia and right-wing extremism remain on the rise. Indeed, one finds that much of people's indignation at exploitation and exclusion has been channelled into political projects that seek to reestablish an imaginary past, to restore a chimerical 'greatness', rather than offer a progressive future. Examples of this abound in North America and Europe, but it is Trump's presidency and Brexit that are the epitomes of this alarming manifestation. Scapegoating immigrants; dismissing the expertise of scientists, academics and journalists; and attacking dysfunctional albeit democratic institutions have become part of mainstream political discourse, to the detriment of us all.

T. Geelan (✉) • M. González Hernando • P. W. Walsh
Department of Sociology, University of Cambridge, Cambridge, UK

T. Geelan et al. (eds.), *From Financial Crisis to Social Change*,
https://doi.org/10.1007/978-3-319-70600-9_13

On the other hand, social movements and rebellious citizens are resisting these developments. Take, for example, the worldwide Women's March on 21 January 2017 that took place the day after Donald Trump was inaugurated as the 45th President of the United States. Welcoming protestors of all genders and ethnicities, its aim was to take a stand against Trump's anti-women behaviour and advocate for the rights of women, foreigners, workers and the natural environment. In the United States, the Women's March was the largest day of protest in the country's history, while in the United Kingdom 100,000 protestors took to the streets of the capital, marching from the US embassy to Nelson's column. Globally, an incredible five million people were estimated to have demonstrated in 81 countries on all continents (including the Arctic and Antarctica), reflecting a level of coordination unthinkable in the days before social media. Indeed, the Women's March appears to have been one of the most widespread and participative demonstrations in world history.

Within this context, our book's overarching idea—that the maturation of a new generation of critical thinkers and activists could provide a fertile source of progressive social change—gives us cause for hope. Paraphrasing Gramsci, our authors have shown that while the old has not yet died, there exists a new world struggling to be born. This has involved actors comprising social movements, political parties and NGOs engaged in conscious projects of social change. The two transformative strategies that our authors have delved into—*interstitial* and *symbiotic*—were drawn from Eric Olin Wright's framework for exploring emancipatory alternatives to the contemporary capitalist system. Both strategies are aimed at promoting and achieving a trajectory of sustained metamorphosis rather than a dramatic rupture with existing institutions and structures. However, they differ in their relationship to current institutions: while *symbiotic* strategies try to use them to advance social empowerment, *interstitial* ones seek to build anew. The advantage of Wright's approach is that it helps to overcome the long-standing antagonism between proponents of each of the strategies by viewing them as complementary and mutually dependent. In light of this, let us now reflect on the import of the contributions of this book in relation to the three challenges we identified at the outset: reclaiming universities, revitalising democracy and recasting politics.

The Future of the University

Across the world, many universities are adopting neoliberal managerial practices and inculcating kindred ideas, but they remain crucial sites of resistance. If we are to reclaim control over how universities currently function, Mike Finn (Chapter "The Never-ending Crisis in British Higher Education") reminds us that there first needs to be a clear articulation about what is wrong. In the case of the United Kingdom, his historically grounded account of higher education reform reveals that the subordination of the university to market fundamentalism is only partly attributable to the rise of neoliberalism in the 1980s. Rather, its origins lie decades earlier with the growing aggrandisement of the state in expanding higher education to increase economic growth and geopolitical power. Thus, Finn argues, the development of any alternative vision for the university requires repudiation of the state's mandate to determine the shape of the university through funding and regulation. Alice Pearson's contribution (Chapter "Consuming Education") adds to this argument by providing ethnographic insight into how the state's marketisation of education appears to be shaping the subjectivities of undergraduates into that of consumers, even when they are protesting the economic theories used by policymakers to legitimise this shift. Focusing on graduates, Eric Lybeck (Chapter "The Coming Crisis of Academic Authority") draws our attention to the ways in which the prioritisation of research over teaching erodes the academic authority of doctoral degrees, degrades the quality of education and turns academics into entrepreneurs beholden to grant-making organisations and academic associations on whom they rely for research grants and publications. The result: a bifurcation within departments, where the elite researchers able to win grants enjoy secure employment, and teaching staff with limited time for research are precariously employed. The primary task, then, is for academics and students to mobilise and wrest back control from the state and the market.

One way forward is Eric Lybeck's proposal to (re)introduce the model of the scholastic guild: a self-regulating community of teachers and scholars that would uphold the value of teaching by helping to identify, insure and support postgraduate students committed to its improvement.

Underpinning its reintroduction is the idea to use the graduate union to create an unemployment insurance scheme that would reduce the risk of unemployment for early career academics transitioning from graduate school to their first secure faculty position—an often-gruelling experience that benefits those privileged enough to be able to hold out until getting a job. Ideally, this would help foster a relational web of solidarity between established and aspiring academics while strengthening the bargaining position of the latter. This strategy is symbiotic, in Wright's terms: it seeks to empower the members of graduate unions, which exist in most universities. Once established on a substantial scale, one could imagine that this new community could broaden its activities. For example, it could enable academics, whose work is often highly individualised, to make demands for greater autonomy and challenge the state's assessment frameworks through the development of alternatives. While Lybeck's attempt to become Cambridge Graduate Union President and implement his platform failed due to the conservatism of staff and students and corruption of the democratic process, there are likely to be other graduate unions and universities much more open and willing to experiment. A vibrant coalition of young academics and students would be pivotal for such a project to be successful.

Another strategy for making knowledge production and transfusion more democratic and egalitarian would be to pursue an *interstitial* strategy aimed at building alternative spaces for research and teaching that exist outside of the university. More specifically, this could involve the creation of autonomous self-owned and self-organised institutions. One prominent example is the free universities movement in the United Kingdom that provides free lectures, discussions and workshops to people at little or no cost. A more radical proposal is for academics, especially early career researchers, to form worker cooperatives in which members own the enterprise, decision-making is democratic, and differences in pay are eschewed in favour of solidarity between workers. These could help support cooperative values and principles—within both the education sector and the economy—and help combat what Alex Simpson (Prologue "Consecrating the Elite: The Cultural Embedding of the Financial Market") calls the 'cultural system of competitive market behavior' that some universities have helped nourish. Indeed, within the arts there are plenty of artist collectives that collaborate in similar ways towards a shared vision. Given the enormous number of PhD students disgruntled with the hierarchy, bureaucracy, nepotism and inequality within the contemporary university, it seems plausible to imagine that there would be a critical mass supportive of, and interested in, participating in such an alternative.

Democracy Now!

Turning to the question of how to revitalise democracy, the authors of the second section to this volume have provided us with some tentative answers. Olga Zelinska's perspective on the Maidan movement (Chapter "Local Maidan Across Ukraine: Democratic Aspirations in the Revolution of Dignity") demonstrates the importance of people's local assemblies, which allow people to envisage different ways of organising themselves. In the Ukrainian context, activists imagined restoring 'people's rule' over political decision-making and budgetary processes through the creation of alternative political institutions such as a new supreme legislative body, the People's Council, with new Regional Councils acting as its foundation. At the local level, they proposed overhauling the representative model of governance, in line with direct-democracy principles, by creating neighbourhood committees and holding regular local referendums on city management. Indeed, people's assemblies have been a prominent feature of contemporary protest and resistance against austerity in other countries such as Greece, Spain and the United Kingdom. The formation of people's assemblies therefore represents a vital first step for any collective effort towards developing an alternative horizon of possibility.

However, as Zelinska notes, the actual implementation of such visions ultimately depends on the ability of activists to overcome the usual barriers to any major challenge to the status quo: co-optation, repression and (geo)political crises. As Benjamin Anderson argues (Chapter "Opportunity in Crisis: Alternative Media and Subaltern Resistance"), while assemblies and other forums such as alternative media can help ignite the radical imagination, it is social movements that are the predominant drivers of purposeful social and political progress. Without traditional political activism—that is, strategic, vigorous and crucially, collective—even the most laudable call to action, cleverly crafted and communicated via social media to millions, is liable to fall flat. Here Steven Speed's riveting account of the battle of Barton Moss (Chapter "The Battle of Barton Moss") shows just how effective participatory forms of protest such as slow walking can be against intense corporate and state pressure. Whether they succeed or fail, though, people involved in the process gain experience and expertise, and organise networks of fellow activists, which are invaluable for future social struggles.

Populism, State Power and Alternatives to Capitalism

Turning to the question of how to recast politics, Mike O'Donnell (Chapter "The Limits of Populism: Mills, Marcuse and Nineteen-Sixties Radicalism and Occupy") has shown how the populist use of the elite/mass dichotomy by the Occupy movement in the aftermath of the 2008 financial crash was also a distinguishing feature of 1960s radicalism in the United States. In light of their shared populist character, he suggests that contemporary social movements in North America and Europe must learn from one of the key strategic mistakes of their predecessor, namely, an inadequate appreciation of the importance of accessing state power. The challenge, then, for critical thinkers and activists today is to recognise this oversight and help progressive political parties articulate a discourse and develop policies that resonate with disaffected right-wing and left-wing voters. Failure to do so will allow the reactionary and authoritarian current within the populist zeitgeist to further undermine institutional democracy. The debilitation of democratic institutions in places like Hungary and Poland is a clear example of this risk. It is especially important to channel the populist impulse among young people towards electoral politics and get them to register and vote, as they are often more progressive than their older counterparts. This was one of the cornerstones of the Labour Party's political strategy during the UK snap election in 2017 in which they increased their share of the vote by an impressive ten per cent. Mulvad and Stahl's contribution (Chapter "The Myth of Bourgeois Democracy") provides theoretical ammunition for proponents of this type of symbiotic transformational strategy by illustrating how the radical origins of parliamentary democracy have been obscured by a false association with bourgeois liberalism. Rather than abandon our democratic institutions at a time of deepening capitalist crisis, they argue, anti-capitalists should instead seek to defend them, reinforce them and re-orientate their interventions.

There are, however, limits to what radical political movements can achieve once in possession of state power. In the case of Greece, Rosa Vasilaki (Chapter "Seeing Like a PIG: The Crisis in Greece as a Tale of Hope and Disillusionment") reminds us how Syriza's coalition government with ANEL failed to challenge the Troika's austerity demands, despite over 60 per cent of the public voting 'NO' at the national referendum in July 2015. The lesson, she argues, is that while Syriza's anti-systemic politics proved effective at disrupting the corrupt political factions that had been dominant since the 1980s, the social democratic alternative it sought to implement did not challenge the system itself. Thus, she concludes, radical politics in the era of crisis need to move beyond seeking corrective measures to contemporary capitalism and engage in un-systemic thinking that identifies and challenges entrenched articulations of economic and state power while enhancing social power. One way of developing a systemic alternative is Charles Masquelier's proposal to organise a large-scale alliance of cooperatives, solidarity economy networks and social movements guided by G.D.H Cole's 'spirit of free communal service' (Chapter "Unleashing the Emancipatory Power of the 'Spirit of Free Communal Service': G.D.H. Cole, Dialogical Coordination and Social Change"). The hope is that once the values and practices of these marginal movements reach a critical mass, it becomes possible to replace the invisible hand of the market with the visible hand of dialogical coordination between producer guilds and consumer councils. What role political parties and other collective institutions such as trade unions should play, and would be willing to play, in constructing such an alternative to capitalism is open to debate.

One thing is clear. The notion that 'there is no alternative' to neoliberalism as the best way for humanity to develop has been challenged. The critical task that lies before us now as students, scholars and activists is to take advantage of this opportunity and help construct alternative horizons of possibility as we have endeavoured to do in this book. Rather than the 'end of history' as Fukuyama observed, this historical moment is a critical juncture, which marks a new beginning. The new generation of critical thinkers and activists engaged in conscious projects of gradual social change is our best hope for envisioning and enacting a future that moves beyond a continuation of the present and a regression to the past. Giving young people the benefit of the doubt and the space to think the world anew is, in this sense, not only desirable but also perhaps our only way forward.

Guide to Further Reading

Brown, Wendy. 2015. *Undoing the demos: Neoliberalism's stealth revolution*. Cambridge: MIT Press.

Hahnel, Robin and Erik Olin Wright. 2016. *Alternatives to capitalism: Proposals for a democratic economy*. London: Verso.

Haivan, Max, and Alex Khasnabish. 2014. *The radical imagination: Social movement research in the age of austerity.* London: Zed Books.

Hardt, Michael, and Antonio Negri. 2017. *Assembly*. Oxford: Oxford University Press.

Izak, Michal et al. 2017. *The future of university education*. Basingstoke: Palgrave Macmillan.

Jones, Bryn, and Mike O'Donnell. 2017. *Alternatives to neoliberalism: Towards equality and democracy*. Bristol: Policy Press.

Klein, Naomi. 2014. *This changes everything: Capitalism* vs. *the climate*. New York: Simon and Schuster.

Lasn, Kalle. 2012. *Meme wars: The creative destruction of neoclassical economics*. New York: Penguin.

Ranis, Peter. 2016. *Cooperatives confront capitalism: Challenging the neoliberal economy*. London: Zed Books.

Rosa, Hartmut, et al. 2015. *Capitalism, crisis, critique*. London: Verso.

Sanders, Bernie. 2017. *Guide to political revolution*. New York: Henry Holt.

Sitrin, Marina, and Dario Azzellini. 2014. *They can't represent us! Reinventing democracy from Greece to Occupy*. London: Verso.

Solnit, Rebecca. 2017. Protest and persist: Why giving up hope is not an option. *Guardian*, March 17. https://www.theguardian.com/world/2017/mar/13/protest-persist-hope-trump-activism-anti-nuclear-movement. 24
Accessed May 2017.

The Free Association. 2011. *Moments of excess: Movements, protest and everyday life*. Oakland: PM Press.

Therborn, Göran. 2013. *The killing fields of inequality*. Cambridge: Polity Press.

Wood, Leslie. 2014. *The militarization of protest policing*. London: Zed Books.

Wright, Erik Olin. 2010. *Envisioning real utopias*. London: Verso.

Works Cited

[Browne Review]. 2010. *Independent review of higher education funding and student finance, securing a sustainable future for higher education*. London: The Stationery Office.

Abbott, Andrew. 1981. Status and status strain in the professions. *American Journal of Sociology* 86 (4): 819–835.

———. 2001. *Chaos of disciplines*. Chicago: University of Chicago Press.

Abu-Lughod, Janet. 1999. *New York, Chicago, Los Angeles: America's global cities*. Minneapolis: University of Minnesota Press.

Adams, Andy. 2014. *Peer group review of operation Mansell anti fracking protest Sussex Police*. Hertfordshire: Hertfordshire Constabulary/Essex Police.

Adams, Richard. 2016. Anti-terror laws risk "chilling effect" on freedom of speech – Oxford college head. *Guardian*, February 7.

Adbusters. 2015. *Get ready for the billion people march*. http://www.adbusters.org/article/get-ready-for-the-billion-people-march/. Accessed 24 Apr 2017.

———. 2016. *Billion people march*. http://www.billionpeoplemarch.org. Accessed 24 Apr 2017.

Adelstein, David. 1969. Roots of the present crisis. In *Student power: Problems, diagnosis, action*, ed. R. Blackburn and A. Cockburn. Harmondsworth: Penguin.

Agamben, Giorgio. 1995. *Homo Sacer: Sovereign power and bare life*. Stanford: Stanford University Press.

T. Geelan et al. (eds.), *From Financial Crisis to Social Change*,
https://doi.org/10.1007/978-3-319-70600-9

Agamben, Giorgio. 1998. *Homo Sacer. Sovereign power and bare life*. Stanford: Stanford University Press.
Ahmad, Aijaz. 1997. Postcolonial theory and the 'post' condition. *The Socialist Register* 33: 353–381.
Alexander, Jeffrey. 2001. Robust utopias and civil repairs. *International Sociology* 16 (4): 579–591.
Alperovitz, Gar. 2011. *America beyond capitalism: Reclaiming our wealth, our liberty and our democracy*. Boston: Democracy Collaborative Press.
Anderson, Perry. 1964. Origins of the present crisis. *New Left Review*, 1/23.
Andriakiana, Eleni. 2016. Public history, 1821 revolution and greek identity. In *Defining identity and the changing scope of culture in the Digital Age*, ed. Alison Novak and Imaani Jamillah El-Burki, 56–80. Hershey: IGI Global.
Appadurai, Arjun. 1986. *The social life of things*. Cambridge: Cambridge University Press.
Aristotle. 1995. *The complete works of Aristotle: The revised Oxford translation*. Princeton: Princeton University Press.
Armstrong, Aurelia. 2008. Beyond resistance: A response to Žižek's critique of Foucault's subject of freedom. *Parrhesia* 5: 19–31.
Atkinson, Joshua D. 2008. Towards a model of interactivity in alternative media: A multilevel analysis of audiences and producers in a new social movement network. *Mass Communication and Society* 11 (3): 227–247.
Atkinson, Joshua D., and Laura Cooley. 2010. Narrative capacity, resistance performance, and the "shape" of new social movement networks. *Communications Studies* 61 (3): 321–338.
Baehr, Peter. 2011. Purity and danger in the modern university. *Society* 48 (4): 297–300.
Ball, Stephen. 2003. The teacher's soul and the terrors of performativity. *Education Policy* 18 (2): 215–228.
Ball, Stephen J. 2013. *The education debate*. 2nd ed. Bristol: Policy Press.
Barron, Anne. 2013. Free software production as critical social practice. *Economy and Society* 42 (4): 597–625.
Baudrillard, Jean. 1994. *Simulacra and simulation*. Ann Arbor: University of Michigan Press.
Bauman, Zygmunt. 2007. *Consuming life*. Cambridge: Polity Press.
———. 2014. *State of crisis*. Cambridge: Polity Press.
Bauwens, Michel, and Vasilis Kostakis. 2014. From the communism of capital to capital for the commons: Towards an open co-operativism. *TripleC* 12 (1): 356–361.

BBC. 2013. BBC survey suggests support for fracking in North West. *BBC News*, December 3. http://www.bbc.co.uk/news/uk-england-25157239. Accessed 24 Apr 2017.

Bell, Daniel. 1988[1960]. *The end of ideology: On the exhaustion of political ideas in the fifties*. Cambridge: Harvard University Press.

Benjamin, Walter. 1968. Theses on the philosophy of history. In *Illuminations*, ed. Hannah Arendt, 217–252. New York: Schocken.

Benkler, Yochai. 2013. Practical anarchism: Peer mutualism, market power, and the fallible state. *Politics and Society* 41 (2): 212–251.

Berman, Elizabeth Popp. 2011. *Creating the market university: How academic science became an economic engine*. Princeton: Princeton University Press.

Berry, Craig. 2014. *Globalisation and ideology in Britain: Neoliberalism, free trade and the global economy*. 1st ed. Manchester: Manchester University Press.

Bettleheim, Bruno. 1969. Obsolete youth: Towards a psychograph of adolescent rebellion. *Encounter* 32 (September): 29–42.

BIS. 2015a. *Fulfilling our potential: Teaching excellence, social mobility and student choice*. https://www.gov.uk/government/uploads/system/uploads/attachment_data/file/474227/BIS-15-623-fulfilling-our-potential-teaching-excellence-social-mobility-and-student-choice.pdf. Accessed 24 Apr 2017.

———. 2015b. *Press release: Student choice at the heart of new higher education reforms*. https://www.gov.uk/government/news/student-choice-at-the-heart-of-new-higher-education-reforms. Accessed 24 Apr 2017.

———. 2016. *The teaching excellence framework: Assessing quality in higher education*. http://www.publications.parliament.uk/pa/cm201516/cmselect/cmbis/572/572.pdf. Accessed 24 Apr 2017.

Blackbourn, David, and Geoff Eley. 1984. *The peculiarities of German history: Bourgeois society and politics in nineteenth-century Germany*. Oxford: Oxford University Press.

Baldamus, Wilhelm. 2010. The sociology of Wilhelm Baldamus: Paradox and inference. Edited by M. Erickson and C. Turner. Basingstoke/Abingdon: Ashgate Publishing, Ltd.

Blee, Kathleen. 2012. *Democracy in the making*. New York: Oxford University Press.

Block, Fred, and Matthew R. Keller. 2009. Where do innovations come from? Transformations in the US economy, 1970–2006. *Socio-Economic Review* 7 (3): 459–483.

Blyth, Mark. 2013. *Austerity: The history of a dangerous idea*. Oxford: Oxford University Press.

Bogdanor, Vernon. 2009. *The new British constitution*. 1st ed. Oxford: Hart.

Bourdieu, Pierre. 1973. Cultural reproduction and social reproduction. In *Knowledge, education and cultural change*, ed. Richard Brown, 71–112. London: Tavistock.

———. 1977. *Outline of a theory of practice*. Cambridge: Cambridge University Press.

———. 1980. *Questions desSociologie*. Paris: Editions de Minuit.

———. 1984. *Distinction: A social critique of the judgement of taste*. London: Routledge.

———. 1987. *Choses dittes*. Paris: Editions de Minuit.

———. 1988. *Homo academicus*. Stanford: Stanford University Press.

———. 1990. *The logic of practice*. Stanford: Stanford University Press.

———. 1991. Le champ littéraire. *Actes de la Recherche en Sciences Sociales* 89 (September): 4–46.

———. 1996. *The state nobility: Elite schools in the field of power*. Cambridge: Polity Press.

———. 1998. The essence of neoliberalism. [Online]. *Le Monde Diplomatique [English Edition]*, December. http://mondediplo.com/1998/12/08bourdieu. Accessed 10 Aug 2015.

———. 2001. *Firing back: Against the tyranny of the market*. London: The New Press.

———. 2011. The forms of capital. In *Cultural theory: An introduction*, ed. Imre Szeman and Timothy Kaposy, 81–93. Chichester: Wiley-Blackwell.

Bourdieu, Pierre, and Jean-Claude Passeron. 1990. *Reproduction in education, society and culture*. London: Sage.

Bourdieu, Pierre, and Loic Wacquant. 1993. From ruling class to field power: An interview with Pierre Bourdieu on La noblesse d'Etat. *Theory, Culture and Society* 10 (3): 19–44.

Briggs, Asa. 1964. Drawing a new map of learning. In *The idea of a new university: An experiment in Sussex*, ed. David Daiches. London: Andre Deutsch.

Brown, Roger. 2015. Education beyond the Gove Legacy: The case of higher education. In *The Gove Legacy: Education in Britain after the coalition*, ed. Mike Finn, 75–86. London: Palgrave.

Buzdugan, Yaroslava. 2012. Legal principles of NGOs' participation in public oversight. *Viche* 12. [In Ukrainian].

Calhoun, Craig. 2012. *The roots of radicalism: Tradition, the public sphere and early nineteenth century social movements*. Chicago: University of Chicago Press.

Callon, Michel. 1988. *The laws of the markets*. London: Blackwell.
Callon, Michel. 1998. *The laws of the markets*. Oxford/Malden: Blackwell Publishers.
Cambridge Dictionary of Sociology (CDS). 2006. *Cambridge dictionary of sociology*. Ed. Bryan Turner. Cambridge/New York: Cambridge University Press.
Campos, Nauro. 2013. What drives protests in Ukraine? This time it is institutions. *VOX, CEPR's Policy Portal*, December 22. http://www.voxeu.org/article/what-drives-protests-ukraine. Accessed 24 Apr 2017.
Campos Lima, Maria da Paz, and António Martin Artiles. 2013. Youth voice(s) in EU countries and social movements in Southern Europe. *Transfer: European Review of Labour and Research* 19 (3): 345–363.
Castells, Manuel. 2012. *Networks of outrage and hope: Social movements in the internet age*. Cambridge: Polity Press.
Castells, Manuel, Joao Caraça, and Gustavo Cardoso. 2012. *Aftermath: The cultures of economic crisis*. Oxford: Oxford University Press.
Centre for Society Research. 2014. *Protests, victories and repressions in Ukraine: Monitoring results of 2013*. http://cslr.org.ua/wp-content/uploads/2014/05/CSR_-_Protests_in_2013_-_29_Apr_2014.pdf. Accessed 24 Apr 2017. [In Ukrainian].
Cetina, Karin, and Urs Bruegger. 2002. Global microstructures: The virtual societies of financial markets. *American Journal of Sociology* 107 (4): 905–950.
Chang, Ha-Joon. 2008. *Bad samaritans*. New York: Bloomsbury Press.
———. 2011. *23 things they don't tell you about capitalism*. New York: Bloomsbury Press.
———. 2014. *Keynote speech*. Rethinking Economics Conference.
Chomsky, Noam. 2012. *Occupy*. London: Penguin Press.
Chopra, Rohit. 2003. Neoliberalism as doxa: Bourdieu's theory of the state and the contemporary Indian discourse on globalisation and liberalisation. *Cultural Studies* 17 (3/4): 419–444.
Christopoulos, Dimitris. 2014. *The 'deep state' in Greece today and the far right: Police, justice, church*. Athens: Nisos—Rosa Luxemburg Stiftung.
Chung, Heejung, Sonja Bekker, and Hester Houwing. 2012. Young people and the post-recession labour market in the context of Europe 2020. *Transfer: European Review of Labour and Research* 18 (3): 301–317.
Cinar, Kursat. 2016. A comparative analysis of clientelism in Greece, Spain, and Turkey: The rural–urban divide. *Contemporary Politics* 22 (1): 77–94.
City of London. 2013. *Key Facts*. http://www.cityoflondon.gov.uk/about-the-city/who-we-are/Pages/key-facts.aspx. Accessed 25 Sept 2013.

Cleaver, Harry. 2012. *Reading capital politically*. New Delhi: Phoneme Publishers.
Cole, George Douglas Howard. 1917. *Self-government in industry*. London: George Bell & Sons.
———. 1920. *Social theory*. London: Methuen & Co.
———. 1937. *Practical economics*. Middlesex: Pelican Books.
———. 1944. *A century of cooperation*. London: George Allen and Unwin.
———. 1946. *Cooperation, labour and socialism*. Co-operative Partnership Propaganda Committee, Sixth Thomas Blandford Memorial Lecture, 23rd November.
———. 1950. *Essays in social theory*. London: Macmillan.
———. 1955. Introduction. In *The social contract and discourses*, ed. Jean Jacques Rousseau. London: Everyman's Library.
———. 1957. Sociology and social policy. *British Journal of Sociology* 8 (2): 158–171.
———. 1980. *Guild socialism re-stated*. London: Transaction Books.
Cole, George Douglas Howard, and William Mellor. 1933. Workers' control and self-government. In *Industry, a memorandum prepared by a group of trade unionists and socialists as a basis for consideration by the working-class movement*, 9, ed. The New Fabian Research Bureau. London: The New Fabian Research Bureau.
Collini, Stefan. 2013. Sold out. *London Review of Books* 35 (20): 3–12.
———. 2016. Who are the spongers now? *London Review of Books* 38 (2): 33–37.
———. 2017. *Speaking of universities*. London: Verso.
Committee of the Regions of the EU. 2011. *Local and regional government in Ukraine and the development of cooperation between Ukraine and the EU*. http://cor.europa.eu/en/documentation/studies/Documents/local-regional-government-ukraine.pdf. Accessed 24 Apr 2017.
Committee on Higher Education [Robbins Report]. 1963. *Higher education: Report*. Cmnd. 2154. London: HMSO.
Committee on Scientific Manpower [Barlow Report]. 1946. *Scientific Manpower*. Cmnd. 6284. London: HMSO.
Constant, Benjamin. 1988[1816]. The liberty of the ancients compared with that of the moderns. In *The political writings of Benjamin Constant*, 309–328. http://www.uark.edu/depts/comminfo/cambridge/ancients.html. Accessed 10 Oct 2013.
CSEP. 2014. *CSEP survey of economics students: Is it time for change at Cambridge?* http://www.cambridgepluralism.org/uploads/1/7/4/9/17499733/report_v14_w.appendix.pdf. Accessed 24 Apr 2017.

Currie, Jennifer. 1999. Why choose a life on the ocean wave? *Times Higher Education*, August 6.

Daily Telegraph. 2016. Worrying populism. *Daily Telegraph*, February 28, 17.

Dawson, Matt. 2016. *Social theory for alternative societies*. London: Palgrave Macmillan.

Dean, Dennis. 1998. Circular 10/65 Revisited: The labour government and the "comprehensive revolution" in 1964–1965. *Paedagogica Historica* 34 (1): 63–91. https://doi.org/10.1080/0030923980340103.

Dean, Jodi. 2013. Occupy Wall Street: After the anarchist moment. *Socialist Register* 49: 52–62.

DeLuca, Kevin Michael, and Jennifer Peeples. 2002. From public sphere to public screen: Democracy, activism, and the "violence" of Seattle. *Critical Studies in Media Communication* 19 (2): 125–151.

Democratic Initiatives Foundation. 2013a. *Prospects for modernization in Ukraine and trends of public opinion*. http://www.dif.org.ua/ua/events/perspekizaclnoi-svidomosti.htm. Accessed 24 Apr 2017. [In Ukrainian].

———. 2013b. *Public confidence in the social and state institutions*. http://infolight.org.ua/charts/riven-doviri-gromadyan-do-socialnih-ta-derzhavnih-institutiv. Accessed 24 Apr 2017. [In Ukrainian].

———. 2013c. Refusal from euro-integration: What next?. *Focus on Ukraine*, November 18–24. http://www.dif.org.ua/en/publications/focus_on_ukraine/zupink-dali_.htm. Accessed 24 Apr 2017.

———. 2014a. *From the Maidan-Camp to Maidan-Sich: What has changed?* http://www.dif.org.ua/ua/polls/2014_polls/vid-maidanu-taboru-do-maidan.htm. Accessed 24 Apr 2017. [In Ukrainian].

———. 2014b. *Maidan anniversary: Public opinion poll and expert interviews*. http://www.dif.org.ua/en/polls/2014_polls/hethrtjhrrhthrtt.htm. Accessed 24 Apr 2017. [In Ukrainian].

———. 2014c. Three months of a Ukrainian revolution: Is this the last straw for Yanukovych?. *Focus on Ukraine*, February 17–23. http://www.dif.org.ua/en/publications/focus_on_ukraine/trhi-janukovicha.htm. Accessed 24 Apr 2017.

Department for Business, Innovation and Skills. 2015. *Fulfilling our potential: Teaching excellence, social mobility and student choice*. London: Department for Business, Innovation and Skills.

Department for Business, Innovation and Skills (BIS). 2016. *Success as a knowledge economy: Teaching excellence, social mobility and student choice*. Cmnd. 9258. London: TSO.

Department for Education and Skills (DfES). 2003. *The future of higher education*. Cmnd. 5735. London: HMSO.

Department of Education. 2016. *Educational excellence everywhere*. https://www.gov.uk/government/uploads/system/uploads/attachment_data/file/508447/Educational_Excellence_Everywhere.pdf. Accessed 24 Apr 2017.

Diamantouros, Nikiforos. 1994. *Cultural dualism and political change in postauthoritarian Greece*, Estudio/Working Paper, Center for Advanced Study in the Social Sciences. Madrid: Fundación Juan March.

Diani, Mario. 2000. Simmel to Rokkan and beyond: Towards a network theory of new social movements. *European Journal of Social Theory* 3 (4): 387–406.

Domènech, Antoni. 2004. *El eclipse de la fraternidad: Una revisión republicana de la tradición socialista*. Barcelona: Crítica.

———. 2009. Democrácia burguesa: nota sobre la génesis del oxímoron y la necedad del regalo. *Viento Sur* 100 (January): 95–100.

Downing, John. 2008. Social movement theories and alternative media: An evaluation and critique. *Communication, Culture & Critique* 1 (1): 40–50.

Duménil, Gérard, and Dominique Lévy. 2004. *Capital resurgent: Roots of the neoliberal revolution*. Cambridge, MA: Harvard University Press.

Dvoretska, Liliya. 2014. *Power to the people: People's councils created in 19 of Ukraine's regions*. http://nbnews.com.ua/ua/tema/112351/. Accessed 24 Apr 2017. [In Ukrainian].

Eagleton, Terry. 2014. The death of universities. *The Guardian*, December 17. http://www.theguardian.com/commentisfree/2010/dec/17/death-universities-malaise-tuition-fees. Accessed 24 Apr 2017.

———. 2015. The slow death of the university. *The Chronicle of Higher Education*, April 5.

Edgerton, David. 2006. *Warfare state*. 1st ed. Cambridge: Cambridge University Press.

Eliassen, Raman, Jostein Løhr Hauge, and Ivan Rajić. 2015. *Fit for a fix: Why the economics curriculum needs a pluralist revamp*. https://www.jiscmail.ac.uk/cgi-bin/webadmin?A3=ind1510&L=HETECON&E=BASE64&P=1574821&B=--Message-Boundary-5594&T=Application%2FOctet-stream;%20name=%22Fit%20for%20a%20fix%20(English%20version).pdf%22&N=Fit%20for%20a%20fix%20(English%20version).pdf&attachment=q&XSS=3. Accessed 24 Apr 2017.

Erickson, Mark, and Charles Turner. 2010. *The sociology of Wilhelm Baldamus: Paradox and inference*. London: Ashgate.

Etzioni, Amitai. 1969. *The semi-professions and their organization: Teachers, nurses, social workers*. New York: Free Press.

Etzkowitz, Henry, and Loet Leydesdorff. 1996. A triple helix of academic-industry-government relations: Development models beyond "capitalism versus socialism". *Current Science* 70 (8): 690–693.

———. 1998. The endless transition: A "triple helix" of university-industry-government relations. *Minerva* 36 (3): 203–208.

Featherstone, Kevin. 2008. 'Varieties of capitalism' and the Greek case: Explaining the constraints on domestic reform. *GreeSe* Paper 11, Hellenic Observatory Papers on Greece and Southeast Europe. http://www.lse.ac.uk/europeanInstitute/research/hellenicObservatory/pdf/GreeSE/GreeSE11.pdf. Accessed 24 Apr 2017.

Finn, Mike. 2002. The new elite. *Guardian*, November 27.

———. 2015. Education beyond the Gove legacy: The case of higher education (2) – Ideology in action. In *The Gove Legacy: Education in Britain after the coalition*, ed. Mike Finn, 87–100. London: Palgrave.

Finn, Mike, and Anthony Seldon. 2013. Constitutional reform since 1997: The historians' perspective. In *The British constitution: Continuity and change*, ed. Matt Qvortrup. Oxford: Hart.

Flank, Lenny. 2011. *Voices from the 99 percent: An oral history of the occupy Wall Street movement.* St Petersburg: Red and Black Publishers.

Fleck, Christian. 2011. *A transatlantic history of the social sciences: Robber Barons, the Third Reich and the invention of empirical social research.* London: Bloomsbury Academic.

Fleming, Andrew 2011. Adbusters sparks Wall Street protest: Vancouver-based activists behind street actions in the US. *Vancouver Courier*, September 27.

Fotopoulos, Takis. 2001. The end of traditional anti-systemic movements and the need for a new type of anti-systemic movement today. *Democracy and Nature* 7 (3): 415–455.

Foucault, Michel. 1972. *The archaeology of knowledge.* New York: Pantheon Books.

———. 2010. *The birth of biopolitics: Lectures at the College de France, 1978–79.* Basingstoke: Palgrave Macmillan.

Foucault, Michel, and Colin Gordon. 1980. *Power/knowledge.* New York: Pantheon Books.

Foucault, Michel, Graham Burchell, and Arnold Davidson. 2008. *The birth of biopolitics.* Basingstoke: Palgrave Macmillan.

Fourcade, Marion, Etienne Ollion, and Yann Algan. 2015. The superiority of economists. *Journal of Economic Perspectives* 29 (1): 89–114.

Fournier, Valerie. 2003. Utopianism and grassroots alternatives. In *Viable utopian ideas: Shaping a better world*, ed. Arthur B. Shostak, 181–189. New York: M.E. Sharpe.

Frank, Thomas. 1997. Opening salvo: The new gilded age. In *Commodify your dissent: Salvos from the Baffler*, ed. Thomas Frank and Matt Weiland, 23–28. New York: WW Norton & Company.

Freire, Paulo. 1970. *Pedagogy of the oppressed*. New York: Herder and Herder.

French, Shaun, and Andrew Leyshon. 2010. 'These f@#king guys': The terrible waste of a good crisis. *Environment and Planning* 42 (11): 2549–2559.

Fuchs, Christian. 2010. Alternative media as critical media. *European Journal of Social Theory* 13 (2): 173–192.

———. 2014a. *Digital labour and Karl Marx*. London: Routledge.

———. 2014b. *Occupymedia!: The Occupy movement and social media in crisis capitalism*. Winchester: Zero Books.

Fukuyama, Francis. 1992. *The end of history and the last man*. London: Penguin Books.

Fulton, John. 1964. New universities in perspective. In *The idea of a new university: An experiment in Sussex*, ed. David Daiches, 1112. London: Andre Deutsch. in Sussex (London, 1966).

Gamble, Andrew. 1989. *The free economy and the strong state*. 1st ed. Basingstoke: Macmillan.

Gatskova, Kseniia, and Maxim Gatskov. 2016. Third sector in Ukraine: Civic engagement before and after the "Euromaidan". *Voluntas* 27: 673–694.

Geiger, Roger L. 1985. Hierarchy and diversity in American research universities. In *The university research system: The public policies of the scientists*, ed. Björn Wittrock and Aant Elzinga, 53–74. Stockholm: Almqvist & Wiksell.

Gerbaudo, Paolo. 2013. When anarchism goes pop. *Open Democracy*. https://www.opendemocracy.net/paolo-gerbaudo/when-anarchism-goes-pop. Accessed 23 June 2014.

Giddens, Anthony. 1991. *Modernity and self-identity: Self and society in the late modern age*. Cambridge: Polity.

Gilmore, Joanna, Will Jackson, and Helen Monk. 2016. *'Keep moving!': Report on the policing of the Barton Moss community protection camp, November 2013–April 2014*. Centre for the Study of Crime, Criminalisation and Social Exclusion, Liverpool.

Gitlin, Todd. 2012. *Occupy nation: The roots, the spirit, and the promise of Occupy Wall Street*. New York: itbooks.

———. 2013. Occupy's predicament: The moment and the prospects for the movement. *British Journal of Sociology* 64 (1): 3–25.

Gorz, Andre. 1982. Workers' control is more than just that. In *Workplace democracy and social change*, ed. Frank Lindenfeld and Joyce Rothschild-Whitt. Boston: Porter Sargent.

Gouldner, Alvin W. 1970. *The coming crisis of Western sociology*. New York: Basic Books.

Gramsci, Antonio. 1972. *Selections from the prison notebooks of Antonio Gramsci*, ed. Quintin Hoare and Geoffrey Nowell-Smith. New York: International Publishers.

Greater Manchester Police. 2014. *Memorandum of understanding between Greater Manchester Police, Greater Manchester Fire and Rescue Service, North West Ambulance Service, Salford City Council, Association of Greater Manchester Authorities, Highways Agency, Igas, Peel Holdings/Estates and Manchester Barton Aerodrome*. Greater Manchester: Greater Manchester Police.

Green, E.H.H. 1999. Thatcherism: An historical perspective. *Transactions of the Royal Historical Society* 9: 17–42. https://doi.org/10.2307/3679391.

Habermas, Jürgen. 1973. *Legitimation crisis*. Boston: Beacon Press.

Hacker, Jacob S., and Paul Pierson. 2010. Winner-take-all politics: Public policy, political organization, and the precipitous rise of top incomes in the United States. *Politics and Society* 38 (2): 152–204.

Hailsham, Lord. 1976. Elective dictatorship: The Richard Dimbleby Lecture 1976. *The Listener*, October 21.

Haiven, Max. 2007. Privatized resistance: AdBusters and the culture of neoliberalism. *The Review of Education, Pedagogy and Cultural Studies* 29: 85–110.

———. 2014. *Crises of imagination, crises of power: Capitalism, creativity and the commons*. Halifax/Winnipeg, London/New York: Fernwood Publishing and Zed Books.

Haiven, Max, and Alex Khasnabish. 2014. *The radical imagination: Social movement research in the age of austerity*. London: Zed Books.

Hale, Sir Edward. 1957. Letter to R. N. Quirk, Lord President's Committee, December 10. National Archives [NA] CAB 21/4627.

Harvey, David. 2005. *A brief history of neoliberalism*. Oxford: Oxford University Press.

Haworth, Susan. 2014. *Re: policing of protest, human rights and justice*. Greater Manchester Association of Trades Councils, July 18. https://netpol.org/wp-content/uploads/2014/08/GMATUC-to-GMPCC-July-2014.pdf. Accessed 24 Apr 2017.

Hayek, Friedrich A. 1944. *The road to serfdom*. London: Routledge.

———. 1993[1960]. *The constitution of liberty*. London: Routledge.

Heller, Kevin Jon. 1996. Power, subjectification and resistance in Foucault. *SubStance* 25 (1): 78–110.

Hillman, Nicholas. 2013. From grants for all to loans for all: Undergraduate finance from the implementation of the Anderson Report (1962) to the implementation of the Browne Report (2012). *Contemporary British History* 27 (3): 249–270. https://doi.org/10.1080/13619462.2013.783418.

Hobsbawm, Eric. 1973. *The age of revolutions*. London: Abacus.
———. 1994. *The age of extremes: The short 20th century, 1914–1991*. London: Abacus.
———. 2005. *Age of Empire, 1875–1914*. London: Abacus.
Hoffman, Jan. 1998. Judge not, law schools demand of a magazine that ranks them. *New York Times*, February 19.
Hoffman, Steve G. 2011. The new tools of the science trade: Contested knowledge production and the conceptual vocabularies of academic capitalism. *Social Anthropology* 19 (4): 439–462.
Hofstadter, Richard. 1967. *The American political tradition and the men who made it*. London: Jonathan Cape.
Holcombe, Randall G. 2010. Pluralism and heterodoxy in economic methodology. *The Review of Austrian Economics* 24 (1): 57–65.
Honcharuk, Nataliya, and Leonid Prokopenko. 2011. The interaction of national government bodies and local self-government: Legal and functional aspects. *Public Administration: Theory and Practice* 3 (7): 31–38. [In Ukrainian].
Horkheimer, Max, and Theodor W. Adorno. 2002. *Dialectic of enlightenment: Philosophical fragments*. Stanford: Stanford University Press.
Horowitz, Irving. 1967. *Power, politics and people: The collected essays of Charles Wright Mills*. Oxford: Oxford University Press.
Hyatt, Susan Brin, Boone W. Shear, and Susan Wright. 2015. *Learning under neoliberalism: Ethnographies of governance in higher education*. New York: Berghahn Books.
Independent News Bureau. 2014a. *The opposition decided to create an alternative government (full text of the Viche Resolution)*. http://nbnews.com.ua/ua/news/110898/. Accessed 24 Apr 2017. [In Ukrainian].
———. 2014b. *The opposition MPs have created the People's Council of Ukraine*. http://nbnews.com.ua/ua/news/111250/. Accessed 24 Apr 2017. [In Ukrainian].
Inglis, David. 2014. What is worth defending in sociology today? Presentism, historical vision and the uses of sociology. *Cultural Sociology* 8 (1): 99–118.
ISIPE. 2014. *International student initiative for pluralism in economics*. http://www.isipe.net. Accessed 24 Apr.
Jacobs, Paul, and Saul Landau. 1967. *The new radicals*. Harmondsworth: Penguin.
Jessop, Bob. 1990. *State theory: Putting the capitalist state in its place*. Philadelphia: Pennsylvania State University Press.

Jizha, Mykola, and Oleksandr Radchenko. 2012. *Public control in the system of public administration as an effective tool of the examination of state-managerial decisions*. http://www.kbuapa.kharkov.ua/e-book/putp/2012-4/doc/2/02.pdf. Accessed 24 Apr 2017. [In Ukrainian].

Johnson, Alan. 2011. The power of nonsense. *Jacobin Magazine*, July. http://jacobinmag.com/2011/07/the-power-of-nonsense/. Accessed 14 Dec 2013.

Johnson, Paul, and Daniel Chivers. 2015. The coalition and the economy. In *The coalition effect, 2010–2015*, ed. Anthony Seldon and Mike Finn, 159–193. Cambridge: Cambridge University Press.

Jones, Bryn, and Michael O'Donnell. 2010. *Radicalism and social movement activism: Retreat and resurgence*. London: Anthem.

Kautsky, Karl. 1964. *The dictatorship of the proletariat*. Ann Arbor: University of Michigan Press.

Kerr, Clark. 2001[1963]. *The uses of the university*. Harvard University Press, Cambridge, MA.

Kirtsoglou, Elisabeth. 2013. The dark ages of the Golden Dawn: Anthropological analysis and responsibility in the twilight zone of the Greek crisis. *Journal of the Finnish Anthropological Society* 38 (1): 104–108.

Kouvelakis, Stathis. 2016. Syriza's rise and fall. *New Left Review* 97: 45–70.

Kovtunovych, Tetyana, and Tetyana Pryvalko. 2015. *Maidan in the first person: 45 stories of the revolution of dignity*. Kiev: K.I.S. [In Ukrainian].

Kravets, Roman, Khomei Oksana, Pasichnyk Andriy, and Valeriya Lopatina. 2016. Grew up in Maidan: Volunteer initiatives two years after Maidan. *Ukrainska Pravda*, February 8. http://life.pravda.com.ua/society/2016/02/6/207741/. Accessed 24 Apr 2017. [In Ukrainian].

Krugman, Paul. 2015. The case for cuts was a lie: Why does Britain still believe it? *Guardian*, May 10.

Kynaston, David. 2002. *The City of London volume IV: A club no more 1945–2000*. London: Pimlico.

Labour Party. 1964. *Let's go with labour for the new Britain: The labour party's manifesto for the 1964 general election*. 1st ed. London: Labour Party.

Lamont, Michèle. 2010. *How professors think*. Cambridge: Harvard University Press.

Langman, Lauren. 2013. Occupy: A new social movement. *Current Sociology* 3 (4): 510–524.

Lapavitsas, Costas. 2012. *Crisis in the eurozone*. London: Verso.

Lasn, Kalle. 2012. *Meme wars: The creative destruction of neoclassical economics*. New York: Seven Stories Press.

Lawson, Tony. 1997. *Economics and reality*. London: Routledge.

———. 2005. The nature of heterodox economics. *Cambridge Journal of Economics* 30 (4): 483–505.

———. 2009. The current economic crisis: Its nature and the course of academic economics. *Cambridge Journal of Economics* 33 (4): 759–777.

———. 2013. What is this 'school' called neoclassical economics? *Cambridge Journal of Economics* 37 (5): 947–983.

Lebaron, Frédéric. 2001. Economists and the economic order: The field of economists and the field of power in France. *European Societies* 3 (1): 91–110.

———. 2006. "Nobel" economists as public intellectuals. *International Journal of Contemporary Sociology* 43 (1): 88–101.

Lenin, Vladimir I. 1917. The state and revolution. In *Collected works, Vol. 25*, 381–492. http://www.marxists.org/archive/lenin/works/1917/staterev/. Accessed 15 Dec 2013.

———. 1918. Democracy and dictatorship. In *Collected works, Vol.* 28, 368–372. https://www.marxists.org/archive/lenin/works/1918/dec/23.htm. Accessed 15 Dec 2013.

———. 1919. First congress of the Communist International. In *Collected works, Vol. 28*, 455–477. http://www.marxists.org/archive/lenin/works/1919/mar/comintern.htm. Accessed 15 Dec 2013.

Levitas, Ruth. 2013. *Utopia as method*. London: Palgrave Macmillan.

Lewin, Tamar. 2013. As interest fades in the humanities, colleges worry. *The New York Times*, October 30. Retrieved 2 November 2013 (http://www.nytimes.com/2013/10/31/education/as-interest-fades-in-the-humanities-colleges-worry.html).

Lindekilde, Lasse. 2013. Claims-making. In *The Wiley-Blackwell encyclopedia of social and political movements*, ed. David A. Snow, Donatella della Porta, Bert Klandermans, and Doug McAdam. http://onlinelibrary.wiley.com/doi/10.1002/9780470674871.wbespm027/pdf. Accessed 24 Apr 2017.

Lipset, Seymour Martin. 1972. Ideology and no end: The controversy till now. *Encounter* 39 (6): 17–22.

London Working Men's Association. 1838. *The people's charter*. http://www.bl.uk/learning/histcitizen/21cc/struggle/chartists1/historicalsources/source4/peoplescharter.html. Accessed 15 Dec 2013.

Losurdo, Domenico. 2011. *Liberalism: A counter-history*. London: Verso.

Luhn, Alec. 2014. The Ukrainian nationalism at the heart of 'Euromaidan.' *The Nation*, January 21. http://www.thenation.com/article/ukrainian-nationalism-heart-euromaidan/. Accessed 24 Apr 2017.

Lybeck, E.R. 2011. For pragmatic public sociology: Theory and practice after the pragmatic turn. *Current Perspectives in Social Theory* 29: 169–185.

MacKenzie, Donald. 2007. *An engine, not a camera*. Cambridge: MIT Press.

MacKenzie, Donald. 2009. *Material markets: How economic agents are constructed*. Oxford: Oxford University Press.

MacKenzie, Donald A., Fabian Muniesa, and Lucia Siu. 2007. *Do economists make markets? On the performativity of economics*. Princeton: Princeton University Press.

Manchester Evening News. 2014. Most fracking protesters are there to 'intimidate the local community' and 'antagonise' the force, police claim. *Manchester Evening News*, January 23. http://www.manchestereveningnews.co.uk/news/greater-manchester-news/salford-fracking-protesters-intimidate-local-6554055. Accessed 24 Apr 2017.

Marcuse, Herbert. 1955. *Eros and civilisation*. London: Sphere Books.

———. 1964. *One dimensional man*. London: Routledge and Kegan Paul.

———. 1969. *An essay on liberation*. Boston: Beacon Books.

Martin, John Levi. 2003. What is field theory? *American Journal of Sociology* 109 (1): 1–49.

Marx, Karl. 1986. The civil war in France: Address of the General Council of the International Working Men's Association. In *Karl Marx and Friedrich Engels' collected works, volume 22*, 307–359. London: Lawrence & Wishart.

Marx, Karl, and Friedrich Engels. 1848. *Demands of the Communist Party in Germany*. http://www.marxists.org/archive/marx/works/1848/03/24.htm. Accessed 15 Dec 2013.

———. 1969. *Manifesto of the Communist Party*. http://www.marxists.org/archive/marx/works/1848/communist-manifesto/. Accessed 15 Dec 2013.

Massey, Doreen. 2013. Vocabularies of the economy. In *After neoliberalism? The Kilburn manifesto*, ed. Stuart Hall, Doreen Massey, and Michael Rustin, 3–17. London: Lawrence and Wishart.

Mavrogordatos, George T. 1997. From traditional clientelism to machine politics: The impact of PASOK populism in Greece. *South European Society and Politics* 2 (3): 1–26.

McAdam, Doug, Sidney Tarrow, and Charles Tilly. 2004. *Dynamics of contention*. Cambridge: Cambridge University Press.

———. 2007. Comparative perspectives on contentious politics. In *Comparative politics: Rationality, culture, and structure*, ed. Mark Irving Lichbach and Alan S. Zuckerman, 260. Cambridge: Cambridge University Press. http://socialsciences.cornell.edu/wp-content/uploads/2013/06/McAdamTarrowTilly07.pdf. Accessed 24 Apr 2017.

McCormick, John P. 2011. *Machiavellian democracy*. Cambridge: Cambridge University Press.

McGettigan, Andrew. 2013. *The great university gamble: Money, markets and the future of higher education*. London: Pluto Press.

Meyer, David S. 2004. Protest and political opportunities. *Annual Review of Sociology* 30: 125–145.

Meyer, David S., and Debra C. Minkoff. 2004. Conceptualizing political opportunity. *Social Forces* 82 (4): 1457–1492.

Miliband, Ralph. 1969. *The state in capitalist society*. London: Weidenfeld and Nicolson.

Mill, John Stuart. 2010[1861]. *Considerations on representative government*. https://doi.org/10.1017/CBO9780511783128. Accessed 15 Dec 2013.

Mills, Charles Wright. 1956. *The power elite*. New York: Oxford University Press.

Mills, Charles Wright. 1959a. *The sociological imagination*. New York: Oxford University Press.

———. 1959b. *The causes of world war three*. London: Martin Secker and Warburg.

———. 1959c. Culture and politics: The fourth epoch. In *Power, politics and people: The collected essays of Charles Wright Mills*, ed. Irving Horowitz, 236–246. Oxford: Oxford University Press.

———. 1960a. Letter to the New Left. In *Power, politics and people: The collected essays of Charles Wright Mills*, ed. Irving Horowitz, 247–259. Oxford: Oxford University Press.

———. 1960b. *Listen Yankee: The revolution in Cuba*. New York: Ballantine Books.

Ministry of Education. 1956. *Technical education*. Cmnd. 9703. London: HMSO.

Mirowski, Philip. 1989. *More heat than light*. Cambridge: Cambridge University Press.

———. 2013. *Never let a serious crisis go to waste*. London: Verso.

Mitchell, Timothy. 1998. Fixing the economy. *Cultural Studies* 12 (1): 82–101.

Moberly, W.H. 1949. *The crisis in the university*. 1st ed. London: SCM Press.

Montesquieu, Charles-Louis de Secondat, Baron de. 1794. *The spirit of laws*. Translated from French, Montesquieu Eighteenth Century Collection Online Database. http://find.galegroup.com/ecco/infomark.do?&source=gale&prodId=ECCO&userGroupName=dkb&tabID=T001&docId=CW3324479092&type=multipage&contentSet=ECCOArticles&version=1.0&docLevel=FASCIMILE. Accessed 10 Dec 2013.

Monticelli, Lara, and Matteo Bassoli. 2017. Precarious voices? Types of "political citizens" and repertoires of action among European youth. *Partecipazione e Conflitto* 9 (3): 824–856.

Morgan, John. 2014. Students at Pearson College get green light for SLC funds. *Times Higher Education*, August 21. http://www.timeshighereducation.co.uk/news/students-at-pearson-college-get-green-light-for-slc-funds/2015273.article. Accessed 24 Apr 2017.

Morrison, Herbert. 1946. Government and the universities: A memorandum by the Lord President of the Council. June 29. National Archives PREM/8/478 [L.P. (46) 160].

Mountford, James Frederick. 1972. *Keele, an historical critique*. 1st ed. London: Routledge & Kegan Paul.

Mozilla Community. 2016. https://www.mozilla.org/. Accessed 6 Feb 2016.

Mudge, Stephanie. 2008. What is neo-liberalism? *Socio-Economic Review* 6 (4): 703–731.

Mullins, Phil, and Struan Jacobs. 2006. T.S. Eliot's idea of the clerisy, and its discussion by Karl Mannheim and Michael Polanyi in the context of J.H. Oldham's Moot. *Journal of Classical Sociology* 6 (2): 147–156. https://doi.org/10.1177/1468795x06064852.

Myseliuk, Andriy. 2010. Ten differences between the systems of Yanukovych and of Kuchma. *Ukrainska Pravda*, July 16. http://www.pravda.com.ua/articles/2010/07/16/5226836/. Accessed 24 Apr 2017. [In Ukrainian].

Nomai, Afsheen. 2011. Adbusters Media Foundation (Canada). In *Encyclopedia of social movement media*, ed. John Derek Hall Downing, 3–4. Los Angeles: Sage.

NUS. 2015. *The higher education green paper in a nutshell.* http://www.nus.org.uk/en/news/the-higher-education-green-paper-in-a-nutshell/. Accessed 24 Apr 2017.

Nussbaum, Martha C. 2010. *Not for profit: Why democracy needs the humanities.* Princeton: Princeton University Press.

O'Donnell, Michael. 2008. Nineteen sixties radicalism and its critics: Utopian radicals, liberal realists and postmodern sceptics. *Psychoanalysis, Culture and Society* 13 (3): 240–260.

OECD. 2012. *Education at a glance 2012: OECD indicators*. http://www.oecd.org/edu/eag2012.htm. Accessed 24 Apr 2017.

Offe, Claus. 1983. Competitive party democracy and the Keynesian welfare state: Factors of stability and disorganization. *Policy Sciences* 15 (3): 225–246.

Oglesby, Carl. 1970. Trapped in a system. In *The New Left: A documentary history*, ed. Massimo Teodori, 182–188. London: Jonathan Cape.

Oleksiyenko, Oles, and Svyatoslav Pototskyy. 2013. "Soft authoritarianism": Yanukovych's regime has chosen the tactics of creeping power usurpation. *Tyzhden*, April 11. http://tyzhden.ua/Politics/77088. Accessed 24 Apr 2017. [In Ukrainian].

ONS. 2012. *Business register and employment survey*. London: Office for National Statistics.

Onuch, Olga. 2014. Who were the protesters? *Journal of Democracy* 25 (3): 44–51.

Onuch, Olga, and Gwendolyn Sasse. 2014. What does Ukraine's #Euromaidan teach us about protest? *The Monkey Cage*, February 27. http://www.washingtonpost.com/blogs/monkey-cage/wp/2014/02/27/what-does-ukraines-euromaidan-teach-us-about-protest/. Accessed 24 Apr 2017.

———. 2016. The Maidan in movement: Diversity and the cycles of protest. *Europe-Asia Studies* 68 (4): 556–587.

Ovenden, Kevin. 2015. *Syriza: Inside the labyrinth*. London: Pluto Press.

Ozarow, Daniel, and Richard Croucher. 2014. Workers' self-management, recovered companies and the sociology of work. *Sociology* 48 (5): 989–1006.

Padgett, Stephen, and William E. Paterson. 1991. *A history of social democracy in postwar Europe*. London: Longman.

Pauly, Louis. 2011. The political economy of the financial crisis. In *Global political economy*, ed. John Ravenhill, 215–272. Oxford: Oxford University Press.

PCES. 2014. *Economics, education and unlearning: Economics education at the University of Manchester*. Manchester: The Post-Crash Economics Society.

Phillips, David. 1980. Lindsay and the German universities: An Oxford contribution to the post-war reform debate. *Oxford Review of Education* 6 (1): 91–105. https://doi.org/10.1080/0305498800060107.

Pickett, Brent L. 1996. Foucault and the politics of resistance. *Polity* 28 (4): 445–466.

Piketty, Thomas. 2014. *Capitalism in the twenty-first century*. Harvard University Press, Cambridge, MA.

Poulantzas, Nicos. 2001. *State, power, socialism, Vol. 29*. London: Verso.

Power, Michael. 1997. *The audit society: Rituals of verification*. Oxford: Oxford University Press.

Psarras, Dimitris. 2012. *The black book of the Golden Dawn: Documents from the history and action of a Nazi group*. Athens: Polis.

Raven, James. 1989. British history and the enterprise culture. *Past and Present* 123 (1): 178–204. https://doi.org/10.1093/past/123.1.178.

RBC-Ukraine. 2012. Parliamentary factions of the Verkhovna Rada of seventh convocation. *RBC Daily*, December 13. http://www.rbc.ua/ukr/analytics/fraktsiya-kommunisticheskoy-partii-ukrainy-13122012114400. Accessed 24 Apr 2017. [In Ukrainian].

Robbins, Lionel Charles Robbins. 1935. *An essay on the nature and significance of economic science*. 2nd ed. London: Macmillan.

Robbins, Lionel. 1966. *The university in the modern world*. 1st ed. Macmillan.

Roberts, Sean, and Oleksandr Fisun. 2014. *Local governance and decentralization assessment: Implications of proposed reforms in Ukraine*. USAID. https://www.usaid.gov/sites/default/files/documents/1863/LOCAL%20GOVERNANCE%20ASSESSMENT%20FINAL.pdf. Accessed 24 Apr 2017.

Robertson, Geoffrey. 2007. *The Putney debates: The Levellers*. London: Verso.

Roszac, Theodore. 1968. *The making of the counter-culture: Reflections on the technocratic society and its youthful opposition*. New York: Doubleday.

Ruggie, John Gerald. 1982. International regimes, transactions, and change: Embedded liberalism in the postwar economic order. *International Organization* 36 (2): 379–415.

Sack, Robert. 1993. The power of place and space. *Geographical Review* 83 (3): 326–329.

———. 1999. A sketch of a geographic theory of morality. *Annals of the Associations of American Geographers* 89 (1): 26–44.

Salter, Brian, and Ted Tapper. 1994. *The state and higher education*. Abingdon: Routledge.

Sanders, Nicholas. 2016. *Report of Regina V Boris Roscin, John Wasilewski, and David Cohen*. Manchester: The Manchester Magistrates' Court. https://netpol.org/wp-content/uploads/2016/01/Judgment-Roscin-etc-130116-Frackers.pdf. Accessed 24 Apr 2017.

Sandoval, Marisol, and Christian Fuchs. 2009. Towards a critical theory of alternative media. *Telematics and Informatics* 27: 141–150.

Satgar, Vishwas. 2014. *The solidarity economy alternative: Emerging theory and practice*. KwaZulu-Natal: University of KwaZulu-Natal Press.

Savio, Mario. 1968. An end to history. In *The politics and anti-politics of the young*, ed. Michael Brown, 32–36. California: Glencoe Press.

Sayer, Derek. 2014. *Rank hypocrisies: The insult of the REF*. London: SAGE.

Schmitt, Carl. 2007. *The concept of the political, expanded edition*. Chicago: University of Chicago Press.

Schulz, Markus. 2015. Future moves: Forward-oriented studies of culture, society, and technology. *Current Sociology* 63 (2): 129–139.

Seligman, Daniel. 1969. A special kind of rebellion. In *Youth in turmoil: Adapted from a special issue of Fortune*, ed. Louis Banks. New York: Time Incorporated. https://www.amazon.com/Youth-Turmoil-Adapted-Special-Fortune/dp/B000ND0N60.

Seymour, Richard. 2014. *Against austerity: How we can fix the crisis they made*. 1st ed. London: Pluto Press.

Shantz, Jeff, and José Brendan MacDonald. 2013. *Beyond capitalism: Building democratic alternatives for today and the future*. New York: Bloomsbury.
Shattock, Michael. 1994. *The UGC and the management of British universities*. 1st ed. Buckingham: Open University Press.
———. 2012. *Making policy in British higher education, 1945–2011*. 1st ed. Maidenhead: Open University Press.
Shaxson, Nicholas. 2011. *Treasure islands: Tax havens and the men who stole the world*. London: Vintage Books.
Shekhovtsov, Anton. 2014. What the West should know about Maidan's ultra-right element. *Krytyka*, February 1. http://krytyka.com/ua/solutions/opinions/shcho-zakhodu-potribno-znaty-pro-kraynikh-pravykh-na-evromaydani. Accessed 24 Apr 2017. [In Ukrainian].
Shepherd, Jessica. 2010. UK universities likely to follow US model, says leading vice-chancellor. *Guardian*, October 8.
Shore, Cris. 2010. Beyond the multiversity: Neoliberalism and the rise of the schizophrenic university. *Social Anthropology* 18 (1): 15–29.
Shore, Cris, and Miri Davidson. 2014. Beyond collusion and resistance: Academic management relations within the neoliberal university. *Learning and Teaching* 7 (1): 12–28.
Shore, Cris, and Susan Wright. 1999. Audit culture and anthropology: Neo-liberalism in British higher education. *The Journal of the Royal Anthropological Institute* 5 (4): 557–575.
Shurkhalo, Dmytro. 2014. Volunteer battalions—Between war and politics. *Radio Svoboda*, August 15. http://www.radiosvoboda.org/a/26531775.html. Accessed 24 Apr 2017. [In Ukrainian].
Skinner, Quentin. 1998. *Liberty before liberalism*. Cambridge: Cambridge University Press.
Sloman, John, Alsion Wride, and Dean Garratt. 2012. *Economics*. 8th ed. Harlow: Pearson Education Limited.
Smith, Brian, and Vanessa Cunningham. 2003. Crisis at Cardiff. In *Managing crisis*, ed. David Warner and David Palfreyman. Maidenhead: Open University Press.
Smithsimon, Gregory. 2010. Inside the empire: Ethnography of a global citadel in New York. *Urban Studies* 47 (4): 699–724.
Snyder, Timothy, and Tatiana Zhurzhenko. 2014. Diaries and memoirs of the Maidan: Ukraine from November 2013 to February 2014. *Eurozine*, June 27. http://www.eurozine.com/diaries-and-memoirs-of-the-maidan/. Accessed 24 Apr 2017.

Solonenko, Iryna. 2016. Reforms in Ukraine: Between old legacies and a new social contract. *Eurozine*, March 17. http://www.eurozine.com/articles/2016-03-17-solonenko-en.html. Accessed 24 Apr 2017.

Spence, Larry D. 1968. Berkeley: What it demonstrates (1965). In *The politics and anti-politics of the young*, ed. Michael Brown, 36–42. London: Glencoe Press.

Spence, Michael. 1973. Job market signaling. *The Quarterly Journal of Economics* 87 (3): 355.

Spivak, Gayatri. 1990. Poststructuralism, marginality, postcoloniality and value. In *Literary theory today*, ed. Peter Collier and Helga Geyer-Ryan, 198–222. New York: Cornell University Press.

Srnicek, Nick, and Alex Williams. 2015. *Inventing the future: Postcapitalism and a world without work*. London: Verso.

Steinberg, Stefan. 2014. Three dead in clash between Ukrainian regime and right-wing protesters. *World Socialist Web Site*. Retrieved from https://www.wsws.org/en/articles/2014/01/23/ukra-j23.html. Accessed 24 Apr 2017.

Stern, Sol. 1970. A deeper disenchantment. In *The New Left: A documentary history*, ed. Massimo Teodori, 153–158. London: Jonathan Cape.

Stiglitz, Joseph. 2009. Moving beyond market fundamentalism to a more balanced economy. *Annals of Public and Cooperative Economics* 80 (3): 345–360. https://doi.org/10.1111/j.1467-8292.2009.00389.x.

Stiglitz, Joseph. 2010. *Freefall: Free markets and the sinking of the global economy*. London: Penguin Books.

Strathern, Marilyn. 2000. *Audit cultures*. London/New York: Routledge.

Streeck, Wolfgang. 2011. The crisis of democratic capitalism. *New Left Review* 71: 5–29.

Suissa, Judith. 2010. *Anarchism and education: A philosophical perspective*. 1st ed. Oakland: PM.

Sviatnenko, Sviatoslav, and Benfold Vinogradov. 2014. Euromaidan values from a comparative perspective. *Social, Health, and Communication Studies Journal* 1 (1): 41–61.

Swartz, David. 1997. *Culture and power: The sociology of Pierre Bourdieu*. Chicago: University of Chicago Press.

Tapper, Ted. 2007. *The governance of British higher education: The struggle for policy control*. Dordrecht: Springer.

Taylor, A., et al., eds. 2011. *Occupy: Scenes from occupied America*. London: Verso.

Taylor, Charles. 1989. *Sources of the self*. Cambridge, MA: Harvard University Press.

Taylor, Astra, and Keith Gessen. 2011. *Occupy: Scenes from occupied America*. London: Verso.

Teodori, Massimo. 1970. *The New Left: A documentary history*. London: Jonathan Cape.

The Economist. 2013. *Ukraine's protests: A new revolution on Maidan Square*. December 7. http://www.economist.com/news/europe/21591217-has-ukrainians-defiance-presidents-european-policy-split-country-new-revolution. Accessed 24 Apr 2017.

The Verkhovna Rada of Ukraine. 1996. *The constitution of Ukraine*. http://zakon2.rada.gov.ua/laws/show/254%D0%BA/96-%D0%B2%D1%80. Accessed 24 Apr 2017. [In Ukrainian].

———. 2010. *The ruling of the constitutional court of Ukraine*. http://zakon2.rada.gov.ua/laws/show/v020p710-10. Accessed 24 Apr 2017. [In Ukrainian].

Thedossopoulos, Dimitrios. 2014a. On depathologizing resistance. *History and Anthropology* 25 (4): 415–430.

———. 2014b. The ambivalence of anti-austerity indignation in Greece: Resistance, hegemony and complicity. *History and Anthropology* 25 (4): 488–506.

Therborn, Goran. 1980. *The ideology of power and the power of ideology*. London: Verso.

Therborn, Goran. 2013. "Global cities," World power, and the G20 capital cities. In *Cities and crisis: New critical urban theory*, ed. Kuniko Fujita, 51–82. London: Sage.

Thompson, Dan. 2014. Three quarters of Mancunians oppose fracking, an M.E.N survey finds. *Manchester Evening News*, March 6. http://www.manchestereveningnews.co.uk/news/greater-manchester-news/three-quarters-mancunians-oppose-fracking-6778067. Accessed 24 Apr 2017.

Tight, Malcolm. 2009. *The development of higher education in the United Kingdom since 1945*. 1st ed. Maidenhead: Open University Press.

Tilly, Charles, and Sydney Tarrow. 2007. *Contentious politics*. London: Paradigm Publishers.

Touraine, Alain. 2014. *After the crisis*. Cambridge: Polity.

Tretiak, Svitlana. 2014. Viche as one of the civil society institutions of modern Ukraine. *Scientific Bulletin of the International University of Humanities*, Jurisprudence (9–1): 56–58. [In Ukrainian].

Ukrainska Pravda. 2011. Court sentence for Tymoshenko: 7 years and 1.5 billion. *Ukrainska Pravda*, October 11. http://www.pravda.com.ua/articles/2011/10/11/6654964/. Accessed 24 Apr 2017. [In Ukrainian].

———. 2014. Putin declared war on Ukraine. *Ukrainska Pravda*, March 1. http://www.pravda.com.ua/articles/2014/03/1/7016683/. Accessed 24 April 2017. [In Ukrainian].

Valevskyi, Oleksiy. 2014. The political crisis of 2010–2013 and the objectives of the new model of public policy. *Scientific Proceedings* 6 (74): 135–144. [In Ukrainian].

Various Authors. 1967[1962]. The Port Huron statement. In *The new radicals*, ed. Paul Jacobs and Saul Landau, 154–167. Harmondsworth: Penguin.

Vasilaki, Rosa. 2017. We are an image from the future: Reading back the Athens 2008 riots. *Acta Scientiarum* 29 (2): 153–161.

Walker, Shaun, and Oksana Grytsenko. 2013. Ukraine protesters return en masse to central Kiev for pro-EU campaign. *The Guardian*, December 15. http://www.theguardian.com/world/2013/dec/15/ukraine-protesters-return-central-kiev-eu-campaign. Accessed 24 Apr 2017.

White, Micah M. 2016. *The end of protest: A new playbook for revolution*. Toronto: Knopf Canada.

Wikimedia Foundation. 2016. http://wikimediafoundation.org/. Accessed 6 Feb 2016.

Wilkinson, Ellen. 1946. Government and the universities: Memorandum to the Lord President of the Council's Committee. July 9. National Archives: PREM/8/478 [L.P. (46) 174].

Wolff, Richard. 2012. *Democracy at work: A cure for capitalism*. Chicago: Haymarket Books.

Wood, Ellen Meiksins. 2008. *Citizens to lords: A social history of Western political thought from antiquity to the late middle ages*. London: Verso.

———. 2012. *Liberty and property: A social history of Western political thought from the Renaissance to Enlightenment*. London: Verso.

Wright, Erik Olin. 2009. *Envisioning real utopias*. London: Verso.

———. 2010. *Envisioning real utopias*. London: Verso.

Wright, Susan. 2015. Anthropology and the "imaginators" of future European universities. *Focaal* 2015 (71): 6–17.

Wright, Susan, and Annika Rabo. 2010. Introduction: Anthropologies of university reform. *Social Anthropology* 18 (1): 1–14.

Wyatt, Chris. 2011. *The defetishised society: New economic democracy as libertarian alternative to capitalism*. New York: Bloomsbury.

Yermilova, Hanna. 2013. Public control in public procurement. *Financial Control*: 24–25. [In Ukrainian].

Yermolenko, Volodymyr. 2014. Dreams of Europe. *Eurozine*, February 6. http://www.eurozine.com/dreams-of-europe/. Accessed 24 Apr 2017.

Zakharov, Yevhen. 2009. *Public control and human rights*. Kharkiv Human Rights Protection Group. http://www.khpg.org/index.php?id=1261552395. Accessed 24 Apr 2017. [In Ukrainian].

Zaloom, Caitlin. 2006. *Out of the pits: Traders and technology from Chicago to London*. Chicago: University of Chicago Press.

Zelinska, Olga. 2014. The prospects of public control in Ukraine. *Open Society Foundation*, NGO. http://osf.org.ua/data/blog_dwnl/Civil_participat_Zelin_artcle.pdf. Accessed 24 Apr 2017. [In Ukrainian].

———. 2015. Who were the protestors and what did they want? Contentious politics of local Maidan across Ukraine, 2013–2014. *Demokratizatsiya: The Journal of Post-Soviet Democratization* 23 (4): 379–400.

Žižek, Slavoj. 1999. Carl Schmitt in the age of post-politics. In *The challenge of Carl Schmitt*, ed. Chantal Mouffe. London: Verso.

———. 2001. *Did somebody say totalitarianism*. London: Verso.

———. 2002. *Revolution at the gates—Žižek on Lenin*. London: Verso.

———. 2007. *Slavoj Žižek presents Robespierre: Virtue and terror*. London: Verso.

———. 2009a. *Violence*. London: Profile Books.

———. 2009b. *First as tragedy, then as farce*. London: Verso.

———. 2009c. *Violence: Six sideways reflections*. London: Profile Books.

———. 2011. *Living in the end times*. London: Verso.

———. 2012. *The year of dreaming dangerously*. London: Verso.

Index[1]

[1] Note: Page number followed by 'n' refer to notes.

T. Geelan et al. (eds.), *From Financial Crisis to Social Change*,
https://doi.org/10.1007/978-3-319-70600-9

R

S

Y

Z